The Tail of the Dragon

D0112815

The Tail of the Dragon

NEW DANCE, 1976-1982

Marcia B. Siegel

Photographs by Nathaniel Tileston

DUKE UNIVERSITY PRESS   Durham and London 1991

Contents

Introduction

TRANSITIONS ARE ALWAYS INTERESTING. They are also the hardest things to see. Transition—from one movement to the next, from one era to the next—can occur in a split second, or it can take a long time, hours, years. Whether the transition is rapid or gradual, we tend to miss it. That is, we see it, but we don't remark it, because we habitually focus on more practical realities. We note that a dancer has changed direction in midair, or that a friend has grown older. But the more startling the change, the more we wonder just how it could have occurred right under our eyes and yet escaped us.

Dance itself is always a kind of transition, an arena where ideas appear, collide, contend, accommodate, and evolve into new ideas. Since this transformation takes place nonverbally, it always remains partly obscured, even magical, to the rational mind of history. Any transitional process confounds history because its outcome is unknown, the significance of its characters is suspended, conjectural. I think one reason dance's history is so scanty, so relentlessly fixated on a few dramatic figures, is that its ongoing life is anchored in the realm of the transitional. By the time historians notice a significant body of new work and label it a trend or an influence, the artists will no longer be experiencing the first, galvanizing charge of dissent. They will have spent their talent or forged into new realms still uncharted by history. By the time history makes its call, the game is over, which is why the public's beliefs about dance trends often lag behind the times.

Dance history is affected as well by the overwhelming and routine loss of the primary evidence on which history is built. Until the universal adoption of videotape to document dance in the last ten years, the making of a thorough record of a dance was so cumbersome that it was only undertaken when the dance had achieved status as a major work. Hundreds of works by major and minor choreographers—everything from sketches and unsuccessful ventures to ambitious commissioned works—are completely lost for purposes of study or re-viewing. We almost never see retrospective showings of a choreographer's work or of the collected work of a "school." On the rare occasions when we do, we are certain to be seeing some falsification of the original work. When a piece of choreography is revived after a season or a decade, steps get remembered slightly differently, style can only be approximated. The initial ambiguities, and often the initial charm, may be lost or deliberately clarified and underlined because posterity's consensus has decreed what the dance "is." I usually think there's more in a dance when it hasn't yet been improved in this way.

How odd it is that the audience knows almost nothing about a new dance work when it is first presented. Of all art forms the most self-evident and the most available to our senses, dance is also the least revealing of its intentions, or even its formal properties. Most choreographers never tell us in words what they "mean" (the ones who do make me intensely skeptical), leaving us to trace their deepest thoughts on the preverbal level of dance itself, if we can. But the audience wants very much to know what it means, which is why people turn to critics to interpret meaning for them, and why the old-fashioned nineteenth-century story ballets are still so popular. For at least the last fifty years, choreographers have turned away from stories and claimed they intended nothing more in their dances than an exploration of dancing. So the spectator reels from credulity to presumption. Cautioned against inferring too much, he or she often suspects that a dance is not just dancing but metaphor, or autobiography, or even ideology. The surface is only steps, but underneath, a more profound text is glimmering. A historian will look back on the dance—assuming the dance remains to be seen—and from a distance determine its significant effects and consequences, its place among the grand schemes and careers of art. Alternative interpretations or images that occurred to us in our initial naive responses will slip away as the historical lens zeros in on an increasingly concentrated, monolithic version of the event.

Unlike historians, critics are almost exclusively concerned with the transitional. They document a series of markers in a day-to-day continuum. They report this ongoing process as a legitimate subject of newspaper journalism, the most marginal and ephemeral and least scholarly of literary forms. Critics try to fathom, above all, what the artist is thinking at the moment of performance and to identify the signs of change, which is to say, the process of dance. Although they are hypersensitized to the present, and don't often venture to contemplate the longer vistas of history, perceptive critics can give us much that history lacks—a sense of what the dance was like in the liminal moment before its outcome was known. Reading their accounts of those here-and-nows, we may be able to see more clearly how events slid slowly forward and lingered behind over the ceaseless flux of days.

The articles in this book were written during a transition between two particularly striking periods in experimental dance: the so-called postmodern period that began in the early 1960s and the contemporary period of the late 1980s to early 1990s, which seems so drastically different all of a sudden. I can't say the eighties and nineties will prove to be influential on what dancers choose to do in the twenty-first century. Nor do I mean to encapsulate the changes I see now as either monolithic or complete. All I can say for sure is that in 1976, when I last collected my reviews for a book, experimental dance looked different and had a different cast of characters and occupied a different place in the overall culture than it did five years later, when my relation to the scene changed because of the closing of the alternative newspaper in which I was able to write about it. I also know that the changes I saw during that period intensified over the following several years, so that the remnants of what was called postmodernism then are nearly as unremarked today as the signs of anti-postmodernism were in 1976.

*

By now the sixties have become remythologized as a fond utopian memory. Now that we "understand" the counterculture, we can accept disorientation and boredom in a performance. We're no longer repelled or frightened by the extremes of countercultural alienation. The fierceness, the passion of protest have been forgotten. The nature of passion itself, and of protest, has changed because of what the sixties ignited. In experimental dance, the shake-up was caused by a most determined rejection of modern dance forms and ideals, what was perceived as an overindulgence in sentiment and ego and a lush theatricality that left the audience passively entertained. The leaders of this rebellion were Merce Cunningham, Yvonne Rainer, Robert Dunn, who sparked the Judson Dance Theater, and some more peripheral but charismatic figures like Anna Halprin, James Waring, and a lot of New York painters, composers, and poets who lent their convictions and their bodies to the indescribable dance events that were going on. Except for Cunningham, who, in a way, kept dancing alive as a respectable possibility for the avant-garde all during the most virulent attacks on the excesses of dance, none of the sixties' new dance standard-bearers appears directly in this book. By 1975 they had all left the dance scene. (Waring died in 1975.) Rainer was making films, Dunn became a movement specialist, and Halprin had channeled the elements of her performance into rituals of community development and healing. The ways in which their creativity diverged from its early explosive manifestations in dance, and the reasons why dance did not sustain itself as a field for their energies, is an interesting study that would probably shed more light on the transition I am documenting here.

That early conflagration, strangely enough, did not consume the dance instinct. In fact, it wasn't really meant to. Rebels are always seen as negative forces, destructive to the status quo. The dance rebels of the sixties were trying to destroy, but they were also looking for new ways to go on, new ways to define dance and to shape it. Responding to the drastic political, technological, and philosophical changes that had followed World War II— the period in which many of them grew up—they overthrew restricting attitudes, forms, systems of training, and modes of performance. Downtown dance in the early sixties was an explosion. But it led almost immediately to some very serious and rigorous work. If someone downtown wanted to call standing still a dance—or pulling a wagon or throwing paint around—there was an audience that would go along with that. And if you could accept seemingly random, nontechnical, fragmented, multilayered events as dance, you might then see an exploration of randomness as dance composition. If a happening could be a theatrical event, why couldn't the disparate, unpredictable elements of a happening, a little more structured, a little more selected, be thought of as choreography? If any body could be inherently a dancing body, the audience could be asked to contemplate ordinary bodies engaging systematically in very mundane activities and find them as interesting as pirouettes. And was it not possible that the subject matter of a dance, its spirituality, its physical presence, could be drawn from sources other than the conventions of the Euro-American past?

As soon as individuals identified the aspects they wanted to work on out of this big, blasted-apart bag of tricks, a process began that was very much like the original modern dance process. Friends got together and worked on problems. After a while they thought they had something to show an audience. In their own studios, or in the streets, in modestly produced performance series in gyms or churches, they did concerts. These groups were not really dance companies. They did not plan to build a repertory. They were doing work, and they went on to do other work. But gradually, the groups became more stable, the works more contained. The originators' ideas became more complex, more technical. Training was needed. If we remember that the most impressive techniques of the modern dance, those of Doris Humphrey and Martha Graham, originated in natural movement such as falling, sobbing, or hand waving, then the evolution of walking and running into the exacting idiom of a Twyla Tharp or a Trisha Brown should not come as a surprise.

Propelled by the energy of revolt, the downtown dancers pursued their individual experiments for a decade. By the mid-1970s they had settled into a pattern that looked more like the conventional dance culture that had provoked the revolt. The downtown scene was again a dance scene, with its own norms and attitudes, its major artists and identifiable styles. It had, by then, been boxed and labeled as postmodern dance—a designation that created convenient boundaries for scholarship and argument. At the same time, traditional modern dance as it had existed before the sixties was losing its individual qualities. With only a few surviving choreographer-centered mainstream companies, modern dance became a more generic system of training and a resource to be recycled and rerouted into the ballet repertory, where new blood is always needed, and into the eclectic pleasure domes of contemporary dance. Perhaps inevitably, the most original downtown dance innovators were also tapped for their novel additions to conventional repertories. These same downtown leaders and their companies have now entered an expanded mainstream of modern dance. The dragon, for the moment, has danced out of sight around the corner.

*

To the extent that the postmodernists had a common ideology, their aesthetic was captured in Sally Banes's *Terpsichore in Sneakers*.* The look was either formal, neutral, spiritedly engaged in compositional problems, and based in more or less ordinary movement behavior, or ritualistic and theatrical but likewise performatively neutral and nonvirtuosic. This tacitly acknowledged style changed severely over the next decade and a half, but not with a bang. Instead of a series of shocks and defiances with clear provocations (the Vietnam War, drugs, the sexual revolution), the eighties turned into the nineties by quiet, almost invisible degrees. Richard Nixon inspired rage; Ronald Reagan spread complacency. It could be argued that in the long run Reagan changed our culture more drastically than Nixon did, but his legacy was hidden under a snuggly blanket of goodwill and paternalism.

The signs of change were appearing in dance work by the mid-1970s. Economics was a major factor, in both positive and negative ways. Federal, state, and local support for the arts reached its peak in the mid-1970s, before the Reagan administration began dismantling and undermining the humanitarian gains won by the counterculture. Subsidies underwrote dance performance and dance touring across a spectrum of taste wide enough to encompass experimental artists. Audience numbers did affect a company's fundability, and box office appeal became important. The scruffiness got cleaned up, the jagged edges smoothed out. In some ways the experimental companies were better prepared to reach a wide audience than traditional groups. They were committed to flexibility, not wedded to proscenium spaces or rigid programming; they could dance in parks or

---

*Sally Banes, *Terpsichore in Sneakers: Post-Modern Dance* (Boston: Houghton Mifflin, 1980).

schools, they could include local performers, improvise, and adapt to the conditions they found. But little by little, the diversity, the unpredictability, the strangeness that was so much a part of experimental dance was tamed and toned down.

As companies structured themselves to go on the road, they had to become businesses, with sound management, publicity, fund-raisers. Dancers had to be paid, so they became employees, not collaborators. Schedules were made long in advance. Presenters wanted old dances that had won quotable reviews and/or steamy reputations. They wanted prestigious premieres of daring new creations; commitments to deliver these new dances had to be kept. So repertory returned, in the form of standard thirty-minute stage dances. The good ones, naturally, were reusable and were maintained as long as they could serve. No more two-hour rambling, intermittently interesting improvisations. No more video intermissions, five-minute monologues, instant replays. No more dancing motorcycles. No more dancing in the trees.

Commissions from ballet companies, many of them in Europe, also helped change the look of postmodern dance. The scale of opera house performing, the expectations and needs of the opera house audience, affected the way the dances were conceived. Choreographers were challenged to make their ideas more spacious, their movement more visibly organized, their performing styles more expansive and extroverted. With ballet dancers or highly skilled modern dancers as raw material, they could transcend their own limitations, augment their movement vocabularies, exploit bodies bred for display.

The generation of dancers they were nurturing in their own companies—the ex-Brown, ex-Gordon, and ex-Tharp dancers who are today's new choreographers—came out with a very different mystique. For them dancing is a goal in itself, lush, prodigal, not always rigorously structured. They aren't problem solvers or obsessive ritualizers. They are expressive, not neutral. They are concerned about issues, but they don't send us out into the streets to protest. They may attack our dearest values, point with derision or shame, but they wish to make us feel sorrier about what we've done to them than about what's wrong with our world. If there's any violence, they act it out, with increasingly dangerous dancing, excessive, invasive physicality, representations of disease and dissociation, not ambiguous metaphors.

*

Dance reflects its society. Thirty years ago its habitat was the counterculture, but today it's no longer on the fringe. How dancers represent themselves now, in fact, is probably determined more than ever by the world at large. Mass media—television and movies, mass magazines, big newspapers, home video, and the astronomically proliferating telecommunications networks—have created an almost irresistible and constantly shifting imagery of performance that weaves together politics, the arts, and everyday life. Dance, the most transient of the arts, responds to this imagery faster than any other art form and is absorbed into it with ease. When the counterculture opened up Americans' attitudes toward the nonverbal and the physical, dance experienced its first widespread popularity. This new awareness welcomed dance as one of many body-centered activities that, potentially, anyone could do and that would be good for your health. Jogging, aerobics, weight training, participatory sports, good nutrition, and dance swept the nation. Today it's impossible to turn on the TV without encountering beautiful young persons flaunting artistic pectorals, undraped cleavages, and sensuous, hard-won sweat. Whether they are selling fruit juice, trying to humanize a public figure, or upping the voltage on the same old soap opera, they pervade our consciousness and influence how we see other bodies on public display. Dancers today, like models or athletes, represent idealized physical types, and to some extent they fashion themselves in accord with popular taste. Even the thin, long-legged ballet dancer goes to the gym to develop her biceps. The relaxed stance and invisible muscularity cultivated by Yvonne Rainer would look freakish among today's tight, intense dancers.

The democratizing ideals which inspired the Judson and postmodern dancers to invent "people dances" and adopt the look of ordinary people on the street have, ironically, assisted in the gradual erosion of high art across American culture. Formalism and experimentation, seen as properties of an elitist and excessively serious art, declined in direct response to the populist imperative. Downtown work acquired narrative, character, verbal texts, pop music accompaniments—every aid to the spectator's comprehension or identification. Dancing itself became only one of many skills the performer could use to beguile and entertain. The eclectic works of the late eighties were spectacles of singing, acting, dancing, juggling, acrobatics, roller skating, trapeze work, and parody of all kinds.

When I reread the pieces in this collection, I am struck by how much we've lost in downtown dance—especially the sense of surprise and adventure, and of being permitted to take part in a challenge. I often did engage in dancerly activities, and in my teaching I stole from choreographers all the time, in search of strategies for helping people to see movement better. I regret the professionalization of the downtown dance scene and the sorting of dancers and nondancers into separate categories again. I miss dances with a concept, and dances that went on for a long time without changing, and dances where, if the choreographer's dog came onstage, it didn't do tricks. I'm growing resistant to dances that are trying to sell me something, and to choreography without dance steps, and to dance steps without choreography.

And yet, every once in a while, someone tries to do a seventies dance. In the past year I've seen, for instance, a piece where the dancers mostly rolled and galloped in the grass on a country estate and a women's ritual piece that ended with bare-breasted odalisques beatifically pouring milk on each other. This kind of work might have been liberating in the seventies. Now it seems naive, even regressive. Nothing reminds us more forcibly than dance of how much we change over time. It is the critic's paradoxical passion to want to capture the moment and simultaneously let it go, to be exquisitely sensitized to the present and even more eager to embrace the future. And that's another thing I learned from the postmodern dancers.

Photographs

1. Simone Forti and Peter Van Riper at the Kitchen.

2. Sara Rudner, 33 *Dances* at Cunningham Studio, Westbeth.

3. Trisha Brown's *Line Up* at Lepercq Space, Brooklyn Academy.

4. Valda Setterfield and David Gordon in *Wordsworth* at
541 Broadway loft.

5. Improvisation with Douglas Dunn (*far right*) at the
Custom House.

6. Twyla Tharp's *The Hodge Podge* at Brooklyn Academy
Opera House.

7. Senta Driver and Timothy Knowles in *Sudden Death*
at Connecticut College.

8. Kenneth King (*left*) and Dancers in *Dance S(p)ell* at Lepercq Space, Brooklyn Academy.

9. Merce Cunningham (*right*) and Company in *Inlets*
at City Center.

10. Jennifer Way, Tom Rawe and Rose Marie Wright in Twyla Tharp's
Baker's Dozen at Brooklyn Academy Opera House.

11. Bill T. Jones at the Kitchen.

12. Andrew De Groat's *Red Notes* at Lepercq Space,
Brooklyn Academy.

13. David Gordon with projection of David Vaughan in
An Audience with the Pope at 541 Broadway loft.

14. Dana Reitz and Malcolm Goldstein in *Between* 2 at
Washington Square Methodist Church.

15. Deborah Riley and Douglas Dunn in *Foot Rules* at Dance Theater Workshop.

16. Karole Armitage's *Do We Could* at the Kitchen.

17. David Gordon's *The Matter* (plus and minus) at
Camera Mart/Stage One.

18. Susan Rethorst's *Swell* at Cunningham Studio, Westbeth.

19. Wendy Perron in *A three-piece suite* at
Cunningham Studio, Westbeth.

20. Susan Eschelbach, Janna Jensen and Charles Moulton
in *Thought Movement Motor* at the Kitchen.

21. Merce Cunningham's *Sounddance* at City Center.

22. John Carrafa, Raymond Kurshals and Tom Rawe in
Twyla Tharp's *The Fugue* at Winter Garden Theater.

23. Laura Dean's Music at Brooklyn Academy Opera House.

24. Deborah Hay in *Leaving the House* at Dance Theater Workshop.

25. Dana Reitz's *Double Scores* at Battery Park Landfill.

26. Charles Moulton and Barbara Allen in *Motor Fantasy*
at Battery Park Landfill.

27. Andrew De Groat (right) and Dancers in *Red Notes/Get Wreck*
at Lincoln Center Plaza.

28. Kenneth Rinker's *Cantata No. 84* at Dance Theater Workshop.

29. Joffrey Ballet in Laura Dean's *Night* at City Center.

30. Blondell Cummings in *The Ladies and Me* at
Black Theater Alliance.

31. Marta Renzi and Cathy Zimmerman in *What Do You Do, Dear?*
at the Kitchen.

32. Yoshiko Chuma's *Champing at the Bit* at St. Mark's
Church parish hall.

33. Simone Forti and Peter Van Riper in *Jackdaw Songs*
at the Performing Garage.

34. Elisa Monte in Cliff Keuter's *Woodblocks* at The Space
in City Center.

35. Twyla Tharp's *The Catherine Wheel* at Winter Garden Theater.

36. Bebe Miller (*left*) and Erin Thompson in *Jammin'*
at Dance Theater Workshop.

37. Trisha Brown and Fujiko Nakaya's *Opal Loop/Cloud Installation #72503*
at Brooklyn Academy Opera House.

38. Lucinda Childs in *Relative Calm* at Brooklyn Academy
Opera House.

Modern Depends on *Where You Start From*

William Dunas: *Solo Dance*, Styrian Autumn Festival
Schauspielhaus Studio, Graz, Austria
Soho Weekly News, 28 October 1976

Word got around before the start of the Styrian Autumn Festival that the London Contemporary Dance Theater, which opened two weeks of "New Dance" from Germany, Holland, England, and the United States here in Graz, represents the latest thing in modern dance.

It's not that Europeans here are credulous—far from it. An exceptionally well-informed and loyal group of balletomanes are commuting two and a half hours each way from Vienna to follow the festival, but their exposure to modern dance has been limited to a few American touring companies. Horst Koegler, the German critic, summed up modern dance on this side of the ocean by saying: "The modern dance is dead. Long live the international style." In Graz, they were ready to believe it, but they may change their minds.

London Contemporary looked like a company without a center. Grounded in the Martha Graham technique, it isn't a direct Graham subsidiary. While the movement style retains some Graham angularity, it's grown smoother, gestural, diffuse. The choreography offers serious content cloaked in mod devices like "mixed media" and pseudo jazz.

Immediately after the second of London Contemporary's tepid programs, William Dunas premiered his *Solo Dance*, and what a contrast. Dunas may be the most puzzling of all seven American choreographers slated to appear here, but in many ways he exemplifies the concerns of all of them.

In an open space, Dunas, tall, curly haired, cherubic faced, and dressed in a tracksuit and white dance shoes, was moving quietly, almost privately, through a chain of steps that looked just enough like ballet steps to seem unfinished. A tape-recorded voice was reading a fragmentary narrative over some Bach played by unaccompanied violin. Perhaps nothing could have denied more conclusively the athletic display and macho posturing of Robert North's *Troy Game*, which the London Contemporary dancers had just performed.

Dunas limits his material severely, refuses to do tricks for the audience. Taking mostly circular or diagonal routes through the space, he runs or hops with baby steps, skimming the floor as if he didn't want to make positive contact with it. He often stands still, making strange, flat gestures with his hands, addresses the audience with arms open in ballet positions and legs incongruously turned in. He slides his feet out to the side in a pale reflection of a dancer's warm-up exercise, emphasizing not the stretching of his legs but the balletic first and fourth positions to which they return. His fingers waggle at random, his body isn't especially careful about the proper alignment. He doesn't seem to be demanding much of himself, except one thing: he keeps on dancing, allowing himself only momentary rests.

When you look at Dunas, you think you've wandered into the room too early—maybe he's just fooling around trying out things, or warming up for something he'll do later. But this is intentional. He's presenting himself as imperfect, deliberately downplayed; he's resisting the overdramatized, overchoreographed seductiveness to which his material leads all too often.

His taped narration—cryptic proverbs, adventure stories and melodrama, sentimental poetry, all excerpts from Dunas dances over the past few years—suggests some great American romantic fallacy to which we all subscribe even if in secret. But instead of trying to match that myth, Dunas makes himself plain, understated. He doesn't save his best side for the audience. He gets sweaty, breathes hard.

He goes on, doggedly, for almost an hour, getting tired and showing it but not getting any more perfect or any more exciting. Near the end, the lights get brighter. He pushes a little harder, becomes a little more animated, jumps a few times, unspectacularly. Then the tape ends and the dance ends and he hasn't done a single pirouette.

I found his performance beautiful and courageous. In spite of a sudden flood of latecomers walking right through his dance to sit down—there had been a scheduling mix-up and a failure of communications, and Dunas hadn't been told—he kept going, refused to lose his concentration or try to win them over.

Dunas, in the sparseness of his material and the discipline he imposes on himself, belongs to a long line of American dance avant-gardists who have always wanted to provide an antidote to the excesses of their time, to counter the dance's decadence, its exploitation of the audience. For me, *Solo Dance* became a reassuring metaphor. No matter how flamboyant and mindless other people's dance may be, Dunas is saying the dance itself still exists as a pure and useful possibility.

Dancing through the Language Barrier

Trisha Brown and Company, Styrian Autumn Festival
Open House, Graz, Austria
ORF Austrian Radio, 21 October 1976

Trisha Brown's image of the dancing figure is different: a woman, not conventionally pretty, neither thin nor fat, and without the taut muscle tone, the extra readiness of most other dancers. The Trisha Brown dancer, particularly Trisha Brown herself, is most of all *present*; she puts herself before you without comment and does what she does. When you first begin to look at what she does—moves rather than movements, separate shiftings of limbs or larger segments of the body into new shapes or positions, one after another in a fluid but mostly unaccented chain of events—it's a little like living where they speak a language you don't know. Out of the stream of German conversation around me I can identify only a few words, and even they are without the rationalizing structure called grammar. But I know the structure is there. And I listen to other things—to the rhythm and formation of the words, the modulation and blendings of voices, the different ways people use the same language. And I understand a lot—quite a lot.

Brown's *Locus*, the second of three dances shown last night at the Open House, eludes detection as a rational plan with specific meanings, although Brown has explained it somewhere and proved it is just that. But if you can't quite see the multiplicity of choices available to the dancers—they can move within imaginary cubes around themselves, cubes of different sizes, and can, in part of the dance, choose to do one of several designated portions of the movement sequence—still you can look at *Locus* for the peripheral information. During the part of the dance that's in unison you can enjoy the phrasing, almost hear the way the movements group themselves, because there's no music to make your eyes lazy or distract your attention. You can take pleasure in the organizing of the stage space into simple patterns and their subsequent disintegration and then the reforming of new patterns. At other times, you can get into the ebb and flow of energy through these loose bodies as they glide from arm gesture to shoulder swivel to displacement of the hip and back into alignment again.

Accumulation and *Group Primary Accumulation* are much easier to translate because the idea is simpler and more repetitive. The phrase accumulates, as one gesture at a time is added to what has been established. When Brown does it as a solo, the additions are sometimes simultaneous with parts of the existing phrase, the connections between gestures can smooth and round off the shapes so they're no longer distinct in themselves. But in the *Group Primary* version, with four women lying on the floor sideways to the audience, each gesture keeps its original shape clearly and enters the sequence consecutively. Since the phrase in this dance contains about forty accumulated small patterns, we get to see each one so many times that we begin to learn the sequence too. And when two stage managers come out and bodily pick up the dancers and move them into other positions—depositing them on their stomachs, sitting them in chairs—we mentally go on with the dance for them until they're settled and able to move their limbs again.

Getting Grander—Minimally

Laura Dean: *Dance*, Styrian Autumn Festival
Schauspielhaus, Graz, Austria
Soho Weekly News, 4 November 1976

Laura Dean's new forty-minute dance, given for the first time here at the Styrian Autumn Festival, has a basic rhythmic pulse, announced in parade-ground shouts at the beginning by the dancers and maintained throughout the piece. The work is called *Dance*, and Laura Dean's idea of dance is a continual series of changing patterns fed by that one driving energy.

Dean began as a minimal choreographer, using walking or hopping and perhaps a single circular or linear floor pattern in each dance. Now her work is more varied, but she's kept the simple, straight line of the body and the direct performer-to-audience presentation that distinguished her work from the start. The dancers support the fast, high-energy flow of their foot patterns by keeping the center of the body stable and contained. They look a lot like folk dancers—though perhaps not having as much fun—and yet there's a stagey gloss to their white satin, sequined costumes, dramatically lit against a black background. The stage atmosphere makes the audience expect unusual events to happen, and instead of the dance droning on at the same level, each small shift in step or tempo or position becomes unusually important.

As the dance begins, the four women and two men dancers are spaced evenly around the stage. After the tempo is established, two musicians reinforce it by playing an eight-count chord sequence on Autoharps. First the dancers quickstep around in a circle, coming down harder into the floor on the first beat of the measure. At smaller and smaller intervals, they change directions and close up the size of the circle, then expand it again as they lengthen the interval between direction changes.

This kind of simple variation forms the basis of the whole dance. There's a section of spinning—all the dancers spinning together, then one and two at a time, tracing clear and repetitive floor patterns. In another section, they look like clog dancers: facing the audience they bob up and down, swinging the legs loosely from the knee, on the rebound from the thrust of the downbeat. With a catch-step to the side, they zigzag and crisscross along diagonal grids. In another pattern they alternate spinning into new positions with little duets in which they clasp a partner's shoulders, huddle together facing each other, and shuffle their feet quickly forward and back.

Always they keep the upper body quiet, reverberating to the vigorous action of the legs, with the arms swinging from the shoulders, hands flinging out to the side or behind, like tap dancers doing a time step. The music changes key and accelerates, and suddenly American hillbilly music and dancing comes to mind, even though the steps are the same as before.

Just when you begin to think there's nothing but legs in this dance, the music changes sharply. In a stunning moment, the dancers reverse roles with the musicians. Instead of the whanging chords made by scraping the hands across the Autoharp strings, the sound becomes a delicate, elfin pizzicato. Now it's the dancers who are doing grand, sweeping chordal gestures, with their arms and upper bodies. The beat is the same as before, but they keep the pulse going with small, gentle inner bounces. The change is so enormous you feel as if the world has flipped over.

It doesn't last long. The musical texture gets thinner and thinner, till it's no more than a single fast-plucked note, and the dancers are standing in place making big spiral gestures. Abruptly the Autoharps are silent, and the dancers begin to sing in the same rhythm. It's a six-part song—each one has his or her own theme—and it has no words except the word "dance." And when all the dancers come to the word "dance" at the same time, the dance is over.

Gestures in Graz

Douglas Dunn: *Early and Late*, Styrian Autumn Festival
Open House, Graz, Austria
Soho Weekly News, 18 November 1976

Even if I hadn't known that Douglas Dunn created *Early and Late* after he arrived in Graz and decided he couldn't perform *Gestures in Red* in the space assigned to him by the Styrian Autumn Festival, I would have known he was dancing about a space he distrusted. Although Dunn's movement seems cool, not overtly expressive, he puts his thoughts and attitudes right on the surface. To me he's incredibly honest, even exposed, about how he feels when he's dancing.

To begin *Early and Late*, he mounted the stage from the audience, where he'd been sitting, and announced his change in program, first in English, then in German. Then he started working in the space, which he'd left bare, with a few leftover appurtenances from the previous day's performance by the German minimal artist Klaus Rinke. Bouncing around on elastic legs, Dunn eyed the space, made a long series of false starts, with the kind of short-of-the-mark testing moves a prizefighter makes, warming up. He flung himself through the space in a series of sprawling jumps. Some stagehands brought in two large flats which they set at right angles, and Dunn took a series of positions determined by this corner. He once did a long, meditative series of such poses, called *Corner Dance*. But here his transitions were restless, sometimes he jerked himself upright or sprang away from the corner as if he'd like to be free of its confines.

Suddenly he pushed one flat over to make a satisfying bang, then hopped up on it after some tentative approaches. On the makeshift platform he did do a few excerpts from *Gestures in Red*: a dance where he rotated his arms from the shoulders, changing direction and coordination without breaking his rhythm; a dance where he shook one hand very fast and gradually allowed its vibration to spread to his whole body; a dance where he rested his forearms on his thighs until they slid off, threatening to pull him off balance.

Later, arriving downstage in a corner, he found some stairs and a door in a wall. There he did a set of variations on whether to continue or make his escape. He'd lunge determinedly at the stairs, panic, whirl down them again, put a hand out the door, reconsider—till he was weaving and feinting in an ecstasy of indecision. When it seemed he might never be able to unwind himself, he called for a screen to be lowered, and a film began of Dunn standing in front of a stationary camera—caught again in an uncomfortable place—having to keep busy with nowhere to go. Sections of the film were intercut with sections of Dunn dancing live; Dunn emerging from a trap in the floor, attached by a rope to the depths below; Dunn posing à la Klaus Rinke—and then dancing—with a piece of wood for a partner.

He made a series of dramatic exits, only to appear again. And finally he began a big, leggy stamping dance, the first one of the night when he didn't seem to be impeded by anything, either the surroundings or any restrictions of his own devising. The stagehands removed the last of Klaus Rinke's props. And then, with no fanfare at all, the dance was over.

Like Merce Cunningham, with whom he danced for several years, Dunn is a wonderful and serious clown and a superbly daring performer. And like Cunningham, he sees his work as an immediate and evolving process, not a job of creating fixed, repeatable stage works. *Early and Late* may never be seen again, since Dunn is working with a group now and doesn't plan any more solo performances after his current European tour. His generosity in making and showing it for Graz is just one aspect of his importance now as one of America's finest young choreographers.

How to Build a Cloud

Robert Wilson: *Einstein on the Beach*
Metropolitan Opera House, New York
Soho Weekly News, 2 December 1976

Robert Wilson's works aren't revolutionary so much as incongruous. Nobody but Wilson has attempted to present minimal art on such an immense scale. Nobody has tackled the mysteries and the dilemmas of mankind more dispassionately, or offered grandiose ideas more modestly. Or perhaps I mean his ideas are modest and his style grandiose.

Einstein on the Beach is an extended meditation on modern life. It slips from one idea to another without necessarily logical connections. It fantasizes, speculates, lingers on some thoughts, reformulates others, follows inspiration till it becomes image. Eventually, it confronts the unthinkable, and then finds a way to go on. For me, the piece was wonderful in all its parts; what I needed was a clearer sense of whose meditation it was, whose mind, because lacking that, the work drifts aloft, unaccountable to either morals or aesthetics. Perhaps the imaginer is Einstein himself, a character who sometimes sits on the edge of the stage and plays the violin. But if so, he represents the arrogant compulsion of "pure" science to pursue ideas to a conclusion regardless of what horrors its discoveries might bring upon the world.

Wilson draws together all the themes of the reverie—science, history, technology, human idealism and fallibility—into the final scene of apocalypse. Up to there, I'm with him. But he doesn't convince me we're going to crawl out of the ruins and be saved by love alone. What about the megalomaniacs with their fingers on the trigger, what about the industrialists and the politicians and the desperate, exploited masses? It wasn't any kindly old dreamer who unleashed that lethal cloud over the globe last week, and it wasn't thanks to him either that, this time, we were spared a radioactive rainstorm.

Einstein seems to me a more varied and interesting piece than any previous Wilson epic I've seen. For one thing, he's chosen his material more rigorously. There may be more objects and people in a scene, but they're not so disparate as before, and they aren't all changing at once. Sometimes he reduces the multiplicity of detail to one evolving image, which lasts so long it acquires tremendous metaphorical power.

His symbols—almost everything in the piece is a symbol of something else—are chosen for their adaptability to many contexts. For instance, hand gestures come in different shapes, all interlinked, and have the small, repetitive, nonproductive quality of what passes for work in the postindustrial society. People stroke tables in front of them as if they were playing the piano or working the console of a huge, delicate machine. People hold up different numbers of fingers or mime doing their nails or washing their hands. But the hand washing takes place at a trial, and the nail filing is the activity of two stenographers. And later, when Lucinda Childs twitches her fingers while delivering a monologue, the business world expands to the counting-out world of technology, the nervous Captain Queeg world of tenuous power.

As in his other works, Wilson manipulates his themes with ingenuity and brilliant stagecraft. To me the most beautiful scene was the one in which the back end of an old-fashioned train recedes imperceptibly against a moonlit sky. Even in this sleeping nowhere, Wilson poses the possibility of evil. A man and a woman come out and stand on the back platform of the train, and after a long, tranquil time in which they embrace, then move away from each other in slow motion, they reenter the car. As they sit facing each other the woman slowly draws a gun and points it at the man. At the same time, a round, ugly black object with lights on it, something like one of those crude bombs in the comic strips, comes down and covers the moon.

Wilson doesn't care so much about the story of a killing; he wants to show, in two ways, the disturbance of a long-established order of things. He does the same thing in the trial scene, where a group of characters repeat their various gestures and sounds but the droning continuum is broken by shouts, words, big motions of falling or changing position. Similarly, Andy De Groat's dancers set up a fairly constant flow of running, jumping, spinning through a big open space, and Sheryl Sutton intrudes on their harmonious universe with a rhythmically eccentric, multidirectional dance.

The pacing of *Einstein on the Beach* was constantly interesting to me. Each scene developed or progressed in a different fashion, some accumulating effects and building intensity to a climax, some moving steadily until one element of change caused a fading away, some keeping a single tonality with interruptions. Wilson may have been influenced in this new shading of dynamics by the marvelous minimal score of Philip Glass. Without resorting to the traditional heartrending devices of romanticism, Glass creates an emotionally rich background of shifting rhythms and sonorities with wind instruments, voices, organ, and solo violin. In his preoccupation with structure, his controlled use of small units of sound and gradually changing textures, Glass couldn't be more appropriate for Wilson. But he adds a certain flexibility and feeling-tone that Wilson hasn't found up to now.

The music isn't just a side dish to the main-course stage event either; it's totally integrated. As in other Wilson works, there's no dialogue; words are used almost musically, to punctuate or thicken the texture of the scene. Glass's music—either wordless or made of syllables or numbers to differentiate tones—is sung by an exceptionally well-trained chorus of about twelve men and women who double as actors and dancers.

And for the first time in a Wilson piece, I find myself remembering individual performances. Lucinda Childs choreographed her own dance on the diagonal in the first scene, a nonstop hesitating run back and forth on three succeeding paths, in which she seemed to be exhorting or haranguing a crowd and not getting an answer, like a sideshow barker or someone demonstrating a potato peeler in a department store. In the last scene Sheryl Sutton danced with two flashlights, like the person who brings the airplane into the terminal, as the spaceship Earth was preparing to extinguish itself. And finally, there was Wilson himself, taking over the flashlights from Sutton and dancing with cyclonic violence, as though his frenzy could bring the whole monstrous thing under control. Or perhaps his mad intelligence was letting the havoc out of its cage.

Dancing the Idea

Kenneth King: RAdeoA.C.tiv(ID)ty
Dance Theater Workshop, New York
Soho Weekly News, 9 December 1976

Kenneth King is enough like Robert Wilson—and enough unlike—to make his new dance, RAdeoA.C.tiv(ID)ty, doubly interesting in the season of Einstein on the Beach. Both men are dreamers who believe in the descriptive possibilities of manipulated language, and in the interconnections among twentieth-century technological artifacts. Both of them conceive of their work as a stage where many theater disciplines can come together, an unformed universe that shapes itself according to each new combination of creative circumstances.

But where Wilson's work comes out as a sort of painting in motion, King's is a dialectical dance. Wilson likes to control his ideas, to put them into forms where their meanings can crystallize and be elaborated on. King gives his ideas their head, lets them flow and bubble and spill away. Like Wilson, he has a delicate sense of the theater, but his images slip out of your consciousness almost immediately. I think of Wilson as a shy man wearing a bold expression, King as an extrovert who speaks in eloquent whispers.

RAdeoA.C.tiv(ID)ty is really several different plays or dances going on at once. Occasionally these threads twist into one another for a while, and then they separate again. There's the dancer's dance, a steady, quiet flow of movement performed by King and Carter Frank, Karen Levey, and Jim Self. Their vocabulary is limited but cumulative. After a long slow opening series of nonstop hand and arm gestures by Carter Frank, in which she stays in the same place but changes her position, other dancers enter and leave, crossing the space with the same concentration on the clarity of their bodies' shapes. A hand is extended from the wings, and Frank uses it to support herself in a continuous series of off-balance arabesques and relevés. Later King comes out and stands with her, sometimes supporting her as she leans and stretches away, sometimes shadowing her spacious arm movements and foot-floor designs.

This material—the self-directed gestures from a firm stance, the casual crossings, the adventures off their center of gravity, and the almost-balletic feet and port de bras—forms the basis for the dancers' activity. They organize it into brief movement games, returning often but unpredictably to the one where they shadow someone else's movement. I can't tell if the dance is improvised, but it has a look of spontaneity, as if the dancers are paying as much attention to each other as the audience is paying to them.

The disembodied hand that supports Frank is one of a series of happenings that look surrealistic when they first occur and later turn out to have been essential ingredients in the "plot" or the movement event. Another is a pair of gloves that appear on Carter Frank's hands when she withdraws them from under a cloth on the floor. Frank backs away from the cloth, and you see that there's a thin cord attached to each finger of the gloves. With Jim Self attending her, she seems some kind of goddess or witch-figure as she leans back, pulling on the mysterious strings, forecasting the slow tippings and leanings people will do later.

During most of the dance, two actors, Tom Cayler and Herndon Ely, appear in standard movie/television poses, costumes, and situations—he wears a trench coat, slouch hat, and shades; she has long tarty blond hair and a minidress; they talk across a dinner table, conversationally, as if, what? He's picked her up and they were trying to get acquainted? They've known each other for ages and have nothing more to say? Except their words are language games, extended puns and stutterings and chains of alliterative nonsense that fall into aphorism as if by chance.

The dancers pick up on this talk occasionally, echoing words, making new thought-chains of their own. With no apparent preparation except you remember that Herndon Ely first appeared inside a prop television set, the actors are dramatically throwing King a $32,000 question. It's something moronic about someone who didn't want our national bird to be the bald eagle. King answers correctly, reading off a piece of paper he received at the beginning of the dance from a sinister character he discovered behind a curtain.

I don't remember how it all comes out, except that the famous person's idea for the national bird was the turkey, and King tops it, suggesting the parrot. What I do remember is what interesting music the words made, the various textures of sound that the dancers and actors produced, some of the messages that popped up. "Besides, if it's really information, there is no content."

And also the way King turned the familiar open space of American Theater Lab into a theater of many and evolving spaces by pulling aside curtains and scrims to reveal new dramas and create new openings through which people could appear and disappear. *RAdeoA.C.tiv(ID)ty* was subtitled *Prologue/ Part I*, and I hope it will be back soon with whatever parts it's missing.

And Now the Weather Report

Simone Forti and Peter Van Riper
The Kitchen, New York

David Woodberry and Richard Peck
112 Greene Street Gallery, New York

Soho Weekly News, 30 December 1976

In the same weekend that David Woodberry and Simone Forti gave their concerts, a friend in Texas wrote that her editor advised her, "Readers these days are so conditioned to cuts and jumps in movies, that writers can insert cutlines when they get stuck with transitions," and someone else reported that the new management of a New York radio station has admonished disc jockeys not to play the same kind of record twice in a row.

Woodberry and Forti seemed, if momentarily, disabled by the short attention span and the undeveloped thought. Both of them, collaborating in part with solo musicians, threw out a few movement ideas that they didn't pursue and were done in less time than a TV program. I wondered why all this pecking and scratching at ideas—is dance now so conceptual that all you have to do is suggest a topic to the audience and let them do the rest mentally? Or if the ideas are too slim to do anything with, what kind of audience would want them?

Puzzling. Because both Forti and Woodberry are dancers who have taken a lot of time to get in touch with their bodies—Woodberry does slow, inner-focused centering exercises, shoulder stands, loosening-up-the-joints rotations as the audience is coming in—when they begin to move, you settle down and get ready for a nice thorough exploration of some aspect of movement. These dancers are so personal, they would seem to have an inexhaustible curiosity about the slightest thing their bodies can do.

For his first dance, David Woodberry put on a down jacket and started himself going by swinging his arms back and forth, with a pleasant swish of nylon against nylon. He tumbled into slow somersaults and falls, the jacket cushioning his impact, and then ran through the space a few times, zigzagging among the imitation Greek pillars that stood down the center of the room. He climbed one of the pillars, fiddled with a wire that distracted him by the ceiling, dropped to the floor again.

In a second part of the dance, which he announced as "How to Stand Up," he pushed himself up from the floor, tilted, lunged, rolled over in various ways, then did a series of gestures borrowed from sports umpires and movie tough guys. Woodberry is an interesting mixture—typical perhaps of a new breed of male dancer. He has the athlete's particular sinewy grace and the sensuality of a mystic. In his contact improvisation with Danny Lepkoff, these two forces were constantly in play.

Once the men established a mutual flow of energy, they moved through a very active and changeable sequence in which not only their roles were always reversing—from carrier to carried, from thrower to catcher—but their relationship kept turning into its opposite. They would drag or pull each other, sometimes quite roughly, make motions of attack and defense, then suddenly they'd be embracing. Not only were the polarities and the quickness of the sudden reversals surprising, but the dancers' resilience and adaptability, their readiness to fend off or grasp, to fall softly or bear the other's weight, was beautiful to watch.

Richard Peck accompanied the closing study, *Improvisation to Recognition of 4 Vignettes*. They really were vignettes, none lasting more than a few minutes. First Peck played the clarinet while Woodberry swung his arms in horizontal arcs. Peck played the sax while Woodberry held two six-foot long fluorescent light bulbs, changing their angle and position very carefully so they wouldn't hit anything and break. While Peck beat a rhythm on what looked like a circular-saw blade, Woodberry and Lepkoff went outside and held up two sparklers against the window of the gallery. Then the dancers came in and strolled self-consciously around the space singing "Swing Low, Sweet Chariot," very hesitantly, as if they'd never done it before, while Peck tried to improvise around them on his sax.

Peck's saxophone and electric piano solos were musicianly and, I thought, far better worked out than anything Woodberry showed that night.

Simone Forti seemed to be a sort of adjunct to Peter Van Riper's instrumental concert at the Kitchen, so perhaps I shouldn't have expected to see a lot of movement. She did one solo sequence, rolling lengthwise into the space, then, after a few long, crouching poses, crawled a few steps and collapsed into soft rolling falls. She exited hitching along on her stomach, arms and legs splayed out to the side, like a crab. Forti has the softest, most pliable body imaginable, but unlike Woodberry she doesn't look elastic. When she falls, she doesn't bounce back, she melts into the floor, sensing and enjoying the contact.

Forti and Van Riper had an amusing dialogue, she on a trombone and he on a soprano sax and later a Rube Goldberg contraption made of plumbing pipes. Sometimes they twittered and honked at each other, sometimes Forti just moaned or blatted like a disconsolate child while Van Riper played a thumb piano with a lovely mellow tone and a piece for several little containers with chimes inside them. His music was interesting and restful at the same time.

Merce in America

Merce Cunningham: *Dance in America*
Soho Weekly News, 6 January 1977

Not that we haven't seen some dance on the small tube, and not, god knows, that I wouldn't like to see lots more work done to find ways of conveying some essence of dance through the living-room medium. But TV dance so far has been pretty disappointing, mainly because so much money has been spent on it and, proportionately, so little of it has really grappled with the limitations—and possibilities—of television.

The same can be said of film, but film is in many ways a more expensive and unwieldy process than television. I would expect video dance to be more experimental—it's more portable, more adaptable, less permanent. But up to now most video dance has used the same two approaches as film dance. You either shoot the dance straight-on as a record of a stage performance, or you try to make something "artistic" in cinematic terms.

The arted-up dance, with close-ups, camera dissolves, dramatic cuts from one action to another, and reorientation of the camera eye to many different focal points, is invariably frustrating to me because it destroys the flow of the dance through space; and the recorded performance, while it has historical value if it's well done, invites comparison to the far more potent original.

PBS's heavily subsidized *Dance in America* series is now in its second year, but the Merce Cunningham program, to be shown here this week and I hope many more times, is the first one to use television as a medium that can give us a completely fulfilled, satisfying dance experience. No apologies, no wishing the performance were live or the screen were bigger. This is not a compromise in either direction—neither a dance made small for TV, nor a TV machinery kept reined in for the benefit of the dance. I suspect the inspired camera work and staging came more from Cunningham himself and his associate, Charles Atlas, than from Merrill Brockway, overall producer of *Dance in America*, who is credited with directing the Cunningham telecast. Brockway's ideas about televising dance have ranged from the parochial and correct handling of Martha Graham to the disastrous conversion of *Billy the Kid* into a movie Western, complete with narration and an almost total erasure of the ballet's innovative style.

What struck me first about the Cunningham show was its absolute trust in the dance. There were no personalities being interviewed, no condescending explanations of what the dance was about to show you, no elaborate visual aids, film clips, sketches, romantic views of rehearsal rooms. It was all dance, from beginning to end, with Cunningham talking diffidently but without affectation for maybe four minutes about his choreography, sometimes against a background of dancing, sometimes off camera.

Of course, it's easier for the Cunningham company to bring this off than most other dancers. They specialize in evening-long Events of nonstop dancing, and although Cunningham's works individually are giants in the American repertory, his company can sustain your attention by just dancing the steps of these ballets in fragmented, overlapping, multidirectional, random sequences. The telecast was very much like an Event, except that material from only one dance at a time was shown, and the activity overall was much less dense, more selective. In all, nine dances were used, including all of Cunningham's feral *Solo 1973*, a substantial chunk of *RainForest*, and a new work choreographed for the occasion, *Video Triangle*. The dances didn't look as they do on the stage or in an open space, but they didn't look like toy versions of themselves either.

Cunningham and Atlas made several brilliantly nonliteral decisions about the video medium. It's not, for instance, a substitute for the eyes of an audience person. The transitions between dances occurred within the camera's space—someone would walk out of the frame and someone else would enter, or the camera would follow someone's gaze and find a new activity going on, or a prop would be carried into the frame, fill the frame, and then be carried out, leaving a new set of dancers behind it. This didn't have the effect of opening up the space, which really can't be done in the small TV universe, but it created a variable energy texture over a continuous time span. What an audience might see peripherally their camera sometimes gave up, letting us retain the image if we could, or returning to it long after we'd forgotten it. This also had a time-altering effect.

Instead of being hampered by the small size of the field, the directors worked with gradations of scale. I've never seen such subtle distinctions made among the subjects in the video field. I know other TV directors have used deep studio spaces and other devices to create the illusion of distance, but Cunningham didn't seem to want to create an illusion. He just diversified whatever he could encompass.

Almost all the group work was done in "layers" of floor depth—not to make some dancers look further away but to make them different sizes, to make a picture with variety rather than one that's crammed with too many things that are too big for it. In the largest, most active ensemble, a section from Sounddance, the camera jumped from one part of the group to another, but I didn't resent it as I usually do. Now I think that was because the camera took on the energy of the dance, a dance about scattering and haste and temporary collecting of individuals. Sudden close-ups in RainForest were like the camera adopting Cunningham's own wariness, his listening glances.

And finally, the camera had become so much another dancer that its tricks too were choreographed. In Video Triangle, it played the game of switching backgrounds, red, blue, green, color-coded to the jumpsuits of three pairs of dancers. Each time the color changed, the dance shifted impossibly too; the dancers were in different places from where they'd been a split second before. It's a dance you could only see on video.

Throughout the first part of the program John Cage's prepared piano score of toneless plunks and dry rattles and much silence gave the dancing a look of quiet seriousness; David Tudor's metallic buzz and resonant whistles built up the intensity later on. As if that weren't enough, Cunningham even dared to offer us some humor, the hilarious Martha Graham parody from Antic Meet. When was the last time a dancer on TV made you laugh—intentionally?

Roz Newman said . . .
Unpublished notes, 14 February 1977

Roz Newman said she'd been disappointed with Summerspace—that it was so much less than in her imagination or her memory she'd hoped it would be. I said how much I appreciated its spareness, that I liked not having everything going like sixty all the time, that a lot of modern dance I see now just tires me out. She said it came from Merce—that idea that you could just keep adding more onto something. She said she'd ruined a dance just the other day by putting more and more in it, trying to "fix" it, until the original idea was gone.

We talked about Merce making so many choices possible—except the choice of selecting, of judging your own output to see that some of it is better than the rest of it, more worth paying attention to. She said how interesting it was to her that Merce had grown up in a world before TV and space travel, a world she couldn't possibly imagine. I said I'd often been bothered that the newer generations are so much less innovative when their world is so much less structured and more mind-provoking—but I realized that to them, that's ordinary. Merce worked in a time of transition and upheaval, so maybe it was *easier* for him to conceive of really revolutionary forms.

Variations for an Invisible Theme

Sara Rudner: 33 Dances
Cunningham Studio, New York
Soho Weekly News, 24 February 1977

Sara Rudner's new hour-long solo, 33 *Dances*, shown at the Cunningham Studio last week, was in some ways a dance of denial—of Rudner conscious of Rudner, keeping Rudner under close scrutiny and control, Rudner working intently on Rudner's material and not allowing herself to pull out all the stops. Rudner can be one of our most high-powered performers, but in this work she curbed her smile, channeled and shaped her energy, almost as if she were another dancer. I felt I'd seldom seen a choreographer working with herself so objectively. The dance was less spectacular, less spontaneous than the extended solo she did last year, *Some "Yes" and More*, but to me it was very wonderful.

There seemed to be only a limited number of movement themes in 33 *Dances*. Not that there wasn't a lot of movement, but the dance included much that I'm beginning to think of as Rudner's basic idiom—fast chaîné turns with far-flung arms; confident, turned-out striding steps and leg gestures; a loosely articulate torso and a mobile head; important pliés and relevés that depend on a strong foot and an amiability about changing her relationship to the floor. These I now take for granted in a Rudner dance, as part of the raw material she works with. They can be brought to the fore, with adjustments of speed and shape, to become the main subject matter of a sequence, or they can be slid in as links between other things, or repeated plainly, as a way of marking time without losing the audience's interest.

Rudner's thirty-three dances were more like little études. She usually started with a simple gestural or propulsive idea and explored it in a number of ways before introducing another motif. What's extraordinary about this is that outlines and sequences from the early studies keep showing up again in later ones that begin with altogether different impulses. Eventually the dance begins to feel like a whole set of embellished tracings of different parts of a single picture that we never get to see. Instead of a theme and variations, it might be called variations for a theme.

Dynamically, the dance seemed to follow a curve, beginning in a quiet, almost contemplative mood, becoming very intense, and then pulling its energy down right at the end. But within this overall progression, it dipped and escalated through every imaginable kind of power.

Rudner likes to play off opposites against each other. One is the disparity between an inward, nonspecific focus and an outward, alert riveting of her attention. We see it in the first dance as she oscillates gently inside her body, feeling a flow, nothing more, then suddenly straightens and looks to the side as if an alien noise had surprised her.

These two constellations of actions are as clear and specific in this elementary form as they are later when she stands twisting her head around to glance sharply at different points in the room, then lets her head go and begins shaking her body violently. Or when, after a sequence of wild head shakes and body undulations, she lies on her back, looking over one shoulder straight into the audience, and carefully lifts her spine in a rippling motion, pelvis to neck and down again. These fixed focuses and calculated displacements of the body sometimes made me uncomfortable. Rudner can be provocative when she pushes herself at you, unsettling when she breaks into what you think of as her easy natural flow to insist on something you've been passing over as a mere transition. Once she looked straight at several people in the audience—I was the first—and made direct, personal contact. The effect was so electrifying that I almost spoke to her right there.

Other times her clarity of gesture is immensely satisfying. She makes a whole scene crystallize just by folding her arms and a beat later starting to push herself backward by pivoting one foot, then the other. Instantly I saw a skating pond. In another sequence, she began in archaic profile—legs going to one side, torso twisted toward us—slowly opened and lifted her arms above her head, hands drooping down, like some maiden in a Nijinsky dance, and, with the hips swinging toward us and the legs turning in, continued to sweep both arms down and curve them around to one side of her chest. Something about the asymmetricality of this, and the gravity with which Rudner performed it the first time, made it stick in my mind. Later she did the whole thing faster, repeated it frenetically, smoothed shadowy segments of it into other movements.

Some of the gestures didn't seem to be made up at all but to evolve by chance. One time, getting up from the floor, she absentmindedly brushed off her clothes. Before we'd had time to decide whether that was intentional, she transformed it into a dance gesture—patting her body all over, the pats spilling down into her feet, where they became little rocking steps, and collecting back in her hands to become a slapping, clapping rhythmic dance.

There were little dances about sudden switches of the whole body tonus, when she would be gyrating almost out of control, then darting across the floor, then sagging, then tensely staring. And there were dances all about one thing—turning dances, rocking back on her heels dances, a ballet dance, a dance where she continually changed her mind. And finally a dance that seemed to recap everything she'd done.

Maybe after all the dance was about Rudner as her own informal self and Rudner as some fictitious characters. I have a feeling 33 *Dances* wouldn't be half so intriguing or coherent in a theater—perhaps because the intimacy of the Cunningham Studio space allowed her to probe both the openness and the mystery of these two personae.

A Taste of Plain

Trisha Brown Company: *Line Up*
Lepercq Space, Brooklyn Academy, New York
Soho Weekly News, 17 March 1977

The concentrated quiet of Trisha Brown's concert at Brooklyn Academy was more or less steadily accompanied by the heavy bootsteps of the departing A & S Generation. Though it drew my attention from the dance, this exodus reassured me. Brown's was about the first dance this year that didn't attempt to be universally soothing, sexy, thrill-packed, or lovable.

This hour-long piece, a compendium of ideas new and old, brief and extended, was called *Line Up*, and it had as a basic motif the simple notion of trying out various ways a body or group of bodies can act out the command, "line up." If this sounds easy, just try asking five people to make a line and see what happens.

Brown's dance has a certain ambiguity about it that provokes your curiosity right away. It isn't exactly dancelike because it doesn't have the taut, goal-oriented decisiveness of most dance, but it has a presence. You would never mistake it for a bunch of people just fooling around. I think Brown likes keeping us off base, likes staying out of the categories, so that we don't start thinking we know what she's going to do next. She's not out to shock us but to engage our interest, a thing that has become rare in dance.

The dancers—Brown and Mona Sulzman, Wendy Perron, Judith Ragir, Elizabeth Garren, and guest artists Steve Paxton and Terry O'Reilly—all come out into the Lepercq Space dressed in white jersey and drawstring pants. They stay there during the whole event, sitting on the sidelines when they're not dancing. They perform with deliberately blank facial and body expressions, concealing impulse and inflection whenever possible, so as not to make drama out of the movement. So the movement comes out very clear, but also at times very dense, because you're left with nothing to hang onto in the way of subliminal clues, like dynamics or personalities or rhythms or entrances and exits or symbolic associations through which you might escape to your own fantasies.

Line Up presents movement in at least three forms: sequences that were improvised and learned so they could be repeated as originally done, actual improvisation with preset movement materials or themes, and set choreography. The memorized improvs included innumerable variations on the idea of lineup. People made their bodies into linear shapes, they made different kinds of pointing, lining-up gestures. They formed a shoulder-to-shoulder line and progressed completely around the perimeter of the space by walking in superimposed arcs around their own body axes and the axis of the line itself, making a floor pattern like a big windshield wiper with five little wipers along the blade.

Or what I just described may have been a set dance, I'm not sure. I have seen some of the things before as dances, like *Sticks*, in which five women slide out from under long sticks held lengthwise, step over them, and slide back under them, all the while keeping the sticks in contact with those of the women at their head and foot. In *Spanish Dance* there's a line of women across the space, all facing the same way. The one on the end lifts her arms overhead and begins to walk with tiny, emphatic steps that displace her hips and pump her knees. She gradually activates the next woman in line as she comes up behind her, and the next, until all five women are strutting front-to-back, like some chorus line caught in a phone booth. In *Figure 8*, to the ticks of a metronome, the five women go, in unison, through a long arhythmic sequence of touching alternate hands to their heads, with their eyes closed. I don't see why, but the fact that they can stay together seems—is—an incredibly exacting achievement.

Brown's way of making movement is modular. Each phrase is self-contained and consistent—whether one part of the body is involved or several, each move takes up its amount of time and is finished. These modules can face in any direction, go at any speed, recur, follow in any sequence. Once having put a sequence together, Brown likes to extend its use in various ways. *Locus*, a dance that was done as a four-part canon a couple of years ago, was performed in Brooklyn by Elizabeth Garren, with Perron, Paxton, and O'Reilly doing their own versions of it at the same time. There was a new kind of *Accumulation*, a form Brown devised in which elements are added to a nonstop movement sequence one at a time. Now Brown was accumulating whole dollops of activity, which the dancers improvised and then went back and rehearsed until they'd learned it on the spot, and three sections of a dance just grew before our eyes.

Another impressive dance was a version of *Solo Olos*, which is three movement sequences that the dancers have learned to do backwards. In performance, Mona Sulzman directs them to "reverse," "spill," or "branch," which they do without hesitation. "Spill," I thought, meant to let the energy of each gesture overflow its original stopping-place, and "branch" seemed to make the dancers go all squiggly at the joints. Anyway, Sulzman in effect choreographs a dance on the spot by playing the performers as if they were a keyboard.

Solo Olos is probably the most difficult of all Brown's dances to watch—you practically have to retain all of it as an after-image in order to see what changes the dancers make in response to Sulzman's unforeseen instructions. But I never did have time to decide if any of *Line Up* was aesthetic or emotionally affecting because I was busy with its construction all the way through. I think sometimes we need work like this to reacquaint us with the materials of art.

Structure as Outpost

Kathy Duncan
The Cubiculo, New York
Soho Weekly News, 7 April 1977

On the cover of the program for Kathy Duncan's solo concert at the Cubiculo there's a beautiful schematic drawing of the structure for her dance, $(ABA)^4$. Around the edge, corresponding to the largest B section of the dance, are written several of Duncan's ideas about choreography, in epigrammatic style—"finding suspense within predictable structures," "avoiding the art that conceals art," "balancing on the edge of control." That she can see her work in terms of these kinds of paradoxes is not unrelated to the fact that Duncan is also a dance critic. The intuitive/creative and the verbal/organizing faculties are closely, even precariously, matched in her makeup, and I suppose it's only another aspect of a tight but chancy logic that she works with composer/music critic Tom Johnson.

Duncan's dance is concerned with structure—you could almost say it's nothing *but* structure, except for those flashes of impetuosity under which the structure breaks down. $(ABA)^4$ was the most tightly conceived of the seven structures on the program. The idea was outrageously simple—like a set of Chinese boxes inside boxes.

Announcing the labels of the phrases as she did them, she progressed on a diagonal across the floor, alternating A-type motifs and B-type motifs. The A motifs seemed to be the variations on throwing herself off balance by flinging her arms out wildly, and the B motifs may have had to do with balancing. What began to happen was that as the ABA sequences accumulated, the sequences themselves took on ABA form, then the first third of the diagonal—several ABAs put together in ABA form—made an ABA form with the second two-thirds, and then the whole diagonal became the A part of an even bigger ABA that had for its middle section a lot of running, tilting, falling, lunging, and flinging movements around the periphery of the space. I counted sixty-four ABA possibilities in the diagram Duncan provided, but during her performance the inevitability, the security of the edifice was so satisfying I forgot its impressive ramifications.

Shoe Shift and *Along a Line* are also fanatically constructed dances. In the first, Duncan takes little backward jumping steps, in regular rhythm, letting one foot lag more and more behind the other until her steps are in exact counterpoint, then closes up the interval again. In the process she shifts the leg bearing the weight of the jump. She slides sideways to the other side of the room, shifting her weight as she crosses a center line; then, after taking off the shoes and placing them carefully on the floor, she slides back again to where she started, again changing the side supporting her weight. She does this four times in four different kinds of shoes, all making different sounds as she stomps in them.

She breaks up a movement phrase into its body-part components in *Along a Line*. While Johnson scrapes out a rhythm on a washboard, she takes eight jerky counts to move each arm or leg into a new position. When she completes the phrase she backs herself up to the rear wall, then carefully lies down on her side, lining herself up with the line marked on the floor. She repeats the pattern, reducing the number of counts to the body part and increasing the number of times she does the phrase, so it comes to look less automatic and more like some of the flingy things she did earlier. I found an odd pleasure in observing that when she lay down along the line, making such a point of her body's alignment, reinforcing her own exactitude, the part in her hair made a curve.

At about this point in the evening, either the structures loosened up or I saw that Duncan was also playing around with a few basic movement ideas the whole time, and I got more involved with the performance images she was creating. In the duet *Broken Mirror Waltz*, Johnson trod back and forth on the center line while singing a wordless phrase of varying lengths in a loud throaty voice and whanging at a guitar. Duncan lurched and teetered and steadied herself by windmilling her arms. Except for one section when they worked in counterpoint, Duncan and Johnson moved/sang or were still at exactly the same times. Yet there was a tremendous contrast between her frail, erratic, highly charged presence and his stable, compact assertiveness.

In *Fall Wall*, Johnson tossed some rubber balls against a wall and let them roll to a stop. Then Duncan came out and keeled over into the wall, braced herself against it, pushed off from it, flopped on the floor—her resistances and density disputing the easy bounce and spin of the balls.

While Johnson blew on a bottle, Duncan stood in one place and made herself repeat a movement sequence that had to do with pointing in the air, hopping in a circle while flailing at the air with both arms and the free leg, and hitching herself around in a circle, dragging one foot, with her eyes covered and her body bent over. At each repetition of the pattern she increased the number of flings or pivots she had to do while supported on one foot. The dance was called Counting Ceremony, but the counts seemed more random than in the previous pieces.

Especially in this dance, Duncan had an air of dogged determination to carry out the challenge she'd set for herself. Often during the evening, she seemed to be in a state of either delicately controlled hysteria or imminent collapse, but she kept going anyhow. The last work on the program, Running Out of Breath, had her jogging around the space while speaking a monologue Johnson wrote for her, which described what she was doing: running and speaking until she ran out of breath. In the intervals between dances, Johnson read her "Ballet Story," wherein a girl named Olga pliés and relevés her way through a timid but mysteriously rewarding youth. It had a ring of autobiography.

Disciplined Upstarts

David Gordon and Valda Setterfield: WORDSWORTH and the motor +
TIMES FOUR
541 Broadway, New York
Soho Weekly News, 12 May 1977

David Gordon and Valda Setterfield enjoy looking outrageous, and for their nonstop evening called WORDSWORTH and the motor + TIMES FOUR they got themselves up in blue and white sweat outfits, blue knee pads, orange athletic socks, and blue suede running shoes, all of which made a really strange effect with Setterfield's porcelain-shepherdess head and Gordon's shaggy black hair and beard. As unconventional as they looked, however, they did some of the most stringent dancing I've seen all season.

Gordon works in a sophisticated, almost rarefied kind of post-Cunningham idiom in which nontechnical movements are arranged in sequentially demanding structures. What's interesting about it is not its plastique or its spatial architecture, but the precision with which it's designed and executed. It has the kind of beauty that scientists mean when they call a complex equation elegant.

Gordon's older dance *Times Four* was sandwiched in between some related ideas titled *Wordsworth*, with a little postscript dance accompanied by motor sounds. At least, that's the way I understood the somewhat peculiar way the evening was described on the program. There seemed to be three separate ideas anyway, though they weren't all presented in neat, self-contained packages. When you think about it, there's no reason a dance has to be delivered as discrete, boxed ideas. Gordon's progression was more like the way we—I—live, doing something for a while, dropping it to do something else, then continuing the unfinished job. It told me something about the way an idea can accumulate energy, focus, force, and sometimes dissipate them, when it's pursued in a concentrated way, and how you can come back to an idea with fresh impetus if you leave it alone.

Times Four is a step dance. Gordon and Setterfield begin side by side and advance a few paces toward one side of the room, retrace their path, make a quarter turn, and do the same thing in each of the other three directions. The dance consists of perhaps fifty different ways of doing this, each variation following directly after the other, the dynamics even, the steps purposely unfancy—stepping or striding forward and back, little runs, hops, pivot turns, and a few cross-legged twisty moves. They only use their arms to support themselves when they fall forward or lie on their stomachs and have to hitch themselves back onto their knees.

They stay in unison the whole time, and eventually you begin to marvel at how they can remember the sequence. Watching it, I could hardly keep track of the directions, let alone the individual patterns, even though each one was done four times. The step designs make so few or such small body changes that it's easier to hear them rhythmically than to see them. Besides this feat of memory, Setterfield and Gordon must have had to use exceptional control to keep from speeding up or allowing any emphasis to sneak into the movement. I wanted to scream or run around the block before they were through.

Wordsworth seemed to be about speaking while moving. Again, there was no attempt to make conventional dance phrases or movement designs, or involve the whole body in a changing activity. The dance was merely a sequence of gestures, each one accompanied at first by a word describing the body part that was moving or the kind of motion: circle, arm, knee, side, straight, breathe. The gestures got a bit more complicated—swing, fall, stare, turn—but they were still non sequiturs.

The audience had been seated in two facing ranks divided by a screen down the middle of the room, which was removed as the dance began, and Gordon and Setterfield started facing opposite sides. At first they followed separate trains of thought, though just the sound of each other's voice tended to throw them off. After getting stuck and unsuccessfully trying to resume a couple of times, Gordon grinned at the audience and said, "We were watching Nixon before the performance," as if that explained everything.

Variations on *Wordsworth*'s theme included a section where they worked in unison or counterpoint but performed different words and gestures; a series of one-beat phrases—let's go—out there—too hot—I don't care—with illustrative gestures, which they recited in canon; a sequence of doing these gestures while giving Shakespeare soliloquies. After *Times Four* they did the gesture sequence in silence but with Setterfield beginning a little ahead and Gordon catching up and passing her, as the stage managers replaced the screens between them. In their separate portions of the room, finally, they did a new gesture sequence—at least, I guess Setterfield, whom I couldn't see, was doing the same one as Gordon—and they accompanied themselves by intermittent humming. By that time they'd already done such phenomenal things that *and the motor* looked pretty tame. Sort of an anti-anti-climax.

Hodge Podge Rampage

Twyla Tharp: *The Hodge Podge*
Opera House, Brooklyn Academy, New York
Soho Weekly News, 19 May 1977

I loved *The Hodge Podge*—or I would have loved it if Twyla Tharp hadn't named the titles of the old Tharp dances it came from, touching off my mania for identification. I couldn't remember some of it later, but the program insisted I had seen part of *Medley* (1969) and some other old things that would have been useful in researching the elusive Tharp, and then I was annoyed that I'd missed them. Again.

*

An opening night with Tharp is no time to get down to the bare Mud.

*

From the time they first announced it, the Tharp "season"—two weekends at Brooklyn Academy—had been one of those events I couldn't keep straight in my mind. Maybe it was just the typography or the layout of the ads that made the project seem disorganized, or maybe it was all those guest stars and pseudo stars appearing on different nights, or maybe it was the schedule of old dances with new names, and parts of old dances, and parts of new dances, and parts of parts of dances that prevented me from figuring out just what Tharp planned to do.

*

The concreteness of Sara Rudner in a black leotard and tights with a white triangle curving over her head like a nun's coif, walking across the stage inside a plywood hoop (Re-moves, 1966). Shelley Washington smashing a red kindergarten chair (Disperse, 1967).

*

Mud. Interesting that the program doesn't say what the ads did: "for Adidas and Pointe Shoes." But the audience starts to yuck right away. I ask my friend why afterward. "Well, it's a parody of ballet, isn't it?" he says. Is it?

*

This article was prepared by formulating approximately 750 words into relatively complete consecutive thoughts, cutting the copy paper into paragraphs, and whirling the strips of paper in a lettuce dryer. The paragraphs were retyped in the order they were removed from the lettuce dryer. A small amount of cheating was allowed in the interest of journalistic neatness.

*

What is a dance?

*

Hermione Gingold will not appear in The Bix Pieces as announced. Twyla Tharp will read the narration instead. Tharp reads her 1971 script onstage for the first time in my experience, reads it very straight and carefully and sincerely, as she no doubt wrote it—and the audience thinks a lot of it is funny. Funny how the actresses who've done it before could control that nervous reaction. By making the speech really artificial they averted our automatic skepticism of anything too gutsy, too personal.

*

A Tharp dance disappears quicker than a snowfall in May.

*

Who is Twyla Tharp and Dancers? Since dancers are the dance so much, especially in Tharp's work, it takes a while just to settle in with them before you can see the dance they're doing. It takes a while to recognize an old dance with new dancers doing it. You absorb what Paul Simon looks like among dancers, or what the newest Tharp dancers look like among the nearly new Tharp dancers and the former Tharp dancers. By the time you get around to the choreography, the dance is over.

*

Stagehands picking up the chair pieces. Rose Marie Wright picking up Tharp's batons in The Bix Pieces. Sara Rudner.

*

Tharp has a lovely way of introducing new dancers to us—making Shelley Washington an instant star in Give and Take last year, for instance. This time, in Mud, a long solo for Richard Colton. He begins with reminiscences of the stable boy's dance from Petrouchka, an old role of his with the Joffrey Ballet, and evolves before our eyes into a Tharp dancer.

*

Tharp doesn't want to get too cozy with us, to settle down and let us know her well. She snatches her work away before it gets too clear in our minds, and the audience loves being let off the "culture" hook. She throws away gems, refuses to dwell on her argument or sometimes even to reveal it, willfully disrupts and diverts serious consideration of her work, puts us on. She gives us the feeling of being an insider—and we haven't had to put in years of rehearsal.

It Isn't Her Name

Twyla Tharp: Mud
Opera House, Brooklyn Academy, New York
Soho Weekly News, 2 June 1977

Mud is not exactly the most prepossessing title for a dance, and after all these years I'm not about to start speculating on how Twyla Tharp arrived at it. I certainly couldn't match it up with that opaque substance you get from mixing water and dirt, even though the dance is an amalgam of ballet and modern movement. Tharp has made other dances in eclectic languages, but Mud is more selective and, as a movement essay, more expressive than they were. It's also less accessible on the surface, which may be why the audience laughed inordinately.

Tharp's choreographic form is never conventional—she doesn't structure a dance according to either the rules of theatrical build, climax, and resolution, or the contemporary style of stringing out events nonsequentially. She's not hung up on things like getting the whole cast onstage for a big finale or distributing movement evenly all over the space. Her movement does not concentrate on placement or orderly progressions in space or even showing the audience interesting body shapes.

I think that the pop idiom is what saved her. By adopting popular music and an easy, vernacular way of moving, she gave the audience a substitute road map to her dances. Whatever people couldn't see in the way of "plot" or virtuosity or emoting, Tharp made up for in casual clothes, rhythms, and textures that are close to ordinary energies. Her dancers look a lot like personages from our pop subculture—rock stars, athletes, models, partygoers. In Tharp's dance, you may not know what's going on, but you recognize the behavior.

Mud has a lot in common with Tharp's other two ballets to classical music, As Time Goes By and Push Comes to Shove, and the choice of Mozart for the two accompanied sections of Mud is not the only similarity. In all three works, she plays around with what can happen when you relax the rules of classical ballet.

Mud is a smaller-scaled work, and it seems to me a less jokey one, more confident maybe. In her wry and understated way, she makes very few outright plays for laughs—one upside-down lift, a few well-timed collisions, that's all. Most of the time she just throws balletic movement on top of feisty, roly-poly stuff that the track team might do when they're horsing around. She works with movement as it comes to mind, fluently, indiscriminately, and always with wit.

The dance does seem to have a progression. When it begins, three women are standing in a ballet-ready position upstage. Before they make a move, Jennifer Way and Raymond Kurshals streak in and out like some unscheduled demonstrators trying to make a speedy pitch before the cameraman notices them and cuts to the main event. Then the music starts—brief dances played by a string quartet—and the women, Rose Marie Wright, Christine Uchida, and Kimmary Williams, dance a sweet, very classroomy ballet that's all out of joint. The women have totally different kinds of bodies and different ways of articulating their pointe-shod feet, their arms and shoulders, their torsos, legs, heads. Their dance splinters off into individual fragments, then reassembles for instants at a time, diverges, comes together again. The dispersals are small but very active, and the reunitings create unusually consolidated pictures even though the motion never seems to stop.

The women gradually make their way across the stage, looking more and more like Isadora Duncanesque nymphs, and then are gone. Immediately, Uchida and Shelley Washington, Richard Colton, and Raymond Kurshals enter and cross to the other side in a speeded-up succession of partnering arrangements—sometimes hitting positions extra hard and breaking them extra soon. Once, as if by accident, they snap into a line and, with two steps and a couple of hand gestures, suggest a Russian folk dance.

When his companions leave, Colton remains to do a solo to some beautiful, slow, almost romantic music. He flips into a few more Russian poses, but mostly his dance is about fluidity, a smooth, circular, but rhythmically alive gliding. Sometimes he starts a gesture a little punchily but lets his aggressiveness drain away into swift, curly detail. For a brief time he's joined by Washington, and then they stroll off together.

A final quartet, Wright, Kurshals, Way, and Tom Rawe, dodge and bump together in a tight group that's continuously realigning itself. The quartet ends and the dance ends as they fall over softly in a pile.

Mud is about Tharp's dancers as much as anything—about all the various places they come from and all the things they can do as individuals. She no longer has to make a didactic point about modern dancers and ballet dancers being able to borrow from each other, as she did in *Deuce Coupe*. Now she shows how they combine forces and energies, how they share their different inheritances. Each section of Mud takes something from the previous one, includes dancers who were used in a different way earlier. At first I thought maybe the dance wasn't finished, it seemed so terse—all the points made in such condensed form and passed over. Now it occurs to me there's a lot of love in the dance. If they didn't fall down from it when they do, we might be overwhelmed with sentiment.

Working the Residue

Senta Driver/Harry, American Dance Festival
Palmer Auditorium, Connecticut College, New London
Soho Weekly News, 28 July 1977

Senta Driver's Sunday afternoon performance at the Connecticut College American Dance Festival opened with Board Fade Except, in which dancers plod around the borders of the stage, throw themselves across it like rolling logs, run desperately without seeming to have any goal. While they do this, lighting designer Tom Skelton calls cues on tape in a long-ago tech rehearsal for a long-forgotten José Limón performance on the very same stage. I kept thinking back over all those years, all those festivals, and feeling an obscure regret: in 1977 all that remains is the effort.

Driver's work eliminates a lot of what dance is supposed to include and then remodels and refines what's left to almost exaggerated proportions. It's condensed and private, like the name she chose for her company, Harry. Watching her choreography, I bounce around between thinking it's bizarre and intractable and makes no sense, and being struck by sudden images that aren't closed off to me at all. When Meredith Monk started, she used to confound me in the same way.

More than specific movements or phrase-shapes, what I'm conscious of with Driver is a sense of the body's weight and a resistance to accommodation of any kind, an almost compulsive patterning of space and of movement sequence, and an inexplicable neutrality of expression that sometimes borders on sternness. Yet an intelligent sly wit jumps out at you, and kinetic surprise seems to be stored in great stockpiles, just waiting to burst through the dancers' reserve. Sudden Death, Driver's new duet for herself and Timothy Knowles (choreographed under a commission from the American Dance Festival) is one of those endurance rituals we've been seeing so many of lately, where the dancers seem to be testing their stamina or virtuosity or the extent to which they dare expose their guts to the audience.

At the beginning Driver and Knowles stride to the center of the stage and lock fists in a brusque greeting, like prizefighters before the bell. Then they position themselves one behind the other along a center line marked by yellow tape and proceed to hurl themselves at high speed through a series of lashing, punching, slamming moves. It's fast dancing done with maximum force and zero subtlety. They face the audience and land square into each jump, lunge, or twist as if it were the climax of a nineteenth-century pas de deux, giving themselves just enough time to adjust their stance before thundering on into another one. They start out in unison, but soon one or the other lags slightly behind, creating a loose canon.

About halfway through the marathon, they both flop to the floor breathing heavily. After a rest period they continue, the jumps getting more dangerous, the throwing around of torsos more complicated. They begin, one or the other, to spare themselves precious energy by slurring through some of the movement, and the dance starts to look more individual. For the first time they seem to be moving closer together, like swimmers or runners at the end of a race who feel comforted by having someone near, even when it's the person they're trying to beat. Suddenly Driver pulls up behind Knowles, grabs him, and kisses him for a very long time on the mouth, as they both stand stiff and gasping for breath. Curtain.

The kiss is a shock, of course, but not because it's any erotic climax. Quite the opposite. The gesture is devoid of all but symbolic sexual content, yet it's as high-powered as a Hollywood clinch. Driver's context makes it something quite other than what it is—another physical feat perhaps, or an act of defiance. A feminist act, I suppose. A reversal of all those male-female encounters where, at the point in the argument when the man suspects the woman is getting the better of him, he hauls her off to bed. Driver disavows the whole arsenal of sexual weaponry, not by burying it but by blowing it up.

Sudden Death is less minimal than some of Driver's earlier pieces—Memorandum, for instance, in which she walks stolidly around in circles reciting a litany of ballerinas' names; or Matters of Fact, where Driver, Knowles, Genevieve Weber, and Jorge Ledesma take turns jumping onto one another's back or hip and being lugged from place to place—but it still is not your average person's idea of a choreographed dance. Gradually she's adding more hyperactivity, more determination, but not an inch of decorativeness or illusion to cover them up.

Has the Piece Begun, or Is This the End?

Douglas Dunn: *Celeste*, American Dance Festival
Connecticut College, New London
Soho Weekly News, 11 August 1977

Douglas Dunn's new piece *Celeste* took me back to 1965, to the first performance of *Variations V*. On the stage of Avery Fisher Hall, Merce Cunningham
and John Cage, Robert Moog, Stan VanDerBeek, Nam June Paik, Billy Klu-
ver, Beverly Emmons, dancers, and musicians created a grand, outrageous
circus-collage of dance, play, film, sound, slides, electronics, and props. At
the end, possibly in ecstasy, possibly in exasperation, Merce Cunningham
rode a bike once through the forest of people and equipment and headed
for the exit, neatly grabbing the woodwork over the doorway and swinging
there like a monkey while the bike coasted offstage. I thought it was the
mixed-media event of all time.

So why was Douglas Dunn doing a mixed-media event at the American Dance Festival twelve years and a lot of housecleaning later? Well, the
scale first, I guess. With the whole Connecticut College campus to work
with, Dunn could let loose the forty-seven dancers he'd been directing
in workshops for the past several weeks. They could spread themselves
out all over the open lawns and the theater besides. He could make his
dance a playground for technical effects by Tal Streeter that included three
movies projected simultaneously with different varieties of distortion, a
giant telephone pole with wires swooping across the landscape, and a
parachute jump.

It takes some kind of courage to let your dance be landed on by two
men from the sky, and in a way, when the circling planes had dropped
their delightful surprise and the spacemen with their multicolored para-
chutes had landed right on the X marked off on the grass for them, there
wasn't much place for the dance to go. But Dunn's idea seemed to be that
the dance could exist underneath and through and in spite of whatever
technical games got played on it.

Celeste is not a dance so much as an improvisational gambit. The performers have worked together in two-hour sessions, gradually accumulating a notebook full of instructions that are supposed to cue them into
movement. The instructions are written after each session and consist of
body-part directions (toe to knee—I'm making these up), impressionistic
or dreamlike phrases (elephant paw), specific tasks (five times around the
edge), ways of thinking about yourself as you're moving (move as if your
clothes are too big), remarks made by the participants during the session
("It's better from across the room").

The performers are free to choose any of these springboards to work with, or any others. They can work alone or together. Only half of them are supposed to be in the space at any given time. Any props they may find in the space are to be considered, but not as props in a dance. Sometimes Dunn moves through the group telling everybody the same thing ("right foot"). One of the performers' choices is not to follow the instructions.

These rules did not become apparent to me in the course of watching the Connecticut performance. Scarcely any order at all was perceptible there. Structured improvisation is a technique used in the last ten years to free dancers from the imposed look of another's choreography, to alert the audience to the realities and choices that comprise a performing situation by building spontaneity into the situation. Dunn had given the dancers in Celeste so many possibilities that they might as well have had none—might have just wandered in, strangers, and done whatever came into their minds.

Outside on the campus, before the arrival of the parachutists, the dance seemed fairly consistent, although so thinly spread out you couldn't always tell who was dancing and who was watching, or if anyone was. The performers limited their movement choices mostly to a few obvious ideas, the kind of thing city folk do when they get in a big open space—running fast and full-out, tumbling and rolling in the grass, playing statues.

Inside, the same crowd, together with twenty white chairs, was jammed into Palmer Auditorium's moderate-sized stage, the various projections, lights, and sounds washing over them constantly. The parachutists folded up their gear and left. This took a long time and preempted a large part of the stage, and their slow, methodical, almost loving way of doing the job made me think of cooking—how you really have to enjoy the preparation since it takes so much longer than the actual meal.

Celeste was not satisfying in that sense. For the hour that the piece dragged on in that space I tried different devices for getting myself interested. I looked at the movies—National Velvet, very weepy; The Thief of Baghdad, with lots of nice, naive early-film tricks like flying carpets, human bats, and a mysterious old man who gestured fiercely and disappeared in a puff of smoke. I looked at the total confusion but it didn't make abstract art, only concrete anarchy. I looked at individual dancers. No one seemed to stay with any idea more than half a minute or so. The ideas were pretty simple and didn't undergo much development. There were people walking back to back, touching, engaging in little races or competitions, falling in piles, lying along the edge of the stage. A man and a woman tried to do a waltz out of step. A man put his head under a woman's long blond hair. People carried each other.

I looked at the movement patterns—there were few. The best sequences were cumulative. A lot of people stood for a while, backs to the audience, and watched the movies. Someone started lining up the chairs; someone else started taking them away. After a long time there was a blackout. The dancers, possibly thinking the piece was ending, galvanized themselves into violent action. The lights returned, and they slumped or twiddled, filling time. They formed two large groups and sprinted several times toward center stage from both wings. The curtain fell, it rose. A 7-Up commercial played on the side wall of the theater.

Of course this kind of thing has "meaning," it means anything and everything. Of course it's nice for the performers to do. It's also a kind of cop-out. Doug Dunn is interested in the different kinds of attention that dancers have when they must make many exposed decisions. He also said somewhere on the sound track that he wanted the performers to make the kind of choices that would give a "look" to the work. To me that means he didn't want to make these choices himself. If the performers didn't want to work in-depth with the material, the audiovisual overload provided them with a kind of camouflage, the instructional proliferation got them off the hook. They dabbled. They played. In that atmosphere, if anyone was being coherent or working their way through something, they were just about invisible.

Doug Dunn is intrigued right now with the idea of accumulating more and more material for the dancers to use. His ongoing piece *Lazy Madge* is not improvised—movement material is set in rehearsal—but the material forms a growing library that the dancers draw from as they wish in performance. What's happened to *Lazy Madge*—it was given in Connecticut after *Celeste*—is that instead of looking more intense, subtle, or profound, it's becoming busy, scattered, preoccupied rather than concentrated. Instead of dancing together, people stand still a lot, making hand and foot designs around their own bodies. *Lazy Madge* seems to be gradually disintegrating, from dance back to the raw materials from which dance comes— unremarkable, unselected, everyday human activity.

The other great moment of Dunn's evening came during *Lazy Madge*, which has only nine dancers. Presumably because the stage had cleared enough to make it possible, a person I hadn't seen before appeared on a bicycle. She rode once around the stage and went out. It was the perfect protest.

My Debut

Unpublished notes, 7 August 1977

Douglas Dunn was one of the choreographers invited to perform in the city-owned Custom House during the summer of 1977. Since he was working with big improvisational forms that year, he announced an open session from 11 in the morning to 6 p.m. every day for anyone who wanted to participate or watch.

Hot & muggy.

Custom House—big arching Romanesque building with an oval marble high dome—circular marble counter & inside the ring a carpeted floor with six huge brass fixtures representing torches (?)—about ten feet high. Dome is beautifully proportioned—WPA frescoes in the ceiling panels look like illustrations from 1941 edition of TRUE magazine. Marble—busts —roman lettering: Verrazano, Cabot, Columbus, etc. Building is not as cool as I'd hoped. I'm wearing my "Only in Austin" T-shirt.

Ask Doug if I can participate. Yes. Watch a few minutes. Doug and three or four others—quiet—posing by themselves—pretty exposed. Do a very minimal warm-up. Doug comes over, says three instructions, ideally simultaneous, get all I can out of:

–Do your instruction (what I decide I want to do; for instance, walk around the edge).

–Do what you need (I interpret that to mean be flexible & be safe).

–Do what the piece needs (Responsibility, at last!).

Decide to make my piece exploring the space & take his "for instance" as an instruction—when I start and when I get stuck I walk around the edge, along the counter, in & out among the torches, and once straight across the center.

For the next two and a half hours I don't remember everything, but:

–Michael comes over & says he'd like to warm up his arms and back— that's his instruction—and can we talk about it. I say, well why don't we ... (moving back to back with him). He says, just what I was thinking. We work for a while, end up in a pile. After a while he suggests we do the same thing in five different places, changing one thing each time. We do, getting sidetracked into a foot-holding game with some other people and an outline-your-shape-in-the-snow game.

–I tell Diane & Jennifer I have never performed before. They are amazed. Later they each give me an initiation dance.

–Once I'm sitting on the counter resting, my feet propped on the ledge. Suddenly they're on a head. A man has been sitting in the cubbyhole under the counter, I didn't even know he was there. His hair is soft & curly. I play with it with my toes.

–Later the same man & Danny come and carry me around the space—I like being carried. People attach themselves to us—it becomes a procession. I begin to feel like a sacrificial victim. "Critic carried to the stake. Dancers have revenge." But absurd—they haven't read my review of Celeste yet. Later we tumble down. Daniel says happy birthday Sandy (?).

–I do a lot of heavy work & rolling around—I'll be black & blue tomorrow. Some man says, you could lift me too. I try. Well I can but there must be easier ways.

–Nat comes. I decide time to leave—going to San Francisco tomorrow. Pack. Organize. etc. Wouldn't mind him taking pix of me working with group. Too bad he didn't come earlier.

I'm not displeased with what I did—had a fine time & enjoyed moving in that space. Learned:

–I was rather timid—not with performing but with that group for the first time. Old questions everybody goes through about improvisation: Trust (I'm pretty good with that)—leadership (stay in the background)—hurt someone's feelings if you'd rather work on your own idea than join theirs.

–Things tended to be either fragmentary or manipulative. Sometimes a "story" got going—I liked that best—(Ruth reading fortunes off the soles of Doug's & Michael's shoes—their feet stuck in the air as they lay on the ground) but didn't last long enough.

–Was barely conscious of the audience and, especially when doing something interesting with someone, unconscious of the other dancers.

–At first I thought what a grand idea & wouldn't it have been nice to have this space to play in all week. Later quite overwhelmed with the responsibility of it—keeping going. I couldn't have gone on another four hours today. But if I'd been forced to—suppose I'd have gotten either more daring with the space and the spectators, or more demanding and serious with the other dancers.

Image Reinforcement

Margaret Jenkins and Company, Summer Dance Festival
Palace of Fine Arts, San Francisco
Soho Weekly News, 8 September 1977

The audience for the eclectic Summer Dance series at the Palace of Fine Arts here was fairly unsophisticated about dance and had no trouble tuning in on the tightly organized if aimless glitter of the popular ballets shown by Pacific Ballet, Oakland Ballet, and Dance Spectrum. But they also reacted with a stir of surprise and pleasure to Margaret Jenkins's Copy, a big, post-Cunningham work that offered none of the ordinary clues to easy viewing.

The dance was a surprise to me too, and so was Jenkins's *Videosongs*, which I saw later in a studio workshop performance. Since I last saw Jenkins's work it's gotten more coherent, more defined, although it retains the spatial and interpretive openness mandated by the Cunningham aesthetic. It seems to me she's started working with one basic tool of any art compositional process that Cunningham purists usually deny themselves—the idea that elements of the composition can be repeated.

A ridiculously simple concept, but it can make a huge difference in a dance that has no characters or plot, where the movement can spew out in all directions and people can be doing ten different things at one time. Because some of these movement events are replays or slightly changed imitations of things seen before, they carry a much greater psychological load than movements that happen only once.

Copy has several sections, each, according to the program, "exploring the various extensions of unison activity—duplication, reflection, and succession." At first, the twelve dancers seem to be a crowd of eccentric strangers, sometimes preoccupied with their own affairs, sometimes running, meeting, separating with no perceptible reason. Gradually we get to know them, not individually but as a group. Their collective behavior begins to seem sensible in its own terms. Enough people do enough of the same things that we can see they have a common purpose.

In a mob scene where everyone seems to be doing something different, we suddenly become aware that two or three people in different parts of the stage are in unison or are copying each other. Sometimes it's only the rhythm of some of the movement phrases that's the same, and it carries like heartbeats under the visual noise. There's one section where four or five people repeat individual phrases we'd seen them do before—over and over we pick them out of the crowd in the same spot, or maybe in a different spot but facing the same way, and it's familiar, friendly, like the refrain of a song with lots of verses. We're pleased with ourselves for being able to recognize so many.

There are big ensembles where people run on and tag someone, who immediately runs off while the tagger continues; a unison dance like something I saw Cunningham do long ago—was it in *Scramble?*—in which people are always leaving as other people come on and replace them. And a big calisthenic session at the end of the dance, where everyone moves all the time and their sequences take them from individual movement into—and out of—total or partial unison.

Jenkins's movement is big, often with rounded or open shapes. The dancers travel a lot, maintaining a very securely placed center to which they can return with sudden ease from jumping or locomotion. The style tends to be rather diffuse in space, but it's sprinkled with small, clear gestures or moments when everything grows still, and these make crystals of very specific dimensions.

Videosongs, given by a group of non-company members who had worked with Jenkins and her dancers for three weeks learning it, was made as a project for commercial television. It's a smaller work, in size, space, and length of the movement sections, than the surging, extroverted Copy. Before the performance Jenkins explained the limitations and challenges of the TV setup and the way she'd structured the dance's eight sections to relate to each other yet be self-contained, so the dance could be interrupted by hair tonic messages if necessary.

The dancers showed some of the phrases from which the dance had been built, then did a short improvisation using the phrase material. This was almost more revealing than the dance itself proved to be, because without a prearranged plan, the sequence still made visual and kinetic sense. Jenkins's movement seems to be all in the same family, so that even when the dancers are doing different things, there's a similarity in the way they distribute their energy and body parts. They seem to be able to fall into similar rhythms quite easily, though their body shapes don't conform to each other. They also use many of the same improvisational tactics—excerpting the phrase by doing it with only one part of the body, lifting someone who continues moving, molding one's body to that of another, and imitating another person canonically. Choreographically, Videosongs employed some of the same devices as Copy, principally the idea of individuals gathering into synchrony and slipping out of it. In both works, there was an interplay of energies and attention that made the dance very alive. The movement isn't tense and high-powered, but it demands that the dancer be in the dance all the time.

Simple ideas take on the aspect of semidramatic encounters: two women move in their own small spheres close together, one of them is always undulating slowly in place and the other ventures away a few steps, but twice—why?—they make the same move together. People intently balance on one foot, other people run in and slide crazily to the floor near them, the person balancing topples to the ground. Three women walk casually around, pausing every few steps to stretch into several common poses they seem to have arrived at by tacit agreement.

The first part of Videosongs was accompanied by a woman's voice reciting some lines about memory. It's a revealing thing, she said, because it opens up "spaces heretofore unrealized." Those are the spaces where Margaret Jenkins is working, and they're ripe at this point.

Twyla's natural instinct . . .

Unpublished notes, 14 September 1977

Twyla's natural instinct for pop (sometimes pre-pop) makes people think she's the crassest of opportunists. Of course she's too smart to let a good gambit slip by, but she doesn't contrive her work to make use of pop. She is just so damned tuned in to the vibes of hustle and flash, she can't seem to avoid getting them loud and clear on whatever channel she's working.

In the video piece *Making Television Dance* she makes her usual quota of outrageous observations—some slightly forced and melodramatic, but most of them coming from that irritated, slightly suspicious place under the skin where most people don't admit they hurt. Studios—the first one she worked in NY—appalled at how small it is, place in the city for the rejected people—poor, disinherited (she doesn't add artists, doesn't have to). "I haven't been here in so long I couldn't find it"—almost choking on the words—is this what success means? Tramping with exaggerated laboriousness up the seventy-nine steps at Franklin Street—it's okay, she's still working there. Ballet Theater—uptown, the big time, sardonic as always about good fortune. Complaining later there's no privacy—a blue TV illusion zapping down like a window shade or a guillotine on a nosy ballet student's face peering in the door.

Harlequinade

Remy Charlip Dance Company
American Theater Lab, Dance Theater Workshop, New York
Soho Weekly News, 6 October 1977

Remy Charlip belongs to the great American tradition of dance clowns, dancers who not only can visualize what's funny, but can move through the implications of what's funny. Charlip's temperament falls very much into the dark side of the spectrum, the introspective, melancholy side. A lot of the time he isn't trying to be funny at all, but something about him—perhaps the extreme clarity with which he defines an apparently capricious line—makes us smile at the same time as we hurt.

Charlip's new company, which just made its debut at American Theater Lab, preserves and extends his quality to a remarkable degree. His concert made me think of some early kind of circus, which wasn't slick and thrilling but was about performers doing roles—a form that could expand or contract indefinitely just so long as the different acts all played by the same rules. Charlip's evening was constructed beautifully, its more or less miscellaneous parts washing up against each other in a rising, then leveling-off tide of animation.

First Charlip gave a very formal welcoming dance, standing in a downlight, lifting his arms, slowly bringing them together and clasping them tight, drawing what felt like the energy of the cosmos into his skull, his eyes, his mouth, his body, and sending it out to the audience with a rush of breath.

Albert Reid and David Hinckfuss began their duet walking in opposing circles, then running, then—after a first, almost violently sudden meeting—beginning to work together. Standing very close, they seemed to be getting the measure of each other's bodies, and soon they were leaning against each other, sometimes with heads together, almost nuzzling, sometimes with totally trusting dependence. The program supplied the information that Reid had stepped into the dance for an injured colleague, and the dance was called *A Week's Notice.*

Eva Karczag choreographed her own solo, *Tendencies,* but it looked a lot like the sketches that Charlip makes and sends to dancers by mail for them to connect in their own ways. At least, the rubbery, twisty positions she passed through looked like the sketches. Karczag first did a sequence in which she flung one arm out behind her, twisting around with it, then swiveling back and extending the other arm ahead. As she repeated the gesture, the flinging-out-behind energy lessened and the thrust to the front increased, until she had inverted the movement. An evolution, where nothing was lost, just rearranged, like an amoeba traveling. Later she did long chains of poses, oozing from one to another, or changing the dynamics of the transitions to make each repetition slightly different.

For tricks, Hinckfuss came out and balanced on a soft rubber ball about eight inches in diameter. If you think that's not much, try it. Then Karczag walked across the space bent over, both feet and hands resting on rubber balls. With each step she slid the ball out from under one foot, catching it as it rolled with a hand that had released another ball just in time for the advancing foot to step on. Sort of a kinetic chicken-or-the-egg situation. Karczag's upside-down concentration made the audience giggle, but her fluidity was virtuosic in a job that someone else might try to solve with super-control.

The evening's big event was *Art of the Dance*, a solo by a different dancer at each performance. It's done on a big sheet of paper, and the dancer's feet are covered with paint. The night I went Sara Rudner had a fine time deciding where and how to dunk her track shoes into the pans of white, yellow, blue, and red. She stomped and slid luxuriously, did an extraordinary dance of making particular parts of her body extremely tense, shuddering-tense, then shaking out the tension in great big swags of movement. Finally she threw herself down and rolled in the wet painting. Afterward David White auctioned off the action-splotched scroll—so much for dance's ephemerality—the proceeds going to the artist's favorite cause. Rudner named Kenneth King, and someone bought it for $52 after a hard-fought competition.

Valda Setterfield, wearing a mannish outfit of pants, jacket, shirt, and bow tie, all in different-color pastel stripes, her silver hair plastered to her head Valentino style, stood in a spotlight and read, in her soft English voice, ten imaginary dances that began with a scenario for the Red Chinese Ballet— "A wicked imperialist stepmother is binding her stepdaughter's feet. . . ."

Charlip did another solo, with a brass rod in his hands, called *Travel Sketches*. The dance consisted of his going from pose to pose with the stick, which could have been anything from a cane to a trapeze to a pool cue to a magic wand. Charlip's poses were never literal, nor were the transitions, which became quite elaborate. But each pose was so definite and so still that it seemed to attract images that had been floating around in my subconscious.

The big dance, the company piece, *Glow Worm*, had Karczag, Hinckfuss, and Reid preoccupied with what might have been the aftereffects of their previous dances, while Charlip darted among them in a long vest sewn with buttons and coins, telling, rather desperately, some kind of story in sign language.

Charlip's concluding solo, *Meditation*, was like an actor's farewell—a

Pagliacci or a Vestris—some genius of impersonation who struts and frets for the last time. But Charlip only drew himself into a few attitudes—a pleading lover, a village idiot, a martinet—so intense and pure his whole body seemed to flood with emotions that were overpowering and not simple at all.

Minimal Differences, Major Distinctions

Judy Padow Dance Company
Dance Theater Workshop, New York
Soho Weekly News, 13 October 1977

Minimalist dances seem to come in two kinds: those that stress choreographic structure and those that stress the body. Judy Padow seems to be in the latter group, but I only realized there were groups when I tried to figure out why she looks so different from the person she most resembles, Lucinda Childs. Padow has danced with Childs since 1973, and like Childs she makes a lot of walking dances. Both of them approach performing with a contained, purposely inexpressive face and body attitude, doing all they can to keep any natural phrasing in the movement from building up psychic or narrative steam. Unlike Childs, Padow doesn't do all this to focus our attention on a particular sequence of steps, evolving patterns in space, or changes of rhythm. During her brief program, continuing through October in the Tuesday Project series sponsored by Dance Theater Workshop, Padow showed four pieces whose interest for me lay not in their ideas, which were quite simple, but in the look of the dancers doing them.

This look is a very strange one—you feel something's unusual about the way they use their bodies, but it's not any isolated mannerism or deficiency or overstressed skill. Padow, who exemplifies it best, is small, with a thin, flat body that shows little of the refinement that usually comes from dance training. She doesn't have that high muscle tonus, that readiness and sense of reserved power you see in other dancers. Her body looks put together with soft, weightless things like marshmallows. While everything else is very easy and flexible, she stiffly pumps her arms back and forth together when she walks, squeezing her chest or upper back between them on each step.

In her solo *Indian Summer*, Padow didn't use her arms this way at all, since the gesture seems to be an affectation of her walking and the dance was completely floor-bound. As she swiveled around, keeping in almost constant motion, she used her shoulders, pelvis, and knees as fulcrum, sliding, telescoping, unrolling, twisting, tilting the rest of her body parts around them. She seemed without bones at all, some new-model human with

360-degree rotation in joints that the rest of us don't even have. It seemed she could change the direction of her gently tumbling, unfolding progress at will.

This sense of attunement to all the segments of the body and the ability to use them independently or in flowing sequence is what Padow shares with the other group of minimalists. She does contact improvisation now, as do all her dancers, Cynthia Hedstrom, Eric Hess, Danny Lepkoff, and Mary Overlie. But Padow is very concerned with how the body looks, where it's placed, what shapes it makes, unlike the contact improv dancers, who don't deal with that kind of programming at all.

In *Cameo*, ten vignettes to short piano pieces of Bartók, the dancers looked strangely childlike, with the mobility of their body parts boxed into the music, one gesture per note, or the force of a step withheld or broken off in order to fit into the metrical line. There were little episodes of polyrhythms—never more complex than one dancer doubling the other's tempo as they chased each other in circles—and occasional moments when two would fall into synchrony while another was doing something else. Sometimes a motif would be repeated with slight variations. The brevity of the musical statements prevented any further development.

Quartet in Unison—actually it was a trio at the performance I saw due to an injury to one of the dancers—was accompanied by what I assume is only a portion of "Victor's Lament" by Philip Glass. The synthesized or organ music has only a few elements—a rhythmic bass, sustained chords in another rhythm, rippling undercurrents, an almost toneless buzz—that recur many times in slightly different combinations and intervals of time. Instead of exploring all this repetition and rhythmic subtlety as someone like Childs or Laura Dean would have done, Padow went about four rounds with the music and ended. Maybe the dance is a work in progress.

Padow, Lepkoff, and Hess executed a stepping, circling pattern with some built-in jumps, in an unchanging chorus line formation. There may have been small variations in their dance pattern, but what struck me was how odd it looked to see three people wheeling around in tight circles around their own axes, always the same distance away from each other, when the steps they were doing had such a potential for traveling through space.

In *Repeat*, Cynthia Hedstrom, in a pool of light against black drapes, walked briskly, in profile, three steps forward, pivoted, three steps the other way, pivoted. She kept this up for a long time, gradually getting a few feet closer to the audience. Then she turned to face us, jumped from foot to foot with large arm swings, for a shorter time. Then she stopped and stood still for a few seconds. Then the light went out. The concentrated smallness of the image she created did funny things to my vision—I kept thinking

I saw her arms move slightly differently, her momentum hesitate for an instant. Once she flicked out of sight, like a couple of missing frames in a movie. But the sequence didn't go on long enough to make any important demands on my perceptions.

Laps

Sara Rudner and Joan La Barbara: *As Is/Layers*, Dance Umbrella
Entermedia Theater, New York
Soho Weekly News, 3 November 1977

Sara Rudner's *As Is* is an hour shorter than the piece she gave at the Custom House at the end of the summer. It's still almost two hours of nonstop dancing, a feat of endurance for both dancers and audience. The fairly elaborate production at the Dance Umbrella, consisting of costumes and set pieces by Robert Kushner and an electronic score by Joan La Barbara, only underscored the physicality of the piece instead of relieving it.

Rudner, one of the best dancers now performing, is possessed by movement. Insatiable. All her recent solos have been marathons, and now she's transferred her superwoman energy to three others, Jean Churchill, Shana Menaker, and Vicky Shick. The four of them barreled and bounced their way through I don't know how many variations on I don't know how many themes and were charging into another one when the lights went out.

In some ways, *As Is* reminded me of Twyla Tharp's concert at the Billy Rose Theater in early 1969. It was Tharp's first appearance as an official, regular modern dance company, although she was segregated within a large season, along with a couple of other "avant-garde" groups. She had an all-girl company then, Rudner was one of them, and they did three grueling pieces that were all movement and no frills. The audience either had to deal with Tharp on movement terms or reject it all.

By now, Rudner's movement looks quite different from Tharp's. You can tell, I guess, that they both came from the same place. Rudner has that finely tuned Tharpian body, capable of balletic extension and balance as well as any combination of kink, bend, isolation, or screwiness. She can make movement flash through her body or spread like honey, make the flow stop, twitch, pull in tight, or jump from one part to another illogically. But Rudner is more placed, more concerned with design, and less indulgent with weight than Tharp—you don't see those sexy slinks or floppy, roly-poly falls that make Tharp so ingratiating. Rudner makes dances from big blasts of pure movement or elaborations on actual movement motifs— like the swimming, jumping rope, and jogging dances in *As Is*. She's not concerned with the insinuations movement can make when it's ambiguous.

Rudner's getting skillful at helping the audience to organize what might become a dizzying array of not-that-different activities. The piece has clearly defined sections, trios and duets that maintain their connection even when the dancers aren't doing exactly the same things, quite a lot of formation dancing, solos that are based on material shown before, and well-timed visual punctuation in the form of particularly emphatic gestures that divide up the long, demanding sequences of movement. After the dance has gone on for a while you can see that there are a certain number of ideas that return over and over: the sports themes I mentioned, a series of isometric moves in which the dancers grip hard in one part of the body till they create such high tension they vibrate, clapping games, calisthenics, and several more complicated sequences of high-energy dancing.

But in spite of the clearly presented structure of the dance, I have trouble hanging onto the specifics of it. It doesn't suggest metaphors to me, or develop into new versions of itself. It's completely assertive in its own presence, but leaves no echoes behind. Rudner does offer some images to us—children on a playground, barnyard animals, long-distance runners or swimmers—but these references are resorted to so often by choreographers that they don't say anything special to me anymore. Certainly not anything poetic or unsuspected. La Barbara chose to accompany these portions of the dance with literal sound effects, which made them seem even more obvious.

Kushner's contribution to the dance puzzled me. There were two curtains, painted in bold, crude strokes with busy overall patterns, sort of floral and carefully sectioned like wallpaper. These flew or slid in and out, as did various black scrims, without any apparent use except to change the dancing area in different ways. For costumes—Rudner almost always changes costumes at least once during a dance—there were a zillion sets of "separates," drawstring pants, shorts, leotards, wraparounds, shirts, and two sets of nameless articles in sequin-black and prints-to-match-the-curtains, which the dancers wore in innumerable combinations. Maybe they were supposed to suggest theatricality and role-playing, or maybe they catered to the universal dancers' fetish for having just the right amount and type of body covering as they go through a day's changes of internal and external climate.

Lately it seems to me Rudner is trying to avoid the feminine stereotypes that a dancer of her looks and magnetism can so easily project. As Is is a very severe dance, not much humor in it and little characterization. It's a dance about dancing the bejesus out of everybody. But in choosing the playful gambits she does as compositional cues, she weakens the grown-up, independent dancer person who's trying to get out.

Slice of the Universe

Kei Takei: *Light Parts 10, 12, 13,* Dance Umbrella
Entermedia Theater, New York
Soho Weekly News, 10 November 1977

By now, everybody must have gotten used to the idea that Kei Takei is dancing the story of mankind, and that each new section of the continuing work
Light is only one speck on the fingernail of the millennia. But I wonder what
it's like to come upon her at this stage, without having lived through the
mystery and pain, the careful rebuilding, the playfulness and socializing
that have gone before.

At this time of *Light*, the world seems to have taken a hostile turn. All
three parts shown at the Dance Umbrella, 10, 12, and 13 (part 11 was done
for the Netherlands Dance Theater, I believe, and hasn't been seen in this
country), are vaguely or openly competitive, even aggressive and territo-
rial. The members of the world are capable of working together, but they're
easily fragmented, and they seem to combine their energies best when attacking someone else. After every series of skirmishes, though, at least one
person escapes alive.

In Part 10, Takei, dressed in white underpants and halter top, with a black
X painted across her whole face, comes across the space warily, as if blind,
occasionally banging two rocks together, like someone trying to scare off
animals in the dark. Two men scramble after her, throwing small stones
along the ground under her feet. She keeps dancing among the stones and
clapping her rocks together, and they keep taking more stones out of sacks
that they carry. A few times she drops one rock. Her tormentors watch
as she gropes for it. Sometimes she finds it, sometimes she doesn't. But
she always stands up again and goes on, clapping her hands together if
she hasn't got a rock, and she leaves the two men behind, staring after her
across the stony space.

The lights dim, and people come and push the stones with pieces of
two-by-fours into a circle at the center of the space. As Part 12 begins, Takei
squats in the center and eight dancers, each with his or her own little pile
of stones, circle around her with a rhythmic stamping dance. Each person
keeps time by bonking two rocks together. Whenever someone drops a
rock, the dance ceases. As if a signal has been given, they stoop down and
scrape the stones on the floor into new designs. When the person picks up
his lost rock, the dance continues, its rhythmic and motor patterns growing more intricate. Meanwhile Takei scurries around pushing their stone
designs into new formations according to some other plan she has in mind.

You can't be sure if the circle dancers are trying to confine Takei to a narrower and narrower space or if she's trying to connect their little stone enclaves to her center-circle. Sometimes the dancers pair off into duets where they shadow box at each other or do little juggling games with their rocks. You can't be sure if they're engaging in a highly coordinated group activity or are on the verge of coming to blows. Finally four of them crowd into the tight circle in the middle, surrounded by the other four. As they stomp and punch at their dance, Takei is quietly making a line of stones, one by one, leading away from the circle and out. The four dancers in the circle shuffle out along this path, and those remaining have taken their place in the center as the lights go out.

In Part 13, Takei and five men come in by the same path. The center of the circle becomes an arena for them, in which they stage several bouts of different kinds of combat—Indian wrestling, knee wrestling, body banging, and more. The fighting is ritualistic. Always the challenger wins, becomes the defender, loses to the next challenger. When they've all had a turn, the last contenders walk around touching the circle of stones gently—making it a little larger each time and fixing any stones that got kicked out of line— while the others sit on the floor and paint red X's on different parts of their bodies with markers they take out of little cloth bags attached to their pants.

Sometimes they all get into the circle together and have group shoving matches until the whole mass explodes and everybody falls outward. A new and rougher war game is getting started when Takei slips away to make another stone-by-stone path, out the other side of the circle from where they entered.

Takei's work is almost an ideal allegorical form. Her materials are very simple, so simple they can mean many things or convert easily into new ones—the circle, the stone, the clapping of the hands together, the idea of arrival or of departure. Her stage is always spare, uncluttered; everything looks all of a piece yet the scene vibrates with things that clash, that cry for your sympathy. The action is obsessively repetitive. There are small variations with each new round of the ritual, but these don't change anything. Rather they make the impact of what you're seeing heavier, by insisting that what you only suspected might be there is there. Is there *too*. The wrestlers not only want to get rid of their opponents but need them to survive; all the fights end with both contestants falling violently; they agree to fight and they lose equally.

A lot of synthetic energy has crept into Takei's work over the years. The dancers sometimes have fake angry or fake surprised expressions, and they sometimes lock themselves together stiffly instead of really struggling. This bothers me unreasonably; the work is so symbolic anyway, it shouldn't matter that some of it only looks like it's happening. I guess the phony intensity of these moments jars against the unassuming power she can draw from basic shapes, sounds, and materials. Anyone can pretend to be theatrical. To make theater from wood and rock and an X and a person squatting is a much greater gift.

Critturs' Gym

Simone Forti, Terry O'Reilly, and Peter Van Riper: *For You*
St. Mark's Church, New York
Soho Weekly News, 8 December 1977

Simone Forti hardly ever actually imitates an animal, but she's figured out how to move the way animals do, with a heightened awareness of body surfaces that seems to insulate her from space even as it's making her contacts with space more palpable. She seems to be able to articulate the parts of her body giving special attention to the weight of each little segment, so that she can look languidly sinuous or make sudden large displacements without hurting herself. There's a certain kind of economy in her movement that you only see in creatures vitally concerned with survival.

When contrasted with another dancer, Terry O'Reilly, in their semi-improvisational collaborative piece *For You*, with musician Peter Van Riper, Forti's approach makes a small but important difference. O'Reilly can handle the soft four-legged stalkings, the no-handed tumbling, the almost-out-of-control spins, the crawling, the giant-step jumps, and the heavy walks that are basic to Forti's vocabulary. But his movement has a subtle tendency for design. He makes it just a tiny bit bigger or more precise or elaborate in space. He is more satisfying to watch in a conventional dance way—he makes the movement more complete, more available. Forti can look awkward sometimes, or as if the movement is thrown away, but she has a special kind of exactitude, an inner sense of proportion and energy as they fit her body. It's not that she restrains herself, but that for her, embellishment is never an issue.

Maybe this is one reason why she doesn't seem to make dances in a choreographic sense, which would require developing, exploring, or somehow manipulating the movement material. In *For You*, the dancers and Van Riper worked in similar ways. They put together repeating motifs from a few basic ideas, the repetitions seldom were identical and seldom lasted very long before the performers would shuffle the elements and drift into a different repeating figure. Van Riper's sequences on soprano and alto saxes and soprano recorder consisted mostly of trilling revolutions in a small tonal range, sustained notes in which he could vary the quality with his body movement, and a few rhythmic phrases. He also played the thumb piano and a pottery cowbell.

At some point each dancer had a small solo—Forti crawled on splayed-out hands and feet, the feet dragging heavily, like a giant crab or a turtle; O'Reilly perched and hovered on one foot or the tips of his toes. But most of the dance was a series of duets. Forti and O'Reilly usually did the same kind of movement independently or worked with the idea of how two individual movers could relate to each other. Sometimes the relating was very close, as in a sequence when they rolled over and over with bodies loosely entwined. Sometimes the contact was more peripheral—rolling over foot-to-foot with their toes touching or somersaulting side by side. Sometimes they did the same thing but didn't touch—a long shoulder stand in which neither one of them seemed to move a muscle while Van Riper strolled between them playing the soprano sax, went over to his corner and exchanged it for the alto, returned to the dancers, and finally finished and left the floor. Only then, as they slowly lowered their legs to the floor, did Forti and O'Reilly show any tension.

Many of their encounters were about meeting and not meeting, being close together or far away, moving in a very similar range of space, shape, and energy without actually falling into synchrony. Often they'd circle each other, coming in so close they'd be back to back, then move off again. Or one of them would take one big hopping step right into the other's territory, and the other would quickly step away. They didn't project that feigned wariness you often see in dancers imitating animals, but they seemed acutely tuned in to each other's position and timing.

Maybe the most intriguing thing about these encounters was the lack of emotional signals. The dancers seemed cleansed of all dramatic intention—even the hostility, affection, alertness that performers usually attribute to the animals they're impersonating. Nor did they evince much more than a friendly enjoyment of each other as partners. Post-Judson neutrality seems to be going out of fashion, but it was nice to come across it again in Forti's work.

Cushioning the Minimalist Pew

Kei Takei: *Light Part 11*
Washington Square Methodist Church, New York

Rudy Perez Men's Coalition
Judson Church, New York

New York Magazine, 27 February 1978

Back in the post-Judson era of the late 1960s, Rudy Perez and Kei Takei were among the choreographers who were redefining the possibilities of dance. They both created highly individual forms and—unlike Trisha Brown and

Laura Dean, two other minimalists who began around that time—have remained pretty much without imitators. They both showed their latest works at two downtown churches recently, Takei at Washington Square Methodist and Perez at Judson.

Dance minimalism started out as an effort to clear away a lot of decorativeness and emotional coloring that had accumulated in the declining period of modern dance. The recovery of the simplest uses of the body in movement allowed people to reexamine the uses of choreography. Perez and Takei both saw a reduced bodily expression as a means of creating theater—an augmented minimalism that grew elsewhere into the spectacles of Richard Foreman, Robert Wilson, and Meredith Monk.

Japanese-born Takei began choreographing in a sort of Oriental crypto-Dada style: I remember one dance in about 1968 that ended when the performers had carefully covered the floor with paper flowers. Soon after that she embarked on what she now says is her lifelong work, Light, a cycle of dances in which the basic materials have remained constant but the ways they're put together and the ideas they convey evolve gradually, acquiring new meanings, losing unneeded ones. At first her work was baffling. People in funny white muslin rompers trudged around with little white packs on their backs. Takei lay on her back and rocked, or squatted and stared into a pool of light. Blindfolded women threw themselves around dangerously. It all went on for a very long time, changing by imperceptible degrees. But now the symbolic baselines have been established, and we see that the packs are any kind of burden, the blindfolds represent handicaps, the danger and the compulsive repetition stand for work, time, any of the inexorable constants under which we live.

In the most recent installments of Light, the performers are drawn to an arena, a ring made of stones that were used earlier for weapons. The eight-member community in Part 11 seems to be trying to pull itself together after the inexplicable stoning of Takei in Part 10. When the dance begins, they've made this ring, and some of them are industriously picking up the stones and putting them in their packs while others dance together in the center. They develop a rather complex, active stamping dance pattern little by little, rhythmically bonking together two rocks that they hold in their hands. Finally, they fling down all the stones they've collected in a spree of dancing. But as the dance ends, they go back to their jobs, carefully collect the remnants of the original ring, and file out.

Light Part 11 was created in 1976 for the Netherlands Dance Theater and this was its New York premiere. Takei has since made two additional parts, in which the tribal energy seems to be building up to another persecution, and Takei and five men engage in several types of hand-to-hand combat.

She sneaks out of the ring finally and builds herself an escape route by laying a path of stones she's filched from the ring.

With both Takei and Perez, I have a sense that they're holding back on movement—they want to limit the body and what it reveals. In Takei's case, this restriction allows her to create metaphors. The images of Light contain a range of human feelings and motivations—greed, obstinacy, craftiness, desperation, resignation, hope—depersonalized but emotionally resonant. When you see a person squatting to pick up a stone, he or she might be about to build, plant, play, or kill, depending on the context. I sometimes think Rudy Perez's holding back is a deliberate attempt to avoid implicating either himself or the viewer emotionally. Never a virtuosic or even a particularly agile dancer, he often depicted himself in the characteristic attitudes of football coaches and construction workers. His dances combined the images of jock stoicism and mechanical everyday gesture, often with slow-motion timing that contained and focused the energy even more.

Now he's working with a group he calls the Men's Coalition, which was featured at Judson Church in . . . Just for the Sake of It and According to What, or Is Dance Really About Dancing. Perez's idea of a male dancing image is highly romanticized and static, a throwback, I thought, to Ted Shawn and the early modern dancers, who didn't try to invent ways of moving like men but wanted simply to show that they were men. Virile poses, muscular simulated combats, with an exalted air of mission hanging about everything. Perez's men's group had all that, but except for a hokey reference to Christian enlightenment at the end of the evening, their mission seemed to be strictly on the surface. Almost always facing the audience, they went through simple movement sequences, working harder and much more earnestly than such movement ordinarily requires. Sometimes someone would eye another man speculatively, but only when the object of his interest wasn't looking.

What makes Perez less convincing than Kei Takei is that he doesn't see the dance as a process. Rather, it's an intelligent collage of ideas that can be suggested by physical positions or actions, or equally as well by music, costume, words. The dance itself has no mystery, it doesn't draw you into its depths; instead it's supposed to trigger you into the depths of your own fantasy.

Unidentical Twins

Viola Farber: *Turf*, Dance Umbrella
Entermedia Theater, New York

Margaret Jenkins and Company
Cunningham Studio, New York

New York Magazine, 27 March 1978

Both Margaret Jenkins and Viola Farber belong to the large family of dancers spawned by Merce Cunningham, but their choreographic ideas aren't much like his, or like each other's. Which is probably as much a tribute to Cunningham as it is to Jenkins and Farber. Cunningham has imparted to all his disciples an attitude of openness toward form and a trust in the power of movement to make its own impression on the viewer. When you look at a dance by Jenkins or Farber, whatever else may be going on in the way of decoration, sounds, words, manipulating of props, the putting on or taking off of more or less relevant costumes, you ultimately have to take the movement into account as a system with its own integrity, its own "meaning."

This was quite a remarkable assertion in the face of the programmatic, psychologically oriented modern dance that prevailed in the fifties when Cunningham's style was developing, and it's perhaps an even more revealing and demanding gift now, when modern dance leads us so often to numb little escape hatches.

Viola Farber's dance has never been especially comfortable or ingratiating to watch. In her program at the Dance Umbrella I felt a bleakness, a resignation, that was harder to take than the hard-driving, existential disengagement of her past work. At one time Farber's dancers would often seem to become possessed by the movement's energy and try to dance themselves into exhaustion. Jenkins's dance runs away with itself too sometimes—something in the Cunningham mystique seems to encourage this total expenditure of physical resources. It's eventually painful to watch, but exhilarating too.

In Farber's company the energy level seems lower now. The spirits, too. I'm not saying her new dance, *Turf*, is a direct expression of the fact that she and the company were forced by a greedy landlord to give up the studio they lovingly built, but its message seems to be issuing from a particularly barren, spiritless place. Even though—or maybe because—there are moments when the dance leans toward a ballet parody.

Turf, for Farber, Larry Clark, Andé Peck, and Jeff Slayton in tracksuits, is accompanied by the Poulenc Organ Concerto and takes place in a no-where of gorgeous light designed by Beverly Emmons. As the music strides vaingloriously in the background, the dancers lurch and fling themselves around, as if their own weight were an insurmountable encumbrance. Rooted to one spot, they strain and pull until one leg comes off the ground, or use all their might to dislodge an arm. But having initiated movement so laboriously, they seem to lose interest, or will, and the limb drops heavily back to its place. They jump doggedly, almost aimlessly, land like sandbags on both feet. Encountering each other, they start some corporate action, then drop it dully as the impulse runs out.

At certain points in the dance, they face the audience and seem to set themselves for giving a more sparkly display, but their effort conveys irony, not self-confidence. After the music ends, they line up and haul themselves, footstep after sodden footstep, toward the footlights.

Margaret Jenkins brought her eleven-member San Francisco-based company to New York for the first time and gave four performances at the Cunningham studio in Westbeth. I find it harder to catch the feeling-tone of Jenkins's work than Farber's. Maybe there's less feeling invested. The dancers seldom initiate movement from the center of the body, they don't put their weight behind what they do. They seem to regard dancing as a more casual thing, with effects that are easier to shake off. Jenkins surrounds her dance with unrelated, possibly even frivolous, stimuli, like the convoluted, evocative language of poet Michael Palmer, exclamatory remarks by the dancers, a taped reading of Wittgenstein's biography. This conforms to Cunningham orthodoxy about all elements of the dance being autonomous, but Jenkins's movements often don't imprint themselves on my imagination with equal insistence.

She's more compositionally minded than most Cunningham descendants. It pleases me to see movement I recognize in a dance—people shadowing other people's gestures, a game of tag where the tagger continues what the taggee was doing (Copy), a hard, angular dance in sophisticated clothes that's done again in shiny unitards, only quieter, blurred, as if half forgotten (About the Space in Between). But her movement seems distracted to me. People are constantly launching into gestures or traveling steps that only progress a little distance before they double back on themselves or switch to another idea. Her dancers' energies don't really build up or subside, except in small increments that cancel each other out.

Maybe you can only be this spendthrift with space when you're really confident about it. Once, in Copy, a dance lit partly by the gray glow of several television monitors, the dancers mill around quite close together. Moving quickly and continuing to make the big, florid arm gestures that are characteristic of Jenkins's movement, they don't shrink in or exhibit any particular caution about bumping into each other. I thought, people in New York never move that way in the dark.

Matters of Merce

Le Théâtre du Silence
Beacon Theater, New York

Merce Cunningham: Events
Roundabout Theater, New York

Kenneth King and Dancers
Lepercq Space, Brooklyn Academy, New York

New York Magazine, 16 April 1978

The French contemporary dance company Le Théâtre du Silence managed to extinguish Merce Cunningham's *Summerspace* before our eyes during its short season at the Beacon. No reason we should have expected a faithful rendition from it, I guess. The French probably think Americans can't do *Giselle*.

After seeing the rest of the repertory Le Théâtre brought for its New York debut—half-assimilated modern dance postures and groupings dubbed onto standard balletic steps, floor patterns, and themes—I could see why it misfired on Cunningham's movement style. But it's harder to excuse its lack of sensitivity to the mood, the texture of this modern dance classic. You have to be pretty out of it aesthetically to throw gaudy green, orange, and red light all over a pastel pointillist backdrop (Robert Rauschenberg), or to play a score in which the notes sprinkle like rain into a pond (Morton Feldman's "Ixion") as if it were something linear written by Liszt.

Come to think of it, the quality of aesthetic preciseness was missing in all of Le Théâtre's work. They seem to be serious, sincere dancers, but their idea about dancing is bland, as if they expect the steps to communicate everything. Well, they come from a tradition where the steps do constitute a solid core of dependable, universally known possibilities. Style to them doesn't mean dance style the way it does to us. American modern dance companies, even the less adventurous ones of today, begin with a certain way they want to move. Somebody, a choreographer probably, or a group of dancers together, says, I want to try making a dance about repetition, or a dance where the movement is all like swinging, or a ballet with all the steps done backwards, whatever, and pretty soon they form a company. No matter what other imagery, logic, or purpose the dance has, it must make dance sense to the people doing it.

The dance sense in *Summerspace*, or any other Merce Cunningham dance, comes from how the dancers put steps together, how they orient themselves in space and time. The French dancers could handle the steps all right, but they looked heavy, uninvolved. They seemed to want to stabilize and solidify each new combination, rather than inscribe it with that particular blend of attention, clarity, and urgency for what comes next that characterizes Cunningham.

But my disappointment with Summerspace came not only because I'd hoped to see at least one piece of fine choreography in this series. The fact is, Le Théâtre du Silence was just about the only place you could see a dance of Merce Cunningham's this season—unless you lived in Boston. Cunningham once more denied his repertory to New York and presented two weeks of Events at the Roundabout instead. Cunningham Events are a little like long dances, but they're not really a substitute. I'm not saying that one is better than the other, but a self-contained, repeatable stage happening has a force, a resonance in our imagination, a "meaning," that can't really be triggered by a one-time-only sequence of movement phrases.

What the Events do exemplify is the triumphant integrity of dancing. In an open space, without benefit of story or mood or climax-development tracks to help us organize what we're seeing, people simply dance things. Of course, what they dance is highly sophisticated—fast footed, articulate, ballet reinterpreted for people who like to get somewhere. The space is very active—often two or three or more separate dance units are going on at a time, and everyone acts as if he or she were the only moving body in sight.

There's an evenhandedness, a downplaying of ego implied in this way of performing, yet Cunningham's dancers come across as very distinct individuals. This season I particularly enjoyed Lisa Fox's calmness and lack of affectation, the way Karole Armitage is gradually introducing her long, balletic body to kinkier manners, and the way Robert Kovich instinctively discovers the phrasing of any movement pattern.

The company as a whole is looking superb now, and Cunningham has loosened up on the almost demonically calculated way he's been choreographing for them recently. He seems to have resumed an interest in partnering work too, after several years. The last two Events contained lots of duets where the dancers had to accommodate to each other by extremely sensitive uses of timing, touch, and position. Sometimes the same duet would be danced by two couples simultaneously, with slight variations of speed. Cunningham himself danced only solos in the Events I saw. Most of his mobility now is in the upper body, but his gestures, his timing, and his concentration make a convincing other kind of dancing—a contrast, no less impressive in its stillness than the activity surrounding it.

Cunningham entrusts the musical accompaniment for each Event to a different contemporary composer. At Event #209 I heard John Cage's "Mesostics re Merce Cunningham," in which Demetrio Stratos produced an astonishing array of sounds and sound effects using only his voice. For

#215 and #216 composer-singer Meredith Monk, with Andrea Goodman and Monica Solem, chanted lullabies and laments, litanies of rage, condolence, and mirthless laughter, sunsets full of birds, and marketplaces full of chattering women.

Kenneth King shares the Cunningham mystique, although he never danced with Cunningham. His performances at Brooklyn Academy were collages of dance, visuals, words, and other elements, not always obviously related. Like Cunningham, he loves found rhythms, and his movement is nonsequential but highly charged. King has the skimming, let-it-go quality of Cunningham, but everything he does seems more predetermined, more significant, though no easier to hang on to. His dances are a mysterious mixture of things theatrical and beautiful, of wit and intellectual provocation and kinetic pleasure—not like a Cunningham dance but like a Cunningham Event carried into a deeper dimension.

I usually have no idea what King's dances are about, but I always think of them as very informational. In RAdeoA.C.tiv(ID)ty a woman reads from some scientific papers of Madame Curie. Dancers in white move gravely in and out of the space, individually and in small groups, sometimes picking up or shadowing one another's gestures, like fugitive images on light-sensitive paper. People in black move across the back of the space in angular poses from antique vases, locked together like fixed, ageless designs. Voices in choral dialogue play verbal games: "Go. go. go be Be. bee go be. Go be. go go be gobe beo goGobe. Go be the Gobi Desert."

In Dance S(p)ell, eight dancers spin and walk in circular patterns while King shows the audience a zany, Duchamp-inspired machine called a "Telaxic Synapsulator." "This is a What Comes After Movies machine." Thin, bearded, possibly crazy, he touts this gadget, which has several rotary parts and no discernible function. "This is a Phobia Fadeout machine." "This is a Brain-to-brain Instant Identity transfer machine." Deadpan, quiet, a tiny thrill of evangelism or trumpery in his voice. "This is a Multiple Foci Focusing machine." I start to see nineteenth-century con men selling patent medicines. And panacea merchants on TV, politicians talking us into new nuclear gizmos. "This is a clean machine." A fanatic, a fake, he offers instant enlightenment, or instant oblivion; which? "This is a dance machine."

Rille

Douglas Dunn: *Rille*
Opera House, Brooklyn Academy, New York
Unpublished notes, 24 April 1978

After last summer's disaster with *Celeste*, Doug Dunn seems to have reversed himself. Everything that *Celeste* did in the way of large, unrestrained, uncensored ideas is now clamped under control. *Rille* is extremely formal, almost didactic at times, everything pulled in—the space, the energy, the interactions. Yet it's not a regressive piece for him. It's just taking a drastically different direction. There's something almost scary about the idea that someone could deliberately make such a shift in his work—choreographers usually evolve more intuitively and gradually.

Rille is a sort of Yvonne Rainer dance—the fulfillment of where Rainer was when she quit dancing because she thought she was exercising too much control over the group. Doug choreographed *Rille*, but it looks as if all the people in it could have thought it up themselves. He managed to keep the feeling of individual assertiveness, yet make his point very clear at all times. (I mean that the points are there and very accessible, though it took me two viewings to "get it," and some people didn't get it at all.)

Yet I didn't really like the piece—both times there were long sections when my mind wandered or I floated near sleep with my eyes open. I think some of this was due to the low feeling-tone of the dancing. Everyone very blank faced (Rainerish) even in the duet episodes, and the dynamics quite moderate and simple. Few explosions or falls or even phrases of any length or complexity. Long times when it seemed there were more people on the stage standing still than people moving, long sequences of two to four or five repetitions of a simple phrase, followed by another series and another, or a person crossing a tiny space with two or three repeats of a phrase, then another person with another phrase, etc. None of these individual statements has any effect on the others, or on the whole quality of the stage. So even though the piece does have an overall shape and development, it never seems to be in the process of developing.

I'm sure *Rille* is an important piece, and that it probably won't be given again. It's important for all the obvious reasons—because it's serious, it doesn't bow to the extroverted, please-the-audience psychology so prevalent today, and it is structured and instructive. I'm fascinated to see what Doug will do next.

Dancing Parttime

Sara Rudner: *Dancing Parttime*
St. Mark's Church, New York
New York Magazine, 5 June 1978

Sara Rudner, a dynamite dancer, choreographs somewhere between the augmented minimalism of the downtown experimentalists and the high-style popularism of Broadway. Rudner's movement is not only highly energized and variable, flowing with ease from big to small, from aggressive to flickering images, but it seems as if her whole body presents itself all the time. She radiates, she makes everything seem momentous, vital. This is a quality I think all great performers have, and it's why you never get tired of watching Rudner dance. But it's highly personal, not something one can train other dancers to do.

Rudner danced for years with Twyla Tharp but stuck to the more austere precincts of creative work when Tharp's dances got more accessible. It seems that dancing *about* something is still not okay with Rudner, and her group works often are relentless. There's a feeling that the dancers are possessed by some demon of motion that commands them to keep on going no matter what, continually whispering new ideas to them that they must carry out. *Dancing Parttime* has slightly more overall shape than her prior group works, but it seems to spread itself open-endedly, geared toward going on rather than reaching a goal. Even when, after an hour of dancing, the five women slowly subside, their energy diminishing along with their space as they sink to the floor, you feel on the next pulse beat somebody could say, "One, . . ." and they'd be off again.

Counting is important in *Dancing Parttime*. Sometimes I don't see why the dancers call out numbers here and there, but other times the counting helps me perceive the compositional idea—as in one sequence where all the women line up along one side of the space and establish a pattern of advancing steps on seven counts, reversing directions and going back to their starting places in four. Later, they play with the phrase, stretching parts of it by repeating some of the movements, slowing down or speeding up the tempo, but always returning the same way to the starting line. More often, though, the movement dictates its own rules, independent of formal counts. Rudner and Jean Churchill chase each other with skittering runs and breakneck baseball slides, so close together that, once, they actually collide. Churchill does a solo circling her arms in growing and shrinking spheres that start close to the body, all the while bending and tilting and weaving till you're sure she'll throw herself off balance.

At some time during the dance, each performer, Rudner, Churchill, and

Shana Menaker, Vicky Shick, and Amy Spencer, has a solo where she flings gestures from what might be ordinary life into space, then goes on without providing us with their context. One sequence looks like an interrupted closet cleaning, another like the windups to a series of moves in some kind of athletic event. Not till the piece is almost over do I suddenly think that the whole package of patterns, games, and variations might have come from the movement material contained in the solo Rudner did at the very beginning.

Multiple Exposure

Trisha Brown and Company
Public Theater, New York
New York Magazine, 28 June 1978

Trisha Brown, who gave four performances at the Public Theater, makes process dances. The dancers are engaged in working out a structure that allows for—sometimes requires—accidents to happen, adjustments to be made, individual decisions to influence the operation. In practice the dance reveals the dancers as much as the dancers reveal the dance.

Brown's new group work, *Splang*, is an exaggerated look at a phenomenon that affects all dancers and critics: the amount of leeway there is in describing movement. Brown gave instructions to Elizabeth Garren, Wendy Perron, and Mona Sulzman as to how to execute the dance. The instructions went like this: "Step forward R, trip, run 3, jab-cross-nod as you back up. . . ." The dance is the three dancers' interpretation of this "score." If you think it produces unison movement, try it on the next three people you get in the same room.

Splang looks like three solos which sometimes almost converge, but it's fascinating what a relatively small range of the choices the dancers make. They look as if they're doing a style, even though Trisha Brown doesn't demonstrate or codify her movement at all in conventional stylistic ways. Her dancers don't seem to move toward or from any fixed goals or body alignings; they're loose and changeable, but even when a shape seems unfinished you can see what it is. Brown and her dancers have an acute ability to perceive a pattern forming and adapt to it, and they seem equally facile with this intelligence in both spacing and timing. They can switch easily from an inner to an outer focus, and in *Splang* this draws the audience's attention to different dancers, helps us find a center of interest even when the action seems randomly organized.

Brown performed her solo *Water Motor*, which seems to be about throwing movement far away, close in, a little at a time, or all at once, but never letting it stop or get completely out of control. And when you see her do the solo *Accumulation with Talking*, a dance that involves adding on and subtracting movements in a continuous, rhythmically repeating sequence while telling stories to the audience, you see that flexibility of moving and thinking together are what she's all about.

Erasures and Afterthoughts

David Gordon Pick-Up Company
American Theater Lab, Dance Theater Workshop, New York
New York Magazine, 16 October 1978

Dance gets distorted and dissipated in two main ways. One is by deliberate upset, strong counteraction, like the therapeutic revolution of the fifties and sixties against the drained, overdecorative formalism of late modern dance. The other is more insidious—a degeneration of the creative impulse through tiny lapses of detail, inadvertent change, elaborations and reworkings of what were once original ideas. At the other end of the continuum begun by Doris Humphrey, Martha Graham, and the moderns, David Gordon is building back up again on the structures stripped bare by Cunningham, Rainer, and the minimalists. In the performance of Gordon's Pick-Up Company at American Theater Lab, I was amazed at how complex and stylized his work looked and—already—how derivative.

I think Gordon is basically a theater person—which didn't necessarily exclude him from the experimental pursuits of the Judson Dance Theater a decade and a half ago. He doesn't have a dancer's body, or even an athlete's, and I find the way he moves the least arresting thing about him. When performing he's always impersonating—often being a version of himself—but he's never *only* himself. He stands eyeball-to-eyeball with the audience in *Mixed Solo*, looks at us frankly, sincerely, confidentially; that is, he *acts* frank, sincere, confidential. But he makes me uncomfortable because he pretends not to be pretending. Later, the people who've been standing in the background watching and wisely remarking on his dance do the same dance, disarming grins and all. *Mixed Solo*, choreographed last spring, is all about the wiles of the performer, the audience's gullible efforts to grasp the profundity we think is there, the ease with which naturalness can be converted into rehearsed material. The dance is circular, airtight, a comment on commenting.

Chair (1974) is a send-up of all the techniques the post-modern dancers used to liberate themselves from the ragged coattails of Graham and Humphrey. Gordon and Valda Setterfield scramble through a long series of moves on two folding chairs. The moves—purposeless but purposefully performed—were supposedly derived from an outlandishly complicated chance procedure. Loaded but irrelevant music ("The Stars and Stripes Forever") plays and does not play. It all seems so much more like a regression to childhood now than it did four years ago.

I think to Gordon words make more sense than movement for conveying ideas. His new piece, *What Happened*, is a sort of choral reading for seven women. In flat, isolated beats, speaking sometimes together, sometimes in a jumble of individual timing, they recite selected words and short phrases, each with an accompanying movement or gesture. It's like a kind of sign language in which the gestures sometimes illustrate or pun the words. Others have used this idea before—Remy Charlip, Trisha Brown, and Kathy Duncan come to mind—but Gordon manipulates the word sequences brainily so that the limited material never quite organizes itself into complete grammatical sentences or whole stories, yet a dense auralvisual texture is created. At particular points the nonsense evolves into Hamlet's "To be or not to be" speech.

Gordon's movement seems deliberately neutral, serving as a sort of visualization of the sound effects, and both elements are meticulously shaped and controlled to develop patterns of unison, echoing, counterpoint, and carefully arranged floor patterns. It's not exactly a dance, but it kept reminding me of Doris Humphrey.

Partly to Mostly Variable

Merce Cunningham Dance Company
City Center Theater, New York
New York Magazine, 30 October 1978

We've gotten so used to Merce Cunningham's Events—choreography presented in any order, any space, in bits and pieces and patchwork combinations—that it's easy to forget his works are not all alike. The Cunningham company's City Center season showed with startling clarity the difference between Cunningham dancing and a Cunningham dance. Of course, dancing in a particular set of costumes and decor, accompanied by a particular set of sounds, looks different from what's simply passing through an unembellished open space. And a title—*RainForest, Inlets*—sets you up for a whole lot more specific experience than an Event #178. But the switch from more or less open-ended and randomly connected movement sequences to a self-contained, finite series of actions called a dance must have as profound an effect on the dancers' perceptions as it does on ours, and the company looked more than just technically potent as it worked with the implicit theatricality and playfulness of the Cunningham dances.

These dancers' usual demeanor is noncommittal. They aim for neutrality, but often they look dead serious or even sour; and sometimes their gaze becomes fixed on some empty area of space for long periods of time. Not responding to the companions with whom they're creating intricate physical patterns, their faces look less alert and intelligent than their bodies. When they get a chance to do the dances as dances, some of the blankness goes away, and there's a shared sense of drama, of fun, of sensuality and intimacy.

Cunningham's range as a choreographer is also much broader than we might expect from the Events, where one kind of movement cancels out another during the egalitarian process of collage. Even when he did repertory more often, people used to identify his dances by their settings, and it's true that RainForest's atmosphere is very dependent on the Andy Warhol silver helium-filled pillows gently bumping through the air against black background and changeable white lighting effects by Charles Atlas. But the dance, choreographed in 1968, also has a very specific movement vocabulary. The body moves from the center with gut-pulling intensity. The dancers work a lot on the floor and, when they're in pairs, with lots of body surfaces in contact. They throw or drag their weight around, often violently. It's easier for animal images to emerge in this dance than in Summerspace (1958), for instance, where the movement is practically all locomotion—running, skipping—with only glancing body contacts and brief resting moments.

With twenty years' dances on view during the season, we could see that Cunningham is usually preoccupied with a particular movement or theatrical concern each time he choreographs. Inlets (1977), visually and aurally influenced by the Pacific Northwest, where it was made and where Cunningham comes from, uses the upper body in much more sinuous, fluid ways than his other pieces do. Inlets is a quiet, almost moody dance. To John Cage's combinations of hollow and rustly sounds, the dancers seem to dissolve and undulate in and out of a fog created by scrims and shifting lights.

But it's an entirely different kind of quiet from the contemplative stillness of Rebus (1975), where, in David Behrman's dreamlike landscape of sustained vocal tones over even more sustained electronic tones, Cunningham as mastermind stands apart from a group of ten dancers. Sometimes he seems to be imagining them, as they freeze in mid-move; other times he manipulates one of them, makes shadowy motions that they fill out and complete, turns his back on their gyrations as if their youthful speed and strength can carry them without his help.

The new Fractions, with Jon Gibson's electronically orchestrated flute solo, reminds me of some 1960s Cunningham works. The company was smaller then, and he was less interested in mass formations and big concerted bursts of energy than he's been recently—in Torse (1976) and Sounddance (1974). Fractions is a dance where many things are going on at the same time. The audience can scan the whole buzzing stage or zero in on one dancer, a choice that's especially disconcerting with something like the totally different simultaneous duets by Louise Burns and Chris Komar, Ellen Cornfield and Robert Kovich. But then Cunningham clears everybody off the stage so we can see Lisa Fox's solo. Fox has a Twyla Tharpian sort of wriggliness in the upper body, an air of slipping through space, but her legs are balletically powerful—a fine contradiction.

Sometimes Cunningham even seems to be choreographing dances to look like Events. We've been looking at the parts of Changing Steps (1974) woven into Events for years, so that it didn't make one cohesive dance when it was all put together, but I found no particular logic in Exchange either. This is Cunningham's latest company work, a big piece using all fifteen dancers. There's a Balanchinian oddness about it—like four couples working first in unison, then two of them starting to do entirely different things from the other two. At some point, everyone goes off and comes back with close-fitting gray sweatpants over their identically colored gray tights. Torsos hang and swing way out, then hunker back into proper alignment. And all the dancers don't gather onstage at once until the very end. That's when I decided that maybe it was a dance about various ways you can amass that many people.

Backwater: Twosome

Steve Paxton: Backwater: Twosome
Dance Theater Workshop, New York
Unpublished notes, 7 November 1978

I found Steve Paxton's improv evening with David Moss, Backwater: Twosome, curiously unkinetic. It seems to me now that almost every time I see Steve dance I have a similar reaction. I always feel he ought to move me more with his dancing, that he's built for more than he's delivered. I guess I have to revise my expectations—maybe for him art consists in not letting loose, in never using everything you have.

Certainly, the main impression I got this time was one of control. Having done contact improv so long, he seems to have gotten down to a science the ability to recover immediately from anything, to land on your feet. This may have started as a way to open oneself up to risk; now it looks like a technique to minimize the effects of risk. He seldom gave his weight away, and whenever he did, he'd quickly let his dancer's stabilizing gear take over and bring his lower body into a secure supporting mode, then he'd continue to hang over or lean out with his torso or head; from there he could look odd or unbalanced but he wouldn't fall.

He seemed to want to undo everything by reversing his tracks, uncoiling his spirals. He'd go through series of tiny, unusual isolations, none, of course, leading to a phrase or a connected chain of movement. Doug once explained to me that the aim of contact improvisation is not to develop structures, not to repeat.

There's always a jock element to the way Steve moves. I suppose it's a combination of his body itself, which is so fit and trained looking, and the casual energy—casual strength & mastery really—of so much that he does. About 90 percent of all he did that evening was unplaced—and then suddenly he'd do something very designed, often very archaic, like slipping his arms up straight and parallel to one side above his head or taking a series of foot-touching sidewards or backwards steps with feet parallel. Then he'd look quite beautiful & quite like Merce for a flash.

Tharpsichore in Brooklyn

Twyla Tharp and Dancers
Opera House, Brooklyn Academy, New York
New York Magazine, 12 March 1979

Twyla Tharp has always preferred making new dances to maintaining an active repertory of older works. During Tharp's uproariously successful Brooklyn Academy season, I began to think she might be right. The older dances not only look significantly different from their original versions, they don't seem as convincing as even the less impressive of her current things. *Eight Jelly Rolls* (1971) and *Sue's Leg* (1974) are terrific dances, full of propulsiveness and stylish wit—I'd rather see them any day than most of what I do see. They've both gotten more refined, more clear, than they used to be. This seems to be the inevitable fate of everything in dance that survives at all, but with Tharp's work it's a major problem because the scruffiness and the blur are part of what endears her to us. Her dances may be brainy, comic, tightly structured, but when we first see them they disarm us with casualness.

Later, the comedy gets broader, the characterization more like characters, and the body language bigger and more precise. The rhythms have
a way of evening out. When *Country Dances* and *Cacklin' Hen* were choreographed, in 1976, the music was played by an authentic bluegrass band.
Now a New York pickup group plays it. The same notes, same tempos,
even the same little yips and shouts are emitted by someone who seems to
be reading them from a score. But the rhythm is all wrong, subtly. Maybe
it's the bowing technique of the fiddlers or the way the phrase is accented,
but it just doesn't feel like country music.

All of Tharp's new dances, where the performers haven't yet gained
complete control over the beat, have a personal play with rhythm that's
disappeared from the older ones. This elasticity, this seeing each dancer
fill out the beat in his or her own way, is one thing that makes her dances
different from something you'd see on a dance floor as choreographed for
Broadway or TV and more like what you'd actually see on a dance floor.

This was most graphically demonstrated in the last part of *Chapters and
Verses*, which is not a complete dance but three sections of a projected
longer work. So far the piece looks like a latter-day *Deuce Coupe*, a review
of the fun, fantasies, and discontents of American youth. The final section
is a long solo for Sara Rudner, who's joined and gradually enveloped by
eleven other dancers, all swooping, sliding, lurching, flinging, and collapsing around to hypnotic disco music. There is a slight edge to the music,
which shifts from phrases of seven beats to six, eight, five, and though the
dancing keeps threatening to revert to a pulsating blob, it never does.

Surprise is the lifeblood of Tharp's choreography. Sometimes she makes
a whole dance about some way-out idea, like Rose Marie Wright's taking
on five men in the marathon *Cacklin' Hen*. Sometimes it's an image materi-
alized from the dance's subconscious memory, like William Whitener's
sweet, gawky dance to the Mickey Mouse Club theme song in *Chapters and
Verses*. And sometimes she just threads clashing ideas throughout an entire
dance, makes them become the dance, like *Baker's Dozen*.

A work for twelve dancers to the jazz piano music of Willie "the Lion"
Smith (played by Dick Hyman), *Baker's Dozen* is an important work and a
compositional advance for Tharp. Beautifully structured, inventively made,
it has, simultaneously, a sense of restraint—of holding back its full forces
until just the right moment—and a sense of unleashing a totally satisfying
flow of movement all the time.

Most of the sections of the dance play with the tension between at least
two ideas. The first section, all duets, seems impelled to move at double
the speed of the relaxed music. The trio section that follows pits exaggerated attitudes of a tango against fast, scrambling partner work. The trios
expand into quartets by means of intricate partner switching. The groups

consolidate into two sextets that seem even more tangled and out of order. But suddenly one of them streaks across in meticulous unison. At last the whole ensemble coalesces, crossing and recrossing the stage in alternate swatches of smooth, strutting unison and jammed-up rough-and-tumble, and against this background each dancer does a brief solo. What an elegant way to show off a company.

I found Tharp's new solo, 1903, both intriguing and curiously moving. I'm still not sure why I had tears in my eyes at the end. Randy Newman sings softly deceptive songs, first ("Sail Away") a bitter advertisement for the cushy American life—to lure the gullible, maybe prospective slaves, across the ocean. Tharp wrenches and thrashes through the space. Newman croons lecherously to "Suzanne"; Tharp does tense, belligerent sexpot poses. Finally, while Newman recalls lazy Sunday afternoons in "Dayton, Ohio—1903," she scoots and slides, suddenly pulling up short to look from side to side, like a little girl in proper clothes listening to grown-up conversation, then flounces into a few more circles, walks off. It seemed to me 1903 tells some hard truths about our fantasies and their fulfillment, about going on with it even if it's not what you thought, and about the grains of romantic illusion that may still cling to the successful performer's Milliskin surface. Maybe it's a chapter from Tharp's autobiography—perhaps all her dance is.

There Are Ethnics and Ethnix

Unpublished, March 1979

One indication that we're in a period of choreographic decline is the rise of the performer. What grabs us now is the dancer, not the dance. Bill T. Jones is one of those extraordinary dancers who can take us to the most extreme limits with complete credibility. You think you're watching him go over the brink of rage or physical control or sanity—and the next minute you could swear he's looking you straight in the eye and telling you the most intimate or loving or shameless things. The dances I've seen him do before seemed so emotionally devastating, I thought he'd have to burn himself out in a couple of years, but in his recent solo program at the Kitchen he seems to have harnessed some of that demonic energy. I'm not so afraid for him anymore—and I guess I'm also a bit relieved; he exacts a lot from the audience as his collaborator and target.

Jones's manic imagination—and the extent of his access to it—often reminds me of the solos of Douglas Dunn. His process of following a train of movement-thought is made visible in Floating the Tongue, in which he improvises a very brief movement sequence, then repeats it several times. As he moves through it, he talks, partly to himself, partly to the audience, verifying the movement facts, commenting on his own performance, releasing whatever associations come into his head about what he's doing. What's on his mind mostly is his family, his friends, race, sex, his dance ancestors and models, the act of performing. It happens so fast, he can't exercise much censorship, and the turns of his mind can be momentarily jarring, funny, shocking, poignant. He exposes himself as such a virtuosic manipulator of audience reaction that I don't know whether to be amused or appalled.

Two of his pieces were process dances. In *Progresso*, he sets out a design of little flags on the floor, bringing one flag out at a time, always retracing his steps along the same path out and back. Later, reciting a long list of gorgeous names, possibly belonging to his childhood friends—Rhodessa, Rhodesia, Vilena, Bill Tass Jones, named after a famous racist governor of Georgia—he gathers the flags into a cluster at the back of the space. He constructs the floor pattern again, this time replacing the flags with little movement incidents. He takes a flying jump off the side of a pillar, somersaults into a split, hesitates at one point along the route to throw a coy look over his shoulder at the audience.

As in *Echo*—a litany of names and impersonations of friends, including himself—his repetitions are enough alike for us to see that they're a sequence, but not identical, so that the sequence infused with his energy becomes a cycle of wildly whipping, falling off, slowly rising, subsiding intensities. In the end of *Echo* he writhes and stumbles, holding a desperate, half-articulate nightmare conversation with his fantasies, somehow wringing the words out of the song, "I'm just a poor wayfarin' stranger."

For a long time, most blacks in dance seemed to have had to prove themselves either by assimilating white styles or by becoming glamorous pop figures. Now there are a few who are working more experimentally and more personally—more on the fringe. Jones's style is confrontational and therefore unsettling. But he's also ingratiating, entertaining, and choreographically substantial. Quite a combination.

I imagine Israel to be a tough, gritty country whose people are made of stronger moral stuff than we are. So I was surprised when the Bat-Dor Company of Tel Aviv turned out to specialize in academic modern dance. The company breezed through here, stopping at Brooklyn Academy just long enough to garner some New York reviews to launch them on a U.S. tour. Like the dance of postrevolutionary Russia, Bat-Dor speaks to a pioneer society not with radical ideas of art but with escapism and romanticized images. The directors haven't sought a new dance language appropriate to their time and their situation, but have borrowed the all-purpose, late-Graham-with-options style studied by Americans who want to get jobs in modern dance companies.

The big work of the program I saw was *Journey*, choreographed by Domy Reiter-Soffer. The piece started out to be rather spare, with Jeannette Ordman, who's also the company artistic director, as a Grahamlike Woman Who Seeks the Essences Within or something like that. But the plot gets murkier, the props more psychedelic, and the apotheosis—the Woman gives birth to a son and immediately becomes enshrined in an elaborate, stage-filling costume—looks something like a 1950s movie musical about fashion photography.

Creative Doodling

Dana Reitz and Malcolm Goldstein: *Between 2*
Washington Square Methodist Church, New York
Soho Weekly News, 10 May 1979

Dana Reitz didn't put any illustrations on the program for her new work, *Between 2*, but some of the notes I took had an odd resemblance to the squiggly drawings she'd used in the past. *Between 2* is actually a collaboration—as I suspect all Reitz's dances are. She shares the space with violinist Malcolm Goldstein. Their ideas mingle, overlap, work off each other. What Goldstein suggests aurally she translates into movement, and the result is so kinetic that my hand draws it quicker than my mind can think up words. Reitz's work is a graphic representation of a thought process. Her method is exactly opposite to that of the post-Cunningham dancers, and its most striking aspect, to me, is its integration, its flow.

In some quarters it's still an acceptable technique to push a movement idea into new territory little by little, enlarging or diminishing shapes, changing the energy qualities, the accents, the phrasing, or in other ways working material into a new form. Merce Cunningham and his followers deprived themselves of this possibility in composition, determining sequence and phrase modification by external, chance procedures—maybe that's one reason why their work sometimes looks fragmentary, undeveloped. Reitz pleases me because her work is logical and also because I feel she's dealt thoroughly with everything she started by the time she's done.

Between 2 is set in dialogue form. Usually Goldstein leads off, playing a nonmelodic motif while Reitz listens. Soon she starts to move, echoing some quality she hears. They each continue until they've satisfied some inner intention, then they pause, collect themselves, begin again. The dance starts quietly, warming up, then blossoms into elaborate tonal/kinetic flights and ornaments.

Each theme may be repeated many times with variations. Goldstein presses the strings into an aria of exaggerated vibrato; Reitz carves big hairpin shapes around herself with her hands and arms. He saws away, making a sound as monotonous and pushy as a motor; she repeatedly folds forward, touching her hands to the floor, kicking or twirling her heels out behind her. Sometimes she throws herself over quite violently, sometimes stealthily, as if trying to sneak up on it; sometimes she taps the floor lightly and bounds off; sometimes she just marks the whole phrase, not touching base at all.

Though the feeling of the dance as a whole is overwhelmingly decorative, Reitz has an irresistible gift for character. It's not her purpose to make character dances or stories, yet the gesture is often loaded, like some arcane form of mime. You also sense an extra significance about what Reitz is doing because she's such a distinctive mover. Naturally long and erect, she seems able to twist and loop her body around in an infinite number of directions and counterdirections. Yet she always seems stable, even rooted, because of a fixed and arresting focus of the eyes and head. You feel she *knows* where she is always, even when her body looks flyaway or distorted. Her dynamic range is quite subtle, moving with ease through different speeds and tensions, and through every variety of lightness—a deft attack, a grazing touch, a skimming trajectory, a soft footfall.

Goldstein's dynamics and his dexterity are a stunning match for Reitz. He can make the bow skitter and whang across the strings while producing the tiniest sounds imaginable. His music too has suggestions of character—his violin can break into wild, sobbing tantrums, puppy yips, wails, and wheezes and can slide like a Japanese flute, play duets with itself in quarter-tones, and thump percussively.

Yet for all their similarities, both in style and intent, the performers remain rather isolated from each other. They always occupy separate areas of the space, moving within small corridors and islands of their own. This sense of being sealed off, of detailing a very specific but very clearly established universe, pervades everything Reitz does. I only realized it the next night, at Merce Cunningham's studio Event. Cunningham did a solo in which he seemed first to detach his arms from his body. Floating above him, connected by what surely were extrasensory means, they probed and palpated the space around him. It seemed to be a much bigger space than he could ever penetrate or use up. A more mysterious space than he could ever really familiarize himself with. Reitz's space is known, used, shown, and, by the end of *Between 2*, full and finished.

After my lecture . . .

Unpublished notes, 31 July 1979

After my lecture at Connecticut College last night, I went to watch a dance class & rehearsal. It appears to meet every night around 8:30 and is familiarly called a stretch class. The teacher, Colette Barry, was setting a semi-improvisational piece on the group, to be given next weekend at a faculty concert. Dressed in an assortment of sweatpants, shorts, & brief tops, the class went through a voluptuous series of stretches, whooping with pleasure when a boy with long black hair & a bandanna on his head began to accompany them dazzlingly on the drums.

The atmosphere, the hour of night, what they did, made it so different from the dancing I'd seen before in that room. (Daniel Nagrin said, "The place is full of ghosts.") And this morning again there wasn't a piano to be heard in Crozier, which was awash with children in a swimming program. The gym, with its dividing wall taken down, was cluttered with gymnastic equipment, and the one early morning dance class was held across the campus in the Williams gym, because people think the studio floors in Crozier are too hard.

Games of Candor

Oberlin Dance Collective
Dance Theater Workshop, New York
Soho Weekly News, 16 August 1979

The Oberlin Dance Collective is a post-postmodern dance company, maybe one of the first. No pickup group or occasional ensemble, it was founded in 1971 at Oberlin College and migrated in 1976 to San Francisco, where it pursues its own dance and dance-related activities, far from the frissons of novelty and economic retrenchment that periodically shake the Soho dance scene. The members attribute much of their dance training to teachers long since quit of traditional modern dance and long since reconciled to the basic rationality of ballet. And the choreographic strategies they employ couldn't have jelled before Yvonne Rainer.

In the two programs they presented at Dance Theater Workshop's Out-of-Towners series, ODC demonstrated not only a common aesthetic, but a common vocabulary of movement associations and patterns with which to convey that aesthetic. Whether choreographed by artistic director Brenda Way, Kimi Okada, Katie Nelson, Eric Barsness, or Pam Quinn, the dances all worked from a balletic body sense—upright torso, strong legs, active arms, all of these relaxed so that the dancer can travel, switch directions quickly, tilt off-center, or even spill. Regular rhythm is essential, so is repetition and variation through repositioning of the same movements. But sequence, build, and development of movement elements are taboo, as, of course, is emoting of any sort.

All nine dancers always look pulled together, inwardly centered, unflappable. But at the same time their performing stance is confrontational. They look the audience straight in the eye, often talking to us as if resuming conversations interrupted but still on their minds. They're not hostile; they're just including us in the everyday business of their lives. The notion that dancers can and even should do this is one basic tenet of minimalism, epitomized, I think, by the calm sincerity of the early Trisha Brown. The Oberlin dancers are less plain, closer to theater, with their verbal anecdotes, mime gestures, the comradeliness among themselves that is allowed to show, and as with all who use literal gestures in dance, they endear themselves to the audience. They bridge the footlights by breaking into our language every so often.

It's not movement that ODC is presenting so much as their own likable, capable personas, being constantly put to the test of structure. This idea is best illustrated, I think, in *Formats*, a series of pieces choreographed by Brenda Way over a period of five years. The three sections shown here required the dancers to be able to do one kind of activity full-out, cut it off on cue, and immediately start doing another kind of activity.

In *Format I* six dancers do swooping, skimming enchaînements, relate personal anecdotes, flounce through jogging and athletic-looking actions, make sounds by clicking, whistling, poking, and slapping themselves, and up and down and back again, switching channels whenever Brenda Way hits a woodblock. She's following a stopwatch, and her time intervals range from a few seconds to maybe forty-five. In *Format II* Bill Irwin and Pam Quinn follow a similar plan, only their movement plots are zanier, and they each have their own timekeeper, Kimi Okada and Eric Barsness, standing in the wings very solemnly with stopwatches. In alternate time slots the dancers rest while the timekeepers rivet their gazes on them and gesture compulsively—Barsness might shake his fourth and fifth fingers, slash the air in front of his chest, pull on his Adam's apple three times, dip his chin, slide his palms down his pants leg, and so forth. Are they giving signals or just doing choreographed nervous activity?

Between these two sections, Katie Nelson (*A Formal Distraction*) starts to sail through some balletic port de bras, stumbles, gets up, falls, starts talking to herself—"I always do that . . ."—starts dancing smaller, jazzy fragments. Then gets it all jumbled up, the falling, the ballet, the jazzing; and she switches from one to the other more often, until she skitters off.

The second time I saw *Formats* I realized that, spontaneous and real as the changes looked, they weren't improvised at all. Some parts of people's stories even came out right to the same word. Nelson fell on the same beat, cursed herself in the same tones. It's disconcerting to find that the vulnerability, the rhythmic togetherness, and maybe even the nice, open faces are rehearsed, not left to chance. ODC is about virtuosity of a certain kind. To them, as to most postmoderns, motivation and transition dilute the clarity of the task. What's wanted is the appearance of spontaneity, the feeling of it, but not the engagement needed to drum it up. You have to be grateful for any product of the seventies that looks nice and stays in the air. Oberlin Dance Collective is one, and I tried not to mind that I couldn't love it too.

Seance with Approving Gods

Toby Armour
American Theater Lab, Dance Theater Workshop, New York
Soho Weekly News, 30 August 1979

There are dancers—only a few—who touch you deeply and remain in your memory for years, forever, yet leave you with practically no concrete information about what they did. They invite us into their private worlds of fantasy, memory, music, and, for moments at a time, remarkably, we seem to be able to join them there. But all we might preserve later is a face, the curve of an arm, the trace left by a whisked-away bit of drapery. Isadora Duncan was one of these dancers. So were Charles Weidman, James Waring, Katherine Litz. These friendly spirits seemed to be looking on at Toby Armour's American Theater Lab concert, even lending her their elusive songs at times.

The performance, which had no title, was a continuous solo to the music of four different composers, played by Richard Busch. But in another sense, the performance really consisted of a long cobweb of a dance by Aileen Passloff, with prelude and aftermath made by Armour.

Passloff's work fits Armour beautifully, makes her look soft, receptive to the images in the air around her, rather than angular and eccentric as she sometimes does. The music, Brahms's Variations on an Original Theme, Op. 21, No. 1, in D, is one of those romantic excursions that start rather quietly and work up to great passionate outpourings before receding into the simpler impulses where they began. The dance follows the same form—but where the music is explicit and full, the dance is understated. The tension between these two qualities, and the effectiveness of strong emotion intersecting with feeling that's held back or merely suggested, is what makes Passloff/Armour's imagery so clear and so inimitable. I think, now, that what's wrong with many Duncan revivers is that they try to "express" it all.

Toby Armour began the evening curled up on the floor, and as Busch played short selections from Bartók and Beethoven, she gradually breathed her way into uprightness, and into space, till, as the Brahms began, she seemed warmed up to give a performance. This, and probably everything I'm about to say, is already too literal. So acute and specific is her reference that she doesn't activate her whole body but seemingly only the smallest nervelets needed to set an idea in motion.

Legs stretched straight along the floor as she sits, she curves her hands above the knees and scrabbles her fingers in the air—perhaps gathering up the music as it comes from the pianist's hands. Seated sideways on one hip, she sharply turns her head and extends one hand in the same direction—and suddenly the room gets about fifteen feet wider. As Passloff's piece begins, she's standing bent over at the waist, both arms dangling to one side, suggesting a Pierrot, symbol of the universal clown-performer. Touching her fingertips together in front of her, she compresses and relaxes her hands, a gesture that recurs in many different sizes and rhythms, implying at times a small instrument—like finger cymbals—or a large one—an accordion—or an expansion into ever wider, oceanic space. She walks in strange ways—bent over at the waist with a flat back and wide, lunging steps—on tiny relevé steps with, I think, wrists flapping.

She commands the space, usually with only a limited number of body parts at a time. Yet you always know how that space is acting on her—whether it's opening out horizons for her or constricting her like a rope around the waist. As Brahms gets heroic, she steps backwards, doing nothing but looking up, looking down, looking up; rolls on the floor, all in a ball, looking up every time she's on her back; kneels, hands behind her back as if they're chained. And as Brahms subsides, she makes her way back to her first theme, the way clowns will draw back into their mask after their adventures, to show you that the mask, the costume, or in this case the body of the dancer, is only a neutral instrument that the gods of theater inhabit as they will.

Busch then plays some more Beethoven miniatures, and Armour rests under the piano, sometimes stretching out an arm to touch the back of the foot pedal. Finally, as a kind of coda, Busch does his own variations on the Brahms, music that sounds at first like an inversion or a distorted replay of what we've heard, and gradually grows into a Schönbergian atonal piece. Armour parallels Busch with a rewired version of some of Passloff's themes, and ends in silence, running-hopping around the space, around, around and out.

Why this one hour of Toby Armour meant more to me than four weeks of thundering Bolshoi, or than most anything currently up there in the dance charts, is not just that she's doing something different, or mysterious, or musical. Armour's way of presenting dance leaves you room, to think, to feel, and to see into spaces that aren't already filled up. I find that a real vacation.

Tropics of Minimalism

Hudson Review, Autumn 1979

Real minimalism wasn't an idea that dancers played around with for very long. Yvonne Rainer's famous manifesto, printed in Tulane Drama Review in 1965, scraped away all the accretions of theatricality, egotism, and sentiment that she felt had been smothering the dance art. "NO to spectacle no to virtuosity no to transformations and magic and make-believe," said Rainer, and no to a lot more. Minimal dance as practiced by Rainer, Deborah Hay, and others had a dry, boring clarity. You knew nobody was trying to seduce you or con you or mystify you. The point was small but unmistakable.

In dance, minimalism worked as a corrective measure rather than an art form. By the time its principles had been enunciated, everyone who had started out to work with plain, non-narrative, nonmanipulative movement was expanding out into the wider realms of mysticism, mixed media, complex structures, or games. By 1971 Rainer herself began using stories, and two years later she made her last dance-theater-film work, This Is the Story of a Woman Who . . ., and segued into filmmaking.

For an idea that lasted such a relatively short time in its crystal form, minimalism has had a powerful effect on our dance frame of reference. This spring, almost by accident, I found myself showing two dance films to a San Francisco audience—Twyla Tharp's Sue's Leg and a new movie of Rainer performing her 1966 cornerstone piece, Trio A. This seven-minute dance is a concise statement of minimalist theory. Wearing a dark T-shirt and sweatpants, Rainer works close to one spot. Her movement consists mostly of folding and unfolding the body in different ways, some fairly intricate but none requiring the specialized apparatus of a trained dancer. Nothing is repeated; the progression is nonstop, there are no transitions or adjustments between the large units of movement, and the dynamics are very even; there's no compositional complexity—only one thing is going on at a time; Rainer's focus and performing attitude are deliberately neutral, aimed straight into the space where she's going. When I realized I would somehow have to relate this plainspoken, radically severe work to Tharp's glamorous Fats Waller dance of 1975, I was a bit worried.

But when I saw the two films together, Rainer looked much less strange to me than she did fifteen years ago. The attitudes of minimalism have filtered into some of our most popular theater dance forms, and none shows them more clearly than Tharp dance. A primary goal of minimalism was to draw attention to the body as a nonvirtuosic movement source—to show that any movement is worth looking at, not just tricks or exaggerated gestures; and a primary characteristic of the Tharpian dancer is his or her familiarity. Tharp attains this look by the use of minimal devices. The clothes are based on streetwear, not dance costume; the dancer's body is easy, sometimes even slouchy, not pulled up and distorted into dancerly grandeur; the focus is inward and the projection modest; the movement flows continuously, not stopping to pose or emphasize, and the dancer is responsive to his or her body weight instead of resisting it. All this makes a Tharp dancer look natural and Tharp dancing look like anybody could do it. We couldn't of course, but the ordinariness provides us with a bridge to Tharp's choreographic labyrinths.

Perhaps because people branched out from it so quickly, minimalism in dance has never become codified. It can mean many things, and choreographers who aren't minimal at all, like Tharp, have incorporated aspects of it. Some minimalist concerns that have appeared in postminimal work include the use of low or no dynamics (Robert Wilson), the use of nontechnical movement such as walking (Lucinda Childs), and the avoidance of predictable or manipulative choreographic forms (improvisational ensembles like Rainer's Grand Union and the second-generation contact improvisation groups). In recent months several postminimalists have shown their work in New York, demonstrating ways that relatively simple movement has become only one element in a much larger complex of ideas, images, and philosophies.

*

Andy De Groat, who made the spinning dances for many of Robert Wilson's theater epics, has been working independently for a couple of years. Using simple steps of walking, running, leaping, turning, and more decorative but sketchily executed arm movements, he's made open-space pieces that are like big ballets without their corsets. The expansiveness of De Groat's movement, the amount of space the dancers cover, the buildups and fade-outs of intensity, all suggest a more formal, conventionalized but not necessarily more meaningful sequence of events than what we're looking at. Red Notes, De Groat's new work, was performed by nine dancers at the Lepercq Space of Brooklyn Academy. His movement language hasn't changed much, but this time the piece is not about movement. The movement is a vehicle for something else. I'm not at all sure what the something else is, but it appears to have something to do with perception. The floor space is marked off with tape in perspective lines converging away from the audience. At intervals, various numbers of dancers walk straight along these lines, getting closer together—and apparently smaller and higher— as they approach the vanishing point, larger and more formidable as they fan out coming toward us.

For the first time De Groat is using bizarre, Wilsonlike objects and events. A Plexiglas table with a pitcher and water glasses on it is placed far away, just where the perspective lines meet, and separated at first from the audience by a scrim. A man shrouded in what might be a blanket, and a woman carrying a lighted lamp cross slowly behind the scrim. Shoes are thrown from offstage into the performing area, and one dancer gathers them up clumsily in her arms, runs with them. Later the scrim goes up and people pause in their dancing rounds to take drinks of water at the Plexiglas table. Through loudspeakers a man reads Gertrude Stein very didactically and insistently; then a fast, propulsive portion of Philip Glass's *Einstein on the Beach* is played. These things all are presented with some urgency or drama. More than merely coexisting with the red-clad dancers who are almost always moving through the foreground space, they interact with and sometimes override the dancers. It might be that the whole dance has to do with the figure-ground duality, the idea that any one of a number of things in our attention field could become a subject, depending on how we focus.

David Gordon's imagination seems to be essentially a linguistic one. Like De Groat he's interested in the blurry borderline between performing and being natural. His movement, like De Groat's, is large and nontechnical, but it is more formal, shaped into quasi-calisthenic units that repeat, run into one another, team up, split apart, but always maintain the same configuration. He rules out succession or development or forced dynamics so that he can orchestrate these units in almost infinite ways.

In the first part of *An Audience with the Pope*, the voice of David Vaughan reads a through-the-looking-glass history of papal audience as performance that in a zany, convoluted way manages to explain, among other things, how the pope's dance became pop dance and what is the origin of the term "the pope's nose." Larger than life-size slides of Vaughan in papal vestments are projected on the wall of Gordon's Soho loft. He appears to be gazing down at the space below, where Gordon is performing a nonstop sequence of walks, hitch-steps, slides, pivots, and drop-rollover-squats. The sequence seems very long, and the activity has such similarity in tone that I can't remember which set follows which. Gordon is joined by Valda Setterfield, and they go through the sequence in unison, except that Setterfield is musing aloud to herself about the pope as private person and performer— "Maybe there are vestments he could wear for tennis, but skiing. . . ."

The whole thing begins again three more times, once as a trio for women in unison, once for two couples, and once for seven dancers. By the time the quartet begins, I still haven't learned the sequence, but it's clear that each couple begins in a different part of it since they're in counterpoint, and at startling moments they fall into unison, acquire a different partner, and continue the counterpoint, without interruption. In the final septet the structure breaks apart even more—into a seven-part canon with individual variations in timing, direction, number of steps repeated—until, at the end, a short period when the dancers just indicate the movements, doing them almost conversationally, the way Setterfield has been murmuring her soliloquy all along.

Gordon seems to make dances as a form of problem solving. He doesn't appear to regard his works as entities that have their own shape and must always be performed in that shape. He adapts, cuts, splices together material for use in different situations, and his New York concerts often seem to be continuous discourses on single ideas even though they may include excerpted or revised versions of older pieces. This spring's program began with a 1972 piece, One Part of the Matter, in which Valda Setterfield, in an old-fashioned wool bathing costume, took a series of poses copied from the body motion studies of photographer Eadweard Muybridge, while on tape Gordon's voice directed her in a not-necessarily-corresponding series of poses. After Pope, the dancers went without a break into a condensed version of last year's What Happened, a fragmented word-movement narrative that must have led to Gordon's development of the pope piece. All three works on this program were concerned with information, conveyed in small segments that insist you deal with movement, spacing, and sounds even while you're struggling to put together a shattered continuity.

*

Another aspect of minimalism concerns pure structure. Having accepted movement in its most basic locomotor forms, people like Trisha Brown, Lucinda Childs, and Laura Dean could concentrate on the sequence and floor pattern and, later, on embellishing the movement itself in various minimal ways. Repetition has been a key instrument for these choreographers. Not only is it the simplest way of structuring movement, it provides an analogue to contemporary rhythms and processes, externalizing our unconscious response to computers and automation. Grethe Holby and Kathy Duncan, veterans of the spinning, stamping marathons of Laura Dean, are both continuing to work with repetition, and in their spring concerts, especially Holby's, I found an even closer relationship to everyday life. With their sleek, shiny drop-dead dancewear, pink and amber floor lighting, and occasionally earsplitting music (one dance was accompanied by Lou Reed's catastrophic "Metal Machine Music"), Holby's dancers brought punk to loft dancing. Indeed, it's not much of a jump from minimal dance to the semihypnotic, pulsing vacuities of disco, or the hyped-up self-destructiveness of punk.

All repetition-minimal dancing has a tendency toward self-punishment. Just setting yourself the task of repeating a step or a sequence of movements for a very long time has the same goal-oriented, endurance-testing competitiveness as our current national pastimes of jogging and calisthenics. Sometimes exhaustion is a point of the dance. Kathy Duncan used to do a piece called Running Out of Breath, in which she did just that, sprinting around the space and at the same time explaining to the audience what she was doing and how it felt. Grethe Holby's new works, Ode and String Out, shown at the Kitchen, seemed constructed so that the dancers would be driven beyond the limits of their strength. As they fought to go on, their movement became distorted in different ways. Some lost their line, sketched in arm gestures, traveled less far, jumped less high. Some seemed to become semiconscious, losing their focus and occasionally their place in the sequence. Because the movement didn't change, you could see the unplanned stresses the dancers put into it as their stamina gave out.

Holby's movement vocabulary is far from everyday. She uses many of the basic classroom steps of ballet, even though some of her six dancers are not exemplary ballet technicians. She considers it a matter of individualism, not a defect, that some dancers are less skilled or less ideally beautiful than others. What she's done to these steps is first to use only a limited number of them, then to present them at steady tempos, mostly quite fast, in successive units, uninflected and without any pauses or transitions between them. Holby also avoids dynamic buildups and stressed phrasing. This was particularly apparent in the year-old Steady State Turning Cycles, which had a score of pulsing synthesizer chords by Richard Peaslee. Circling with large sliding steps and little leg gestures from ballet, the dancers covered a lot of ground in formations of three and four; but though they kept in time with the music, they held back from the thrusting-subsiding momentum it suggested. And in the Lou Reed piece, β HookUp, they threw themselves to the ground, rolled over, sprang up again, as if violence was as commonplace to them as entrechats.

Kathy Duncan strikes me as one of the few dancers who hasn't diverted minimalism or absorbed it into work that has other concerns. If anything, Duncan seems to be cutting out some of the more interesting maximalisms that may have inadvertently crept into her work over the years. Her new dance, An Hour for Piano and Dancers (Tom Johnson), was given at American Theater Lab by Duncan and five other women, with Yee-Ping Wu as pianist. Like the music, the dance is an uninterrupted sequence made of a very few basic motifs that keep combining and recombining to create different atmospheres. Duncan's entire preoccupation now seems to be with balance and unbalance as produced within a walking pattern. The dancer throws her body forward or teeters back, then makes a business of recovering without allowing herself to be pulled into any new movement designs or directions. The speed of the original step, the force of the impulse by which she disturbs her balance, and the upward or downward tendency of the step at the moment of deviation all determine how far and how drastically the dancer oscillates before returning to stability. Both the walking and the falling occur in all kinds of spatial groupings and at different speeds.

I think it's Duncan's single-mindedness that impresses me most in this dance. It colors the dance unmistakably with intensity and contrast. The dancers focus in front of themselves, seldom acknowledging each other directly though they often work in close unison. They move in straight lines, keep a contained, unaccented flow of energy going. Those moments when they pitch forward or stagger back seem either highly dramatic or highly arbitrary. After a while you realize that the fall is not going to be really dangerous—the body always catches itself before going very far out of control, sometimes the flailing-up arms or the shoved-forward pelvis don't actually displace the center of gravity. But the walking suggests a constancy, uprightness, and control that the falling always contradicts, and there's one section where the impulse escalates into lurching, convulsing violence. The women at various times looked to me like lost little girls, like comrades in some faintly unpleasant, demanding, but virtuous enterprise, and like neurotics whose survival depended on deliberately destroying order and proving they could get it back.

Two-Finger Tunes and Concertos

Jane Comfort
Kiva, New York

Diane Jacobowitz
Dance Theater Workshop, New York

Soho Weekly News, 20 September 1979

Diane Jacobowitz and Jane Comfort have danced with some of the same downtown choreographers, but their common experience has led them into vastly different territories. The two women's styles, shown in their performances last weekend, could represent completely opposite poles in the range of possibilities available to the minimalist point of view. Comfort is plain, straightforward; she presents her ideas openly and without guile so that they acquire all the significance they're entitled to, maybe more than even she expected. Jacobowitz is distracted and distracting, her ideas laid waste by extraneous pleasantries.

Under the general title *Solos and Duets for Hands and Feet*, Comfort began with her 1978 *Steady Shift*, a standing-in-place dance. Facing the audience and shifting from one leg to the other with a pronounced sideward hip thrust, she gestured along and across her body with her arms. Since she used the steady pulse of her leg shift as a guide, so did I, and I was soon silently humming the phrase her arms made, as the left, then the right swept up to the opposite shoulder, cut across and out to the side, and continued on down. At first the pattern was quite even and predictable. After a few repetitions she switched to another gesture pattern, then another and another, each with a slightly different rhythm, which made my silent song change its shape easily. But there came a phrase—I think by now she was getting a bit more complicated and her hands twisted around each other somewhere in the center before going their separate ways—when I noticed a tiny hitch in the right-left symmetricality of my inner echo. Everyone has a slight difference between left and right sides, and just as I was thinking this fractional disparity must have been unconscious, Comfort made a gesture with her right hand totally different from that of her left.

At this point Comfort started to lengthen the phrase even further, from the identically repeating one-two, and the longer two-part two, by connecting two or more of the arm paths we'd seen, taking a longer and longer multiple of the initial weight-shift cycle to get back to what could be a beginning. Until there seemed so many different phrases and so few repeats that maybe there wasn't a beginning but only a pulse. Then she went back to her very first repeated phrase a few times and stopped. People told me afterward that they had perceived intricate mathematical formulas in the dance. It never even occurred to me to count.

In *Gyre*, Comfort and Daniel McCusker jogged together around in a circle, changing their relationship—ahead or behind, inside or outside—every few steps. This dance too maintained a steady pulse. The steps varied from running steps to sideward steps to backward running, and the circle track evolved gradually into a tight circle, two adjacent circles, and McCusker looping big and little circles around Comfort. Imperceptibly the whole plot reversed itself and they ended circling backwards into the spot where they'd entered.

Comfort is experimenting with sign language as a movement resource, and in *Sign Story* Marjorie Gamso read a text about women's roles from Gertrude Stein while Comfort stood and gestured each word. The gestural shapes were clear and unusual, and Stein's poetic repetitions made for some dancelike phrasing. But at this stage the dance is pretty static and literal, while the words, parceled out and uninflected by Gamso, have an arch modernity that I read out of Stein when I have her all to myself. *For the Spider Lady* finished the program, a brief solo in which Comfort stretched and pulled herself off balance into very extended and distorted counterdirections. A sort of winding down, it seemed, from all the previous containment.

It's hard to describe Diane Jacobowitz's movement—or any other element of her work—because she seems determined to interfere with her own consistency. She has that upper-body-mustn't-know-what-the-lower-is-doing look of some post-Cunningham dancers, notably Kenneth King, with whom she's danced for a couple of years. But for some reason, perhaps his grave refusal to play up, King convinces me that there's a plan behind all his scurrying about, while Jacobowitz just seems to scurry about. She opened with *Rough Cuts*, which she called an "overture." Dancing solo

and accompanied by Tom Wachunas, who played the guitar and sang in exaggerated Bob Dylan style about a bird on fire—or rather a buhd own fah—
Jacobowitz introduced and just about exhausted her movement repertoire.
This consisted of fussy, steppy steps in emphatic second or first relevés,
rushing back and forth along the same path, and other balletic maneuvers
done for their own sake; pushy gestures of the torso and arms unaccompanied by footwork; and odd traces of mime behavior—a funny face, a
skewed pose, a trace of action with an invisible prop.

Two video monitors flickered throughout this dance with a film of four
dancers doing a dance that might have been related to the one Jacobowitz
was doing, but the pictures were so small I didn't pay much attention to
them. In the next dance, Mudsong, four dancers did something that might
have been related to the dance on video but they didn't capture my attention sufficiently to tell. They were accompanied by Jacobowitz, Wachunas,
and Susan Greenblatt, who played and sang the bottom part of "Heart and
Soul," those elementary chords that kids thump out ad nauseam when they
don't know how to play the piano. Mudsong was a very long dance in which
very little seemed to happen, and it irritated me more than I thought any
dance could in September.

The last two items on the program irritated me less because, I guess,
Mudsong had softened me up. White Tar was a parody of punk. This seemed a
bad idea since punk is already a parody of some other kinds of pop. Lecture-
Dem in Geeneewannaland was a parody of dancers trying to explain what they
do to audiences, using made-up words and motions for the real ones so
earnestly delivered on such occasions. The jokes are sometimes funny, but
the targets are too easy. Jacobowitz is a dancer I've enjoyed in King's work
and that of others. She has a good musical talent, humor, and, I suspect,
a latent romanticism. There were times in Lecture-Dem in Geeneewannaland
when she and Linn Walker jibbered quietly to each other while Wachunas
strummed something harmless and I thought of the kind of atmospheres
Meredith Monk can create. For some reason Jacobowitz doesn't want to
put all that talent out there on its own. I have no idea why.

Pulling Apart Together

Douglas Dunn: Foot Rules
Dance Theater Workshop, New York
Soho Weekly News, 27 September 1979

Costumes are getting to be a big item on the downtown dance scene. Since
Twyla Tharp made sweat glamorous, the idea of a basic working uniform
for studio concerts has evolved to include Milliskin, glints of gold jewelry,

and sensuous layers of fabric. For *Foot Rules*, Douglas Dunn and Deborah Riley wore an assortment of locker-room gear, beachwear, underwear, and unclassifiable garments in curdled colors, designed by Mimi Gross Grooms. Dunn's dance, however, apparently had nothing to do with the bizarro tinge of these costumes. This was only one of many contradictions in the new duet; I even thought the dance might be about contradictions, or about trying to reconcile them. I may be imposing a critic's logic on some other kind of process. And yet . . .

What came across to me most strongly was the difference between the two dancers. Dunn and Riley are both skinny, wiry physical types; both are dry, noncommittal performers. Their actual movements appear to be similarly conceived and made, yet Dunn's dancing simmers with character, drama, foolishness, irony that he can never completely suppress. At the moment Dunn seems to be interested in choreographing body shapes and gestures more than expansive spatial or rhythmic patterns. When he dances, these designs seem to emerge out of an ongoing movement or thought process. They travel with him, out of and back into the surface of his motion, like whitecaps on the ocean. Riley's gestures seem to be both the reason for her motion and its end result. You see her dancing as a succession of events, landmarks that make a flat terrain important.

Riley gives her movement almost no nuance or development. She knows where she's aiming, and she goes directly there, then goes on. Dunn flavors his designs with ebbs and flows of speed, anticipatory tremors, little aftershocks of movement fluttering out his fingertips. His torso is extremely articulate—it seems his body hardly ever works in one straight unit, but tilts, caves in, leans out over itself, twists or curls against itself.

Foot Rules is perhaps the hardest to follow of all the dances I've seen by Dunn, though it's always easy to look at. I think this is because there's so much movement in it and so little obvious structuring of the movement material. Occasionally in the first two of the dance's three sections you see things that seem to refer to earlier things, but mostly the clues to an overall plan seem to lie in the dancers' relationship to each other. They work separately but usually at the same time—isolated but connected by some obscure telegraphic attraction, as when Riley stands upstage and flaps her arms up and down, *Swan Lake* fashion, and a second later Dunn, diagonally downstage from her, wheels in a circle, answering her message by flying, not by kneeling in princely adoration. There are moments that seem very long and still, when they meet and match actions, often in mutually supporting/repelling poses.

In the second part, their attraction grows more aggressive. From different sides of the space they challenge each other with urgent foot-slaps on the floor. They join hands and swing in a circle, pulling away from each other, flung sometimes to the ground when they break contact. Several times he lifts her, carries her around like an unwieldy piece of baggage that wouldn't be half the struggle if he'd keep her still instead of changing her position all the time. Later she twirls him round and round, finally pushing him almost out of the space, then stalks away, hands on head, like some triumphant but guilt-ridden Martha Graham heroine.

In the last part of the dance their polarity and their accord are most emphatic of all. They sit on chairs at the sidelines watching each other's solos. One by Dunn is all perturbed circlings with tenuous references to more conventional dancing—a suspenseful slow plié down to the ground, a twittery toe dance with his hands clasped behind him and his face lifted angelically. In another solo he sits or lies on the ground, though that implies a much more static position than he ever takes, his arms busy with a long series of mime gestures, all different, all suggestive, but none representing anything you ever quite saw any person do. One of Riley's solos reminds me at some point of something Dunn did earlier, a hopping turn with one leg sweeping wide around her body axis, and I begin to wonder what other concealed correspondences might have slid by me in the last hour. They do a final duet of glancing unison and inversions of each other's movements. Then Dunn drifts away leaving Riley to finish. Whether this is a nod to women's liberation or a throwback to women's exploited ballerinahood, or whether it has nothing to do with any of that, I'll probably never know.

Beadwork and Fringe

Rosalind Newman: Cairn
Emanu-el Midtown YM-YWHA, New York
Soho Weekly News, 4 October 1979

Rosalind Newman is obsessed with movement. Not just any movement, but movement that's decorative. Her new dance, Cairn, is like one long cadenza in search of a theme. There were some recurring ideas in the dance, besides the idea of perpetual motion, which I suppose is a theme in itself. But curiously, as some shapes or patterns echoed through the piece, they seemed to lose quality instead of gaining it. The question of why my eye didn't welcome the repeated image intrigued me. How does, or doesn't, anarchy become art?

Structure is no longer considered essential by many postmodern dancers, and "just dancing" has been all right for a long time. But while Newman reminds me of two of the most successful practitioners of antistructure, Louis Falco and Merce Cunningham, she exhibits neither the psychologically suggestive groupiness of Falco nor the austere selectivity that makes Cunningham seem to intend themes and designs even when he claims none.

Cairn is a long piece, broken by an intermission. The first section is danced in silence, the second to a series of piano-drone studies by Charlemagne Palestine. The seven dancers are distributed in apparently random order and groupings—a duet might grow into a trio but it might as easily continue, supplemented by another duet or something else; a solo can break off to become a momentary partnership; a solo, a duet, and a larger group can be going on at the same time. There doesn't seem to be any continuity about the way these events lead into each other. No group logic demands that at two or three moments, and nowhere else, the entire ensemble should line up evenly across the space while one member, usually Newman, dances a specially lit solo in the center. Or that the group should stumble upon unison movement at the very end, like the four typing chimpanzees and the works of William Shakespeare.

Newman's movement doesn't have a lot of curlicues or rhythmic intricacy, but it's elaborate in its own way. With her small flexible body and musical phrasing, Newman can change directions, shift her balance, make large gestures faster and more smoothly than any dancer I can think of. When she puts this virtuosic speed on other dancers, they can seem finicky or pressured. They have to make steps smaller in relation to their size, they flatten out curves, bang their arms through space, turn corners on a dime. The men look especially awkward, not playful but childish, with their pitter-pattering feet and slashing arms.

Whenever Newman's dancers work together I get the feeling of casual game playing. Two people join hands and a third throws herself across the bridge; they run a few steps, trade roles. People fall against each other like a pile of spoons, roll off the pile. They seldom move in real harmony—or even real competition. Everything in Cairn seems to be taken on the run, but then you wonder why, if this person is in such a hurry, she pauses to throw the audience a pas de chat or fling her leg up in an arabesque. As the dance went on, the idea of momentum grew more and more important to me. Jumps, lifts, even arm and leg gestures seem to need the power of a windup to get them going. People dash across the space in order to dash back the way they came. They lean artistically off balance in order to right themselves. They hurl themselves at one another, sometimes landing in a contrived lift—across the partner's back for instance—and sometimes making a calculated miss.

The activity is furious, pointless, yet it doesn't look hostile or even depressed. Or friendly either, for that matter. Working for speed and change, the dancers seem to withdraw inside themselves. They're isolated from one another, even when they're working in groups, wrapped in contemplative personal skins that they create with their constant self-touching, framing, steadying arm gestures. Their faces seem unimportant compared to their bodies—their identity, their intention, less memorable than the prodigality of their action.

Keeping House among the Pines

Kei Takei: *Light Parts 4, 5, 14*, Dance Umbrella
Camera Mart/Stage One, New York
Soho Weekly News, 18 October 1979

Kei Takei's epic *Light* has moved into a domesticated phase. Like a condensed history of some undiscovered race, *Light* has gone through periods of bleakness, communality, and aggression. In the latest installment, Part 14 (subtitled Pine Cone Field), the population of Takei's world has paired off and is beginning to make nesting moves.

The piece opens with John de Marco unfolding a wad of cloth hardly bigger than a flag that has been placed in the center of the space. It's folded in triangles, origami style, and de Marco ceremoniously lifts one corner after another from the center and opens the material to reveal another folded layer underneath. When he finally gets the sheet spread out flat, it covers almost the entire space. Three, then two other dancers come in with their own smaller bundles and unfold them to make five overlapping squares on top of the big one. It's partly the tidy, ritualistic way they undo these many folds that makes me think they're making a particular space for themselves, perhaps a more permanent one than the ring of rocks they laid out then scattered or rearranged in other parts of *Light*.

After they've got the forest cleared, so to speak, two couples appear with big baskets of pinecones strapped to their backs. Side by side, each couple steps back and forth in a sort of treadmill rocking. From time to time they gesture in ways that suggest farming tasks to me; between stints of striding and flinging they huddle together or crouch down. Sometimes a few pinecones fall out of their baskets and lie around them on the ground. And all the time they vocalize together with a rhythmic "haw!" as if they're trying to discover language by imitating birds. Finally they sink to the ground, each couple on one of the small cloth squares, and John de Marco, who has been watching them, gathers up the corners of each sheet, fallen pinecones, dancers, and all, and ties them in housewifely bundles like laundry.

Three women and a man come in with packets of sticks tied on their backs. They seem more forceful than the first group, stamping and shoving their fists at each other, punching the air with pistonlike arms, and punctuating their labors by blowing the air out of their puffed-up cheeks. Eventually they too drop to the ground and are wrapped and tied in three clumps by de Marco. Then Takei and Kiken Chin dance among the five white-shrouded hulks, sometimes taking separate paths, sometimes meeting. They hold their mouths open and stretched into tight O shapes and call wordlessly to each other. A man and a woman sing quietly from under one of the sheets, and slowly the lights go out.

I've seen all the parts of Light as they were made during the last ten years, and the more Takei adds to it, the more potent the work as a whole becomes. It's like some modern myth building up under our eyes. Takei reminds us in a program note that it's in part the life of herself and the performers, but it's more than just a poeticized document. New episodes are added and old ones recalled, but the meanings of the past chapters aren't fixed at all, even though the events and objects in them remain the same. Takei has a remarkable gift for choosing simple but loaded imagery. In Light Part 1, three women plodded around with packs on their backs. Who they were and where they were taking the packs we didn't know, and still don't. But in those first years the packs were made of cloth and filled with something soft but burdensome. The women looked sad. I sometimes thought of war refugees, especially in one performance when someone bent under an enormous pack and a trick of lighting made person and pack together resemble a mushroom cloud. Later the packs became bags filled with weapons; now they seem to be associated with clearing and cultivating land. And the people themselves get done up into cloth bundles.

Some parts of the story are told more often than others, and they change quite a lot. Light Part 5—the holding-each-other-up-until-they-fall-down trio—grows more grotesque and arty. The men, now Maldwyn Pate and John de Marco, labor to get into odd positions and make horrified faces. Takei stays apart from them most of the time, straining upward, and only occasionally clamps herself onto a leg or arm of one of the men like a drowning person, and she lets go her grip and goes sprawling long before they do. I don't like Part 5 much now. It's too ghastly and artificial for my taste, like Victorian religious paintings.

Part 4 has changed too, mostly because the elfin Takei now skips through the role created by the much more serious, possibly even malicious Carmen Beuchat. As the mastermind who fits together big white slabs of a jigsaw puzzle, she increasingly limits the space of five other people, who are allowed to walk only on the bare floor, until they vanish in a blackout just as Takei puts down the last piece. Once the puzzle is complete it makes a square in the larger space that's the same size as the unfolded sheet in Part 14. When I saw the white expanse for the second time that evening, my mind doubled back and I wondered if this new section might be a flash-back in the story, to a world starting to civilize itself only to be snuffed out by an ice age.

Pleasures of Perversity

Senta Driver/Harry
Lepercq Space, Brooklyn Academy, New York
Soho Weekly News, 1 November 1979

The name of Senta Driver is writ as large in the ads this season as the cryptic name Harry, Driver's company. This is not the only indication that a slight thaw has tempered the resolve of this most resolute postmodernist. For reasons of her own, Driver has adopted a series of uncompromising positions that tend to obscure her message even when she most wants us to understand what she's doing. I think she has a near-fatal pedagogical streak that often makes her seem to spend more time telling you what the dance is about than dancing the dance. Her new works, *Simulcast* (choreographed with Peter Anastos) and *Primer*, go light on the rationalizing and are easier to take.

Primer, like its name, is quite a didactic piece, but in resisting her verbal impulse, Driver lets us look at the dance as if it were no more than dancing. Each section seems to begin with a rather simple idea that proceeds into increasingly intricate or demanding activities. There's a tremendous amount of "material" in the dance, and it's treated as material, to be shown and passed by or maybe to be used later in another fashion.

Although Driver's basic tools are simple, the speed and complexity with which she develops them can make you wonder how a minute before you were thinking it was elementary. In one of the early group sections, Nicole Riché, Jeffrey Clark, and Rick Guimond skitter around the space with accelerating and decelerating footsteps—these are done in the same meter so the dancers have to suspend and spread out their steps on the slow ones, creating a strong contrast to the tight little fast ones. They make sudden explosive jumps straight up in the air. They throw their upper bodies forward violently and roll back up the spine with equal force. Some time later, they're kneeling on the floor jerking their pelvises forward in little convulsive spurts and circling their arms from side to side.

Except for some fluent passages of weighty twisting and tossing, Driver has a tendency to use the body in a very contained, controlled way, the torso almost monolithic. Only one thing is usually going on at a time, though it may be strenuous. In Primer a lot of attention is given to the feet, to jumps that stress landing, to the varieties of step that feature special parts of the foot. Riché does a solo in which she stands on the very front part of the balls of the feet and the toes. Up there, she doesn't do anything else, and you're almost forced to consider those strange, unwavering, elongated feet as aesthetic realities in themselves, which you never do in ballet where they're always engaged in making flashier things happen.

There's a lot of other stuff in Primer. Falling and carrying, rhythmic counterpoint. But what stays with me after it's over is a sense of the dancers' bodies—sturdy and earthbound, full of potential grace and determined to overcome it. Irony is always implicit in Driver's dance because she always reminds you of what the dancers are not doing, specifically ballet and the more refined types of modern dance. So it's not surprising that she's collaborated on Simulcast with Peter Anastos, one of the most subtle and inspired ballet parodists now at work. Anastos created some of the cleverest works in the repertory of the Ballets Trockadero de Monte Carlo, of which he was a codirector and principal ballerina until last spring.

Simulcast begins with Driver and Anastos in a role-reversal duet that starts with emphatic gesticulating in a language as clear to them, if not to us, as ballet mime. They're accompanied by a sound track of a TV interviewer gushing questions that are answered in monosyllables by Anastos and with windy seriousness by Driver. Their dance gets more physical, they act like partners, but they're not particularly choosy about which one is doing the hauling around and which one is being hauled. None of this so far looks much like ballet or even dance, but as the piece goes on it blossoms into a ballroom scene, almost contemporary. Driver wears a pink ruffly formal just like the one I loathed but wore to my high school senior prom.

Driver and Anastos do a series of variations to Mozart's variations on "Ah, vous dirai-je, Maman," an extension of the galumphing heel-toe dancing of Primer, in which some sudden soft hand gestures by Driver look unreasonably lovely. Finally the principals, backed up by Riché, Clark, Guimond, and Peg Conner Hewitt, perform a send-up of Swan Lake Act 3, the part before the Black Swan and all the terpsichorean fireworks. Anastos is the hapless prince whose Graustarkian mother (Driver) tries to marry him off to any available male, female, or whatever. Anastos is a wonderful foil for Driver, gesturing ineffectually and rolling his eyes in futile protest.

Far from Denmark

David Gordon Pick-Up Company,
The Matter (*plus and minus*), Dance Umbrella
Camera Mart/Stage One, New York
Soho Weekly News, 13 December 1979

Coming back to Gotham from anywhere is not easy, but after a week in the cozy arms of Denmark's nineteenth-century choreographer August Bournonville, it's going to take time. Like a lot else in New York this week, I saw David Gordon's *The Matter* (*plus and minus*) as some weird inversion of the world of Bournonville. Some of Bournonville's most charming compositions celebrate the Danes' love of travel, their attraction to the exotic behavior of people who live where there's no snow or winter-long darkness. The dancers depart from their own tidy and complex dancing to dress up as Spaniards, Neapolitan fishermen, vaudeville darkies, and let rip with the pyrotechnics that Bournonville style normally keeps under restraint.

David Gordon's intention is not to spice up a too-tame existence, but to make even the exotic seem drab. He uses virtuosic skills to do it. This is not so perverse when seen as a logical development of the avant-gardist revolution of fifteen years ago. The plainness that was needed as a corrective to hype and overdecoration in dance has now become a theoretical substructure for many people. The natural set of the body, the unstressed transition, the neutral, private face are as essential to the look of post-modern dance as the turnout and the pulled-up chest are to ballet. Any discussion of postmodern dance today, I suppose, is really about where the individual choreographer goes from there.

David Gordon's twenty-two dancers look a lot like ordinary people wearing their ordinary everyday clothes. But quite soon you discover they're real dancers. The motley assortment of clothing blends curiously in color and style. It turns out to have been Selected and Coordinated by Suzanne Joelson. Gordon and Valda Setterfield—he informs us rather possessively in his program note that she's his wife—do a duet made of a series of very convincing, even erotic embraces. Just at the climax of each clinch, slides flash on the backdrop showing different views of them in the same pose. Then one partner slips out of the grasp of the other, leaving him or her encircling thin air.

A lot of this concert seemed to be about freezing and prolonging the postures of natural movement. Ain Gordon sweeps out a prop doorway, stopping at the end of a stroke for what seems like a whole minute before continuing. David Gordon arranges chairs, cardboard cartons, large quilted pads in the center of the space, pausing after he's placed each one, not to inspect its position but to get us to notice both it and himself in the act of positioning. Later, big groups of people make accidental-looking tableaux, leaning and twining around each other, holding someone overhead in a chair.

Several times masses of people cross the space and stop in attitudes of going. The stopping poses seem as calculated as they are meaningless. Toward the end, the mass freeze consists of small groups, facing each other and sometimes touching, looking almost conversational, almost like snapshots. But somehow the groups haven't got the right focus or immediacy either then or after they leave one by one and come back to the same positions dressed in bathrobes and nightgowns. Although you see them getting into and out of these positions, once they've congealed there doesn't seem to be any reasonable explanation why they should have been caught like that.

This is not true of Valda Setterfield's reproduction of the poses from Eadweard Muybridge, the photographer who made multiple shots of people in motion. Maybe that's because Setterfield tries to capture the particular intensity that belongs to each act of running, throwing, bending over. Gordon, discussing the poses with her on a sound track, is too knowing, placing disproportionate importance on something basically pointless. He *wants* the process to sound contrived. Setterfield takes it seriously. Somehow she redeems a lot of Gordon's artful objectivity, his implicit exploitativeness. When, at the beginning of the piece, the first notes of La Bayadère Act IV begin to play and you see Setterfield come out slowly with a line of people behind her, you get Gordon's whole joke. The Kingdom of the Shades is a famous ballet image, twenty-four women coming down a ramp doing arabesque after arabesque. But for Setterfield the image is full of meaning, even feeling. So is the end of The Matter (plus and minus), when Prokofiev's "Death of Juliet" music plays, and she's picked up and held high overhead by five people like a corpse in an old-fashioned ballet.

There seemed to be less dance in this performance than is usual for Gordon, and what there was was downplayed. Gordon did a solo of offhand poses, not exactly finished or connected, while singing snatches of something like "In the Mood" in a whiskey tenor. The other dancers did what might have been the same dance or something derived from it, all together but not in unison, during what was announced as an intermission. Later five women did a sequence of vaguely sexy gestures that might have been derived from that, while the others made a big tableau with props. Throughout the concert, my eye kept wandering with relief to whatever was moving that seemed to be motivated and sequential: Ain Gordon's shadow on the wall as he paced inside his prop doorway before his entrance; Setterfield and later everyone else changing clothes at the side of the space; audience coming in late or leaving early. Maybe Gordon meant for me to notice all that too. I hope so.

Mauve Punk

Karole Armitage: *Do We Could*
The Kitchen, New York
Soho Weekly News, 20 December 1979

If we have to start differentiating the varieties of punk now, Karole Armitage's *Do We Could* probably belongs somewhere at the soft end of the scale. The piece began with a slam and ended with a mannerly farewell. I figured maybe the punk was an affectation, a chance for some nice, clean dancers to get their hands dirty. The dancers—Armitage is a member of the Merce Cunningham company, Deborah Riley and Michael Bloom have both danced with Douglas Dunn—were dressed in those goofy, unbecoming clothes of punkdom. Armitage was all in black—tight cotton pants, a blouse, soft heelless boots. Riley wore black espadrilles, a black skimpy skirt slit way up on both sides, and a sleeveless white T-shirt. Bloom had on black basketball sneakers, black pants, a white shirt with the sleeves cut off, a black tie, and black-rimmed eyeglasses. All of them had their hair plastered down except for Armitage, who has a crew cut, and all their hands were freshly gloved in paint—yellow, blue, and purple.

They exploded out of that slamming door into the light and walked very fast around the room, the kind of racers' walk that makes your legs stiff and your torso gawk way out over them. The dancers looked a little like scared chickens, I thought. As they skittered around they made peculiar little hand gestures or jabbed at the air with their upper bodies. After a certain amount of time, they'd all come to a halt, rest a moment, then begin again. At each interval they seemed to be adding one gesture to the sequence, but their movements were so erratic and spastic that it didn't seem to count. They got a little winded during this section, but they didn't really push themselves. Paint started getting smeared on their clothes as their hands brushed against their bodies, and once Riley leaned on a pillar and left a good set of purple handprints.

In other sections of the piece, they stalked around like zombies, their hands flapping, their heads and arms jerking. They clustered indecisively together, sometimes appearing to lean on each other, sometimes pulling away, but how long they could sustain this supporting structure didn't seem to be an issue. For long periods of time they stood in one place, dropping into unresilient pliés and jerking their limbs and torsos. Again, sometimes I thought they were trying to hang loose from one particular joint or throw their weight just so far and stop it, but that didn't seem to be a consistent pattern either.

Another "theme" of the dance was to clutter up the space. The Kitchen space is permanently obstructed with pillars anyway, and I did think maybe Armitage was underlining a point there. The dancers would periodically interrupt their quasi-tasks to drag some unnecessary and inefficient-looking piece of equipment into the space where it would block their way—a two-by-four with a crude lamp on the end and a long cable trailing, a large reflector strung on a rope, stuff like that. But since they didn't seem particularly concerned with moving through the space in any special way, the junk just sat there and looked junky. Charles Atlas's patchy, low-wattage lighting made it all one piece with dingy Broome Street out the windows.

The dancers looked very different from one another. I sometimes thought they weren't all doing the same dance or that they were improvising or playing Follow the Leader Not Too Closely. Armitage is tall and spidery. Riley is strong and tense. Bloom's body doesn't settle properly into its skin when he finishes a move, he has to adjust it bit by bit, and it often fights him, giving off involuntary little flicks and knobby tremors on the way to an uneasy repose. Bloom was kind of the comic of the piece, peering around at the others as if checking their scene and perhaps finding it no more reassuring than his own.

While they were doing a long series of in-place thudding gestures, we could hear someone dragging something heavy up the Kitchen's back stairs and around the outer rooms, and finally knocking on the door near the audience. Armitage went and opened it. A man walked in with a hand truck, coats and a briefcase loaded on it. He unpacked while the dancers relaxed. He took out a water jug and glasses, paint can, paint thinner, paper towels, candles. He lit two candles and recited a few words of a possible poem. Then they all cleaned up the space, wiping the floor, painting over Riley's handprints on the pillar, putting the awkward props back where they'd been at the beginning. Armitage and Bloom toasted each other with water. Then they all put on their coats and left. It was the most resolute thing they'd done all night.

Minimalism Meets Maximalism

Meg Harper: *Bad Moves/Was*
Cunningham Studio, New York
Soho Weekly News, 3 January 1980

Although Merce Cunningham has had a fundamental influence over the thinking of contemporary dancers, many of them have outstripped him in violating traditional concepts of what dance is. Cunningham broke up the natural flow and sequence of movement with his isolations, chance methods of creating movement structures, aleatory spacings and environments, but he never really abandoned the notion that dancing is a total, rhythmic engagement of the body with space. In being objective about the things that move and how they move, he didn't seek to limit movement, only to clarify it, diversify it. In fact, in recent years Cunningham's movement has become more complex in terms of spatial direction, phrasing, simultaneous but contrapuntal combinations of body parts, and it's less random looking in floor pattern and overall composition.

One whole wing of the postmodern dance establishment has used specificity and selectivity to pare down movement choices, to work within very restricted allowances of body parts, action, timing, and space. You'd think the two points of view were incompatible, but Meg Harper has managed to adopt them both. Harper, who danced with Cunningham for ten years, learned Lucinda Childs's minimalist spectacle, *Dance*, this fall when one of Childs's dancers was injured. In *Bad Moves/Was* she seemed to be exploring some minimalist possibilities with a Cunningham-wide vocabulary.

The uninterrupted hour-long performance consisted of a dance on a line (*Was*), preceded by *Bad Moves* in sketch form, then followed by the sketch elaborated. Both dances appeared to be based on similar movement ideas—simple locomotive steps, often with a plié or relevé as the main point of emphasis; even rhythms that changed mainly in terms of speed, seldom in intensity; occasional resting postures in which her body didn't look anything like the way it did in motion. She used her arms a lot, often moving them symmetrically from the shoulder joints; although her gestures differed slightly, she seemed to be always opening her arms, never closing them or curling them around the body in any sort of decorative way. She didn't always move in a straight line across the room, but she usually looked as if she intended to.

Was, the more minimal of the pieces, was easier to follow, since it was confined to the center line down the length of the Westbeth studio and was made of gradual shadings and expansions on the basic forward or backward plié/relevé step. First Harper merely added pivot turns to the step, increased the size of it, doubled the speed. Later on she lengthened or interrupted the regular pulse of the step by touching the traveling foot to the standing ankle or by describing a circle on the floor with the working foot as it advanced. Still later she made almost a phrase by taking a couple of tiny running steps and a hitch-fall, or a hop, jump, and a little lunge onto the forward leg.

In *Bad Moves* no such developmental sequence was evident. Harper just made variations on the step, did them, dropped them, went on to something else. Parts of earlier things would recur, like a vibration of the hands, a jerky sideward twist of the head as she turned, a semaphorelike unfolding of an arm, but the whole dance didn't seem to have a single thread of progression running through it.

Occasionally the dynamics would build up, without any inherent reason, then subside, again without apparent cause. Harper's performing style throughout was contained, moderate, smooth. Her idea was to keep going except when she had to rest. She never seemed to let the movement evoke her comment, take her out of control, persuade her to flash on the audience.

Toward the end, Harper stood perfectly still while Alicia Bridges on tape sang a disco number about getting into ACKSHUN! The song played again and she faced the audience and turned some side steps she'd done before into big leg gestures thrown from the hip, sidling little hip wiggles, and shoulder slants, as if she'd had a delayed reaction to the music's invitation. A disco dance surely, but one safely confined, reduced to a few suggestive lines. Rather than bursting through the carefully inscribed patterns she'd laid out, Harper was content to stretch them a little.

Papyri

Wendy Perron and Susan Rethorst
Cunningham Studio, New York
Soho Weekly News, 20 February 1980

The new dances of Susan Rethorst and Wendy Perron are like ancient manuscripts written with great intensity but now partly disintegrated. They may be beautiful to look at but their message is indecipherable. The most interesting question about Rethorst and Perron is why do I get the idea there's a message? Both women are devoted to the post-Cunningham ethic of not "using" one's choreographic material. A movement phrase is allowed to repeat any number of times, but once it's been presented it's replaced by another which is apt to be completely unlike it and certainly mustn't resemble it enough to seem like an ornamentation or a second thought. The idea of progression, especially in Perron's work, is also taboo. If any movement results in anything or contributes to anything that appears later, it isn't evident. Nor does the dancer deliver these units with any performance comment that would emphasize some of them and thereby diminish others. They're all clear and complete and equal. I look at these linear dances with expectation and a constant sense of loss. Each movement erases the one before. It's like reading a language you don't understand.

A three-piece suite, Perron's choreography "with contributions from the dancers," consisted of two duets and a solo by Perron. First Kyle deCamp and Paula Clements enter like zombies, on the balls of their feet, one step at a time, with arms stretched stiffly down to their sides. They move in brief capsules of gesture, mostly doing the same thing. Looking inward, they seem to be enclosing their own bodies with odd tracings of arms and legs. Sometimes these moves might refer to past activities—putting clothes on, using some kind of exploratory instruments like telescopes—whose function has long ago become obsolete.

Margot Crosman and Susan Rethorst come into the space, and they all lie on the floor in pairs, raising themselves partly off the ground as if awakened from sleep, then lying down again—over and over. The first duo leaves, and Crosman and Rethorst work close together, also frequently in that same casual unison. For a while they converse in complicated two-arm gesture-sentences. Then they move around a bit more. They seem rougher, riskier than the first pair. They fling their weight around, fall on each other once or twice.

Then they leave and Perron makes a lurching, collapsing entrance, circling the space until she stumbles to the floor. Her dance seems to alternate between the contained carefulness of Clements and deCamp, and the more vigorous, less controlled ventures of Crosman and Rethorst. Sometimes she stands and makes large, inward-leading gestures in which the hands don't finish defining the space the arms are carving out. Sometimes she makes slow, meticulous ripplings of her spine or whole body. And sometimes she slides or falls fast and dangerously. Even the quiet parts are so intense, I feel she must be telling me something, but each move denies the one before. At some point, she backs up to a wall of mirrors. Taking one step at a time to the side and tapping the mirror with her hands, she quietly gets out a sentence: "no words tonight here doesn't mean no voices."

Susan Rethorst's piece, Swell, is more structured visually but no less cryptic. As the lights come up we see nine women sitting on the floor, spaced around. Before we grasp what they're doing or who they are, all but one of them get up and stand along one wall for a long time, slowly turning to touch the wall or cup a hand to their own bodies. This may all be a prelude to the main part of the dance, in which the women move out onto the floor and begin doing various sequences in groups of two or more.

The dance is surprisingly choral. There's usually more than one small group moving at a time; often the group is split up so that analogous sequences happen in different places with a contrasting one between them. Women unobtrusively break away from one group and join another, changing both the design and the rhythm of the space. Rethorst's movement is less self-contemplative than Perron's. It seems more purposeful; people often seem to be going from one place to another. The movement is bigger, not so gestural. In fact, a lot of it involves the whole body folding up or twisting askew.

During one long period of time, they all sit on the floor facing one end of the space. One move at a time, in threes, fours, together, they curl up on their knees, sit back, sink to the side, always looking straight at the audience when they face us. Each woman has her own look—one is calm, one slightly quizzical, one maybe covering some inner agitation. But the variety is in their collective variety, like the multiple shades of mauve, brown, and black in their warm-up clothes, not in any one person's changeable reaction.

All the entrances and exits in this performance were either extremely peculiar or extremely reticent, almost stealthy. Rethorst's women, near the end, began a sort of rumbling all-fours walk toward one corner, gathering in a close group, then flowing out onto the floor again. After some more moves that I can't remember, they seemed to form a line that threaded around the edge of the space, bunched itself up in another corner, and shrank away out a door. It was as if they'd formed some strange organism seeking a way out. And at that last moment I realized I didn't remember seeing anyone walking upright on her two feet at any time during the whole dance.

Hurdling through the Limelight

Charles Moulton: *Thought Movement Motor*
The Kitchen, New York
Soho Weekly News, 27 February 1980

Nontechnical movement has been working its way toward some kind of dance form, and Charles Moulton's *Thought Movement Motor*, with scarcely a dance step in it, had everything a dance has except sequential shape. Moulton and his partners, Susan Eschelbach and Janna Jensen, executed small units of activity, in no perceptible order, taking definite breaks in between to rest and assume positions for the next set. These strung-together tasks had the air of naturalness and challenge you see in sports or stunts, but the movement itself had that other, exacting quality that belongs only to stage performance. The combination was curious and fascinating—not least of all because Moulton was able to sustain the dual nature of the event through an hour of ramifications.

Like a dance, *Thought Movement Motor* kept its ideas confined to a few basic categories that got worked over and turned this way and that. It might have been called Three Themes or So and Variations. There was the step-pattern theme, basically a walking dance, in which Moulton would set a tempo by snapping his fingers and occasionally calling out counts. Then the dancers would move briskly into space, usually keeping together rhythmically and in formation, but sometimes separating into counterpoint.

Sometimes their steps were very big, almost sprawly, and involved rapid switches of direction, crisscrossings, and near-collision courses. Sometimes they were syncopated with little jumps and turns. One six-count combination seemed to contain all these possibilities, shuffled and spun out in succession.

There was the helicopter theme, basically a spread-out pivot turn, that could get flung among some walking or running steps but could also be done in the air or upside down. Moulton could toss off one of these and land in a sliding fall; he could spring up into one from the floor by pushing off from one hand. He could stand and do it backwards.

There was the fall and support theme—a visualization of the idea of a trio of equals. In one gambit the dancers simply let themselves pitch forward or back onto another person, usually in some regularly timed sequence. Complications could be built in, like recovering from a back fall and running around to the end of a line to be ready to catch someone else.

Another set of arrangements, also based on the idea of bracing against one another to provide support, kept the fall carefully controlled. Someone would sit on the floor and hold someone else's foot, bracing against the other foot, and slowly lower him or her while preventing a disastrous skid. Eschelbach held the crooked-back elbows of Moulton, who faced away from her, and, straddling his legs, lowered him straight down to the floor. There were also trio versions of this possibility. In one, Eschelbach stood in the middle with Jensen and Moulton canting out on either side and Jensen, on the floor, eventually pulling both of the others her way. Together they looked like a sailboat heeling over. One of the nice things about these sections was the way Moulton allowed himself to be supported by the women. He really did conceive the work equally, not making it easier for the females or holding back to spare them.

Moulton moves with the physicality and spaciousness of an athlete and with a precise sense of gradation in his contacts with the ground. He could suddenly turn a running step into a base secure enough to swivel around or jump from, and he could land on a dime or come down loose enough to roll right into a fall. He must get some of his rhythmic flexibility from Merce Cunningham, with whom he danced for a few years, but the relaxed, unplaced look of the movement, the ease of the way the trio works together, is very un-Cunninghamlike.

After a five-minute break, there was a sort of coda. To ticktock electric organ pulses by A. Leroy, the dancers played an intricate game of passing three rubber balls from hand to hand. A bit like juggling, the game had the rhythmic and spatial acuity, the pleasing refinement of sword dancing or Chinese acrobatics. They missed a few moves, stopped, discussed what they'd muffed, started over. And still it looked like a performance.

Mediadance

Joan Jonas: *Solo Hits*, Intermedia Art Festival
Guggenheim Museum, New York

Meredith Monk: *16 Millimeter Earrings*

Soho Weekly News, 5 March 1980

Joan Jonas's Guggenheim Museum performance during the recent Intermedia Art Festival consisted of four pieces made between 1972 and 1979 under the title *Solo Hits*. Odd how many of the pieces shown in this festival were revivals. For almost two decades we've been told avant-garde work should be disposable, even deliberately self-destructing. Repertory is supposed to be a bourgeois limitation, and if you preserve a performance experiment you might inhibit its therapeutic value. Yet this season some of the major iconoclasts of post-Judson dance are reviving their early works. Of course, it must be easier to get public funding to reconstruct a known antiestablishment dance, one that didn't touch off the revolution, than to finance a new one that just might. I even heard Yvonne Rainer is doing a remake of *Trio A* for Dance in America, with big dance stars in the roles created by herself, Steve Paxton, and David Gordon. Can this be true?

Jonas's works, performed with linking interludes of sound and projected images, ran together almost imperceptibly. Her consistent subject over the years seems to have been the identity of the performer as threatened and expanded by the devices of replication: film, TV, and also simpler modes of reproducing images, like drawing. In one way, she's hardly there at all, except as a target, an object to be cycled through the machine and consumed. In another sense, though, she's Megawoman, purveyor of a thousand identities, all of which could only have come from herself.

The performance is about who she is, or about the ambiguity of who she is. Sometimes she looks middle-aged and plain. Sometimes she looks young and glamorous. She puts on masks and becomes smoother, more opaque. I don't know what she looks like. I'd never recognize her on the street.

But not only has she a multiplicity of faces. There in the center of the media and gadgets, she makes sounds that get modified or blended with recorded sounds; she dances witchy dances that conjure up films of volcanoes. Fragments of her flicker and pulsate and drown out the whole of her standing ten feet away. She shows you herself through many eyes. Who's to say which is the real one? The naked woman who scans every inch of her body through a pocket mirror sees a self we can't see—but we see one that she can't. At one point, she beats a rhythm with her hands as a video camera films her. The video monitor shows her hands on a split, sliding screen, so that the rhythm on the screen is different from the rhythm she's "actually" producing.

At the end she undresses a skeleton, tenderly lifts it from its stand and carries it like a baby, telling it a story. She puts a punched tape into a music box and cranks it, singing a lullaby to the tune it plays. She takes the tape out, flips it over, puts it through the music box backwards, and sings a different tune to the same notes played in reverse.

Media itself has this intriguing dual capability. It's fantastically change-able, fleeting, not bound to the physical limits of time, space, volume, and it can transform its subjects in the same ways. At the same time it can fix and preserve an image to create a very narrow, inflexible, and long-lasting version of truth. Perhaps the continued existence of the films that were part of many recent avant-gardists' work has helped them see their work as more permanent, more like a painting or a sculpture.

The Intermedia festival also showed a record film of one of Meredith Monk's earliest dances, 16 Millimeter Earrings (1966), newly shot by Robert Withers and incorporating most of the original footage of the piece. This dance too was about multiple identities projected by Monk live and Monk on film, sometimes simultaneously. Earlier and more primitive techni-cally than Jonas's work, 16 Millimeter Earrings used theatrical and dramatic devices like costumes and fake flames, but employed the camera mostly in straightforward close-ups, with film images thrown directly onto props like a lamp shade. Manipulations of Monk's image were achieved mostly through cutting—time-lapse montages, split-screen images—rather than through distortion of the picture such as blurring or fast zooms. And Monk still uses film in this relatively uncomplicated way.

Both Monk and Jonas as performers are quite passive, allowing them-selves to become objects of the camera's (or the audience's) gaze. But their methods are different. With Jonas, the emotional or aesthetic message comes from the technical changes the media can work on her neutral sur-face. In 16 Millimeter Earrings, Monk's fingers slowly claw a red Dynel wig into a snarled web of fibers. In her Quarry the camera stares at a group of people huddled in a cave, then slowly withdraws until they become flecks in a rock pile; later it glances across lifeless bodies floating in still, clear water. With Monk, the content of the image is always stronger than anything the technology does with it.

Higher Math

Merce Cunningham Dance Company
City Center Theater, New York
Soho Weekly News, 12 March 1980

Suppose you're ideologically and aesthetically committed to experimental choreography, as Merce Cunningham is, and suppose you've been choreographing regularly since 1953 on a steadily evolving and growing population of dancers. Cunningham has not been in the business of erecting monuments all these years, or even stylstic tin roofs under which his dancers can shelter awhile. He has no repertory to speak of except for his current work, and that's always pushing beyond itself. Unlike any other formally organized dance company, Cunningham's dancers are groomed to do the unknown, rather than to reproduce a body of previously composed work or carry out new work in a previously determined idiom. His working process is to set up problems that challenge himself and the dancers; he figures the audience will follow along somehow.

The City Center season included mostly recent work, and, whether because of the way Cunningham is choreographing now or because his production elements have fallen into a pattern of bland obstreperousness, I found I was observing the performances as if they were the more loosely structured, evening-long occasions that Cunningham puts together for any sort of open space, called Events. I was aware, for instance, that *Roadrunners* had some jokes in it and might possibly have been making fun of Martha Graham; and that *Locale* was made for small groups, in color-coded costumes, that recombined in various pleasing ways; and that *Duets* had an interesting score (by Peadar and Mel Mercier) made from the sounds of Irish jigging and clog dancing. I noted that in the revival of *Landrover* (1972) I missed Carolyn Brown not so much for her superb dancing as for the mantle of composure that she used to spread over the whole dance. I knew that I should be examining all these new or restored works for their specifics, but it was the way the company was dancing that claimed my attention.

As Cunningham grows older and more distant from the physical capacities of his dancers, he seems to want to push them into realms of accomplishment more arcane, more exacting than he himself ever achieved. The willing dancers of the present company make it possible for him to test the wisdom of age on the bodies of youth. This season there were times when I thought he'd been making deals with the devil—or maybe that he *was* the devil.

As his own participation becomes more restricted, Cunningham bothers less about the most obvious distinctions, cares more about minute variations. All the new works, like *Torse* (1976), which is the signature piece of this period, use virtually all fifteen dancers but feature none of them and offer an incalculable number of changes on a limited assortment of elements: body positions, direction, rhythm, repetition. The six-person works *Rune* (1959) and *Inlets* (1977) seemed unusually human scaled and spacious in this context.

Cunningham has never been a choreographer of large structures, but— perhaps by accident—his most satisfying dances have exhibited coherence in overall shape as well as the smaller inner workings. The end of *Place* (1966) is different from, and a consequence of, the beginning. *Winterbranch* (1964) and *Summerspace* (1958) are like beautiful orchestrations of a few movement melodies. *Landrover* closes with a neat reference to its opening. I don't see Cunningham selecting and arranging his material on this level anymore.

The body, which he long ago found out how to segment in unusual ways, is now a finely tuned machine, able to break up into several simultaneous and unrelated systems or a succession of isolated moves that skip from place to place like a connect-the-dots puzzle. This movement used to make sense somehow, or the dancers made it make sense, but when I think back on the new work, I see tiny particles, pinpricks of action. The dancers seem to be moving in a frenetic fog of instructions, perpetually stimulated and perpetually listening to some interior program that they dare not lose track of. They don't look as if they're dancing. In fact, they could be avoiding dancing in case it should confuse them.

Too many promising young dancers who join Cunningham now decline into expressionless flaccidity in a few seasons. Some of them look sullen, others mechanical. They lack joy or cheerfulness; they lack a sense of alertness to each other, to the dance around them. Their field of awareness extends to about arm's length, whether they're unfolding an arm or taking a big running jump. They dance with unrelieved virtuosity. You can admire them but they don't ask it.

The things that looked most alive to me this season were the duets, where having to coordinate with a partner seemed to give the dancers something to focus on besides their inner battles. Cunningham is especially good at partner work, though it's seldom remarked. Partnering evokes qualities he doesn't call for often from the individual dancer: body plastique, dependency, sensuality, risk, a tuning in to the ensemble. His new *Duets* reminds me of *Septet*, the limpid work he made on his first company, in which he seemed to be discovering the rest of the human race.

Duets is simply that, six couples who work only with each other and alone onstage except for fleeting appearances by other couples. Each pair has a different quality, or might have if the dancers allowed it to show. I especially enjoyed the springy playfulness of Robert Kovich and Louise Burns, but the other pairs were either temperamentally ill-matched or simply didn't try to sell it.

Cunningham's trickster-clown persona has always crept around the edges of his dance. We see him in this guise now and then, slyly changing clothes or shadowing other dancers or making quiet mischief in a corner, but he's never transferred this wit to the other dancers. He doesn't encourage them to find identities of their own, either, and except for a few hardy individuals like Kovich and Burns and Chris Komar, they don't assert themselves. Duets seemed to cry out for ego-interpreters, but Cunningham these days gets more of a rise out of the camera—as in Charles Atlas's idiosyncratic films of Locale—than out of his own dancers.

Mediadance

Merce Cunningham and Charles Atlas: Locale
Soho Weekly News, 2 April 1980

Merce Cunningham set a precedent by programming a whole concert of his films during his City Center season. This represents quite a turnabout for Cunningham, who a few years ago was resisting efforts to show his company on film because he feared it would distort the audience's expectations for live dancing. Then he took some time off to learn about film and video techniques, and he's since collaborated with Charles Atlas, either as cofilmmaker or choreographer, to make some of the most effective dance ever put on the screen.

Atlas's film of Locale gave me many things to think about, though it was almost impossible to see. His concept for the film was to move around while photographing the dancers. Moving cameras can make me dizzy in the best of times. When they surround a fixed point or pan around from one, I'm often impelled to give up my own sense of center and submit to an external motion that I can neither predict nor control. Atlas's lens moves, and it looks at moving dancers, and the camera itself moves as he travels with it through space. Looking at the image that results I not only lose my own center, but have to let the image go at the same time I'm perceiving it. Critic Arlene Croce admitted that her initial enthusiasm for the film faded some after viewing it on the big screen—she'd seen it first on a monitor. I haven't yet seen Locale in TV-size, but I imagine it would be a whole lot easier to encompass if it didn't take up your whole visual field.

Locale intensifies the mortality of dance, and of Cunningham's dance in particular. Stressing the immediacy of each dance gesture, its discreteness and uniqueness from all its fellow gestures, Cunningham fosters the gesture's ephemerality. In his dance, we're always encouraged to see each moment with at least as much attention as we gave the previous one. Atlas's *Locale* makes your whole field into a sort of peripheral vision—a blur, a sensory experience almost without form or definition. Halfway into the film, the camera quiets down. It stops zooming around and reconnoiters more slowly, even pausing at times to inspect one group of dancers thoroughly. You get intervals of orientation, recognition. You begin to follow. Then the camera-eye moves off and the facts dissolve again.

I'm assuming, of course, that the "facts" of this dance are those of a conventional dance: that it consists of people in a fixed and clearly defined space; that they move and are still, and that the viewer can distinguish between these two states and can define the source and intent of the movement; that the movement has finite beginnings and endings; that the dancers have specific identities and relationships to each other. What a lot we take for granted.

Atlas assumes none of that. Because he moves his camera around, and because he's shot the film at different times against different backdrops, you're never sure where the dancers are situated, or from what angle you're seeing them. Often you can't even be sure what they're doing because the camera grazes their moving forms only long enough to extract a charge of energy or a sense of something streaming off into one direction or another. Sometimes the camera itself carries the motion from one dancer to another, leaping across empty space. Eventually, I could almost look at the film like a light show, except that I felt a vague sense of betrayal toward the dancers.

Interestingly, we got a look at *Locale* from several perspectives. Cunningham made a proscenium dance out of the choreography after the film was done. Shown on the City Center season, the dance seemed to be making a point about small numbers of dancers grouping and regrouping in different combinations, as if Cunningham wanted to reestablish their collective order after all that cinematic chaos.

From the outtakes of *Locale*, Charles Atlas made a second film, *Roamin' I,* documenting the filming process. Intercut with shots from the *Locale* film were black-and-white scenes of Atlas gliding around the studio, camera on shoulder, followed by acrobatic helpers who shoved the cabling out of his way, and by dancers whose off-camera moves, entering and leaving Atlas's frame, were sometimes more agile than their dancing. This ballet of the production crew is always fascinating to me. I love seeing the workaday and theatrical functions overlap and mesh together. Maybe I'm caught in our widespread passion for documentation. ABC's documentary on the vast facilities, equipment, and personnel it invested in covering the Olympics made the athletes seem small and insignificant. Yet, if you think about it, the athletes are all the more remarkable because they haven't got any technical slaves to lift them off mountains, race them down hills, or spin them over the ice.

Maybe the stupendous resources involved in all media lead inexorably to their upstaging or trivializing their subject matter. Director Herbert Ross told Tom Buckley of the *Times* there wouldn't be much dancing in his *Nijinsky* film "because the choreography of the period before World War I seems very dated now." Whatever dancing survived Ross's ruthless cutters has been sanitized by contemporary choreographer Kenneth Macmillan, assuring that audiences won't be able to judge the obsolescence of Diaghilev's finest hours for themselves. *Nijinsky* is even more of a betrayal of dance than Ross's *The Turning Point* because it portrays real people. According to this latest fable, Nijinsky's dancing is to be remembered only as a by-product of a tragic love life and a doomed ego. And I thought it was about art.

Fugues and Fights

Twyla Tharp and Dancers
Winter Garden Theater, New York
Soho Weekly News, 9 April 1980

Twyla Tharp certainly has reached the point in her career where she could afford to coast. One of the things that makes her very special to me is that she keeps on taking risks. And I don't mean risks like producing three weeks in a big Broadway theater during a subway strike. Tharp is still the most surprising person in all of dance, I can't even predict where one of her bombshells will burst. The season's most amazing experience for me was the transformation of *The Fugue* with its first all-male cast. Choreographed in 1970, *The Fugue* is Tharp's most rigorous surviving work, a last, pure indulgence in composition before she turned to the broader demands of theater dancing. An exercise in counterpoint, the dance is merely a series of variations on a movement theme, presented without music, in strict linear sequence, with no elaboration or artifice. The women who originally performed it (Tharp, Sara Rudner, and Rose Marie Wright) wore boots and black gauchoish costumes, and some people saw the dance, with its miked stompings, precision timing, and ramrod poker-faced attitudes, as a feminist tract.

Tom Rawe, Raymond Kurshals, and John Carrafa now perform *The Fugue* in gray pants, gray long-sleeved sport shirts, and brown street shoes, and they not only redefine the dance, they redefine male dancing. To see men move like this—fast and precisely, with infinite modulations of weight and body plasticity, and also wearing the garb of ordinary men—is as great a revelation as seeing Fred Astaire for the first time. I don't know if Tharp intended to soften the dance this way, or if it occurred naturally. The men are more at ease with their own strength, they can swing or slouch through transitions that the women had to struggle with more determinedly. But the more I think about the season, the more impressive Tharp seems in terms of how she presents the male image.

American men have emerged from the seventies less tough, more vulnerable. The *Times* fashion section colors them rugged but pastel. Dance's men can now accept roles as stars and sex objects; they've gone jock and they've gone unisex. But Tharp is the only choreographer I can think of who gives her men their total physical potential without asking them either to promote or deny sex. Her men and women dancers confront each other, and us, on equal footing—sex isn't particularly an issue, which somehow gives everybody's sexuality more scope.

You can see this latitude reflected in the solos Tharp has choreographed for different types of men. Larry Grenier's in *As Time Goes By* was one long, lazy, almost giddy string of spirals. Mikhail Baryshnikov in *Push Comes to Shove* veered from explosive bravura to exaggerated nonchalance. The new *Brahms' Paganini* opens with an extended aria for Richard Colton. Like those I just mentioned, and like so many other showpieces Tharp has given to men and women, it's almost a catalogue of the distinctive things this dancer can do, in whose pages we also read his temperament, his personality.

The solo is unrelenting, an endurance test. Tharp has picked up the almost masochistic virtuosity in Brahms (Books 1 and 2 of his Variations on a Theme by Paganini), the unending, even tortuous flow of ideas. Colton rips through huge jumps and extensions, finicky cascades of foot and hand gestures, turning sequences with expansions or diminutions of size and speed, sprinkling it all with reminders of the folk dances that are part of Brahms's language. He does it all in high energy, even the comparatively quiet parts, scarcely pausing for thought between bursts of invention. The florid romanticism of it is extraordinary, especially for a man in sports clothes.

Tharp's movement vocabulary doesn't change much from one dance to another, but I've begun to feel that what she's choreographing is different states of mind rather than different environments or situations. Her dances leave me with specific emotional residues and often very little information. The second half of *Brahms' Paganini*, for instance, seemed negligible the first time I saw it—after Colton's brilliant display, just a lot of contentiousness and unflattering, bunchy fashion costumes by Ralph Lauren. On second look, though, the contentiousness came across as a response to the music, a further exposition of what Colton had been doing, only transferred to two couples and a single woman. It's like some romantic ballet—I thought of Eliot Feld—gone amok. The couples (Shelley Washington, Raymond Kurshals, John Carrafa, Shelley Freydont) clamp together, push away roughly, strain for ever more complex and ostentatious lifts, more dangerous athleticism, while Jennifer Way thrashes and yearns in the outfield.

Brahms' Paganini was the only new piece among the season's short works, yet everything looked fresh to me. I've never seen a better performance of Eight Jelly Rolls except maybe my first time in 1971, but then, everything of Tharp's is an earthquake the first time. And Baker's Dozen, at the end of a feisty program that began with Ocean's Motion and Brahms' Paganini, seemed even more serene and beautiful than it had last year when it was new.

Tharp has never viewed her own repertory as a sacrosanct thing. In fact, what happens to Tharp's dances after they're made can be seen as a process quite as creative at times as the choreographic process itself. Her dances change in ways as simple as acquiring new costumes, and as drastic as being totally reworked or heavily edited. Because she keeps her repertory in this slightly precarious condition, her works never look studied or fossilized; her dancers never look bored.

I suspect too that she has an irresistible urge to clean things up. The second time around a Tharp dance usually looks tighter, less messy than the first. The point gets clearer, pointier. I felt this way about Deuce Coupe II, the cut-down, simplified model of the great Beach Boys ballet she made for the Joffrey in 1973. The current revamping, or Deuce Coupe III, for Tharp's company alone, brings back much of the old piece, yet views it at a distance—it's more like a memory than a revival.

Tharp has restored most of the original numbers and the original shape of the dance—a kind of antiphonal coexistence between ballet dancing and vernacular concert dancing. But the new version has a finish to it that I find almost unpleasant. Rose Marie Wright, playing the ballet spirit whose formal presence affects the whole ballet, is almost a caricature, in a sylphide dress the size of a beach umbrella. The graffiti painters now are real artists, and they execute a handsome mural of 1960s slogans, designed by Robert Huot. The dancers look comfortable with the music, not galvanized by it as they once did.

For ten years Tharp has been the preeminent choreographer of pop music, and she's often used it to say something about the young. Deuce Coupe no longer seems to be a dance of adolescents, and neither does Ocean's Motion. I didn't see the Chuck Berry dance during the few months of its earlier existence in 1975. I'm willing to believe it was minor Tharp but timely. Seeing it now, the movement seems internalized, the dancers self-absorbed and aggressively isolated from each other. Near the end of the dance, a second group of five dancers joins the original five. Each one is dressed identically with someone in the first group, and what they do is an exact mirror image. The sudden introduction of this most basic of structuring devices is a shock in itself, and the effect grows even more astonishing as Tharp maintains the idea through lineups to much more casual-looking spacings on the stage. People drape their arms around each other's shoulders, saunter aimlessly; their opposite numbers are doing the exact same thing in an overlapping layer of reflection. The mirror-chorus has been added since the first version of *Ocean's Motion* and tells us as much about Tharp's development as it does about an increasingly straight younger generation.

Remembrance of Pratfalls Past

Twyla Tharp: *When We Were Very Young*
Winter Garden Theater, New York
Soho Weekly News, 16 April 1980

When We Were Very Young, Twyla Tharp's new evening-length brainchild, isn't a dance. It isn't a play, or a musical, or a recitation, or a cabaret. What it most resembles is a circus, and I suppose that's why its emotional import sneaks up on you, and why you remember the end so much more forcibly than a lot that leads up to the end. Like a circus it covers its heartache in boppy disguises, piles on stunts even if they don't go together, is good-natured in its cruelty and relentless in its efforts to please. And, at rare moments, it leaves itself mercilessly exposed.

Practically everyone has mixed feelings about this work, which is experimental in ways few but Tharp ever attempt. She invents new forms by mixing known forms, deals with information not usually transmitted through dance, and presents radical concepts in a popular setting. In this piece, Tharp is not so much eclectic as overinclusive. Some of its parts don't match. I dislike John Simon's brassy, two-bit Broadway score and the yelling that accompanies it so much of the time. Santo Loquasto's modular cardboard box constructions, handsomely lit by Jennifer Tipton, are almost too beautiful, too elementally functional. The piece is all contradictions, and is about contradiction. Oddly, it works as a whole though all its pieces don't.

Perched above the stage in a spotlighted nest, Thomas Babe and young Gayle Meyers play a father and daughter talking about the father's boyhood and family memories, specifically his recollections of his mother. The writing, by Babe, is impressionistic, psycholiterary, rambling from traumatic incident to seemingly pointless detail and back again. Babe uses the standard devices of fiction to recall the past—old photographs, snatches of nursery poems, generational similarities and overlaps. Although the script would probably read all right, it isn't easy to follow the first time. But literature does seem clumsy and intrusive when you're used to the evocative modes of dance, and there were times when I thought Tharp and the dancers could have said it all without any words. They not only illustrated Babe's narrative but gave it depth.

Babe's mother, as he tells it to Meyers, is a lovable kook with a fatally destructive ego split. She yearns to be perfect, but she can't get within ten feet of respectability before the walls start closing in on her and she goes off on a toot. Tharp shows the development of this character on two, possibly three levels, also overlapping and woven together without pauses except to shift scenery. First there's a fairly literal representation of Jane's escapades—the family (Tharp and Tom Rawe, Katie Glasner, and Raymond Kurshals) as a battlefield only slightly more under control than the anarchic world out there where she seeks liberation and eventually death. The family characters are at times represented in depersonalized form by surrogate dancers dressed in white acrobat gear. These beings do most of the dancing; they are a distillation of the characters' best and worst qualities.

Then there are the even less realistic fantasy figures who exist outside of the characters and represent their wishes, their ideals, and maybe their fate: a solemn juggler (John Carrafa) who at the end tosses Jane the implements of her life—a baseball cap, a teddy bear, sunglasses—and leaves her with arms full and nowhere to go; a Little Match Girl (Shelley Washington), forever shivering in the snow outside the rich kid's window; the inexorable army of taskmasters who keep marching through, chanting verses that Jane can never remember the right words to.

Jane's nuttiness and her horror of confinement get more and more violent. She dreams of dead children, but instead of being at peace, they're beautifully imperfect. She gets drunk on her thirty-ninth birthday and declares a momentary truce in the matrimonial wars. After making violent love to her husband—they bang away at each other after a wrestling bout in the shower—she runs away again. This time she doesn't come back. Among her wild-living friends down at the end of the town, something happens to her that's too terrible even for Babe to explain. He finds her in the hospital and watches her life signs finally give out. The piece ends in a long apotheosis that swerves between pandemonium and desolation, till Tharp/Jane solves her dilemma by dropping off the edge of the stage into the dark.

Are we supposed to take this piece personally? Advance interviews indicated it's a fusion, with artistic liberties, of Babe's and Tharp's autobiographies. I think Tharp is trying, rather desperately, to express through narrative dance things she doesn't reach in her other choreography. But when she must portray a specific character, she's self-conscious. She plays Jane as frenetic, wired, like a punch-drunk prizefighter. Her timing and physicality make her a spectacular comic ordinarily, but this clowning is hyperactive and seldom truly funny. The kids are goofballs, Danny the husband a shambling lecher. But the perfect angel-couples are blank and almost mechanical, no improvement.

Tharp plays the danger, and the desolation, at high and higher voltage. The piece is full of armor plate, bristling with defenses. People fight, people make love; in both actions their bodies are hard, their contacts more like fending off than giving in. The noise is deafening. Jane's need to bust out is furious, insatiable; her capacity for quiet seems mixed with a fear of death. I'm moved by Jane's tragic end because Tharp has been killing herself and the dancers for two hours to move me. And because Tharp has to struggle so with her own feelings before she can reveal them. Perhaps the energy of that struggle is what propels her creativity—Jane says, "I know the right way. I just don't want to *do* it that way!"—but I wish it were easier for her.

Professional Prophet

Kenneth King and Dancers
Cunningham Studio, New York
Soho Weekly News, 23 April 1980

Kenneth King has taken on the job of prophet. For years he's been warning us, advising us, needling us about the terrible shape civilization is in and the many things we could do about it. He probably knows we aren't listening, but he goes on anyway. Like a true professional, he's cheerful and patient about this work that never gets done with, and he keeps on offering the human race new ways to save itself. At various times he's suggested computers, language, ultrasophisticated machines and media, counterespionage. Now it's astrokinetics.

Astrokinetics has something to do with projecting the body's energy into space to make more room for ourselves. Sounds like dancing. Sounds like space colonization. King is thinking about both in his new dances, *Space City* and *Blue Mountain Pass*. *Space City*, part of an in-progress film project King is doing with Robyn Brentano and Andrew Horn, was a solo by King that seemed to consist mostly of long sequences of movement evolving by small but dramatic degrees from apparently abstract beginnings. He would balance on one foot with arms stretched out to the sides, gradually changing the position of his hands and free foot until he looked more like he was yanking himself off balance than holding himself on. He'd be jogging in that casual, energy-conserving way joggers have, then he'd shoot a glance out to the side, the glance would become a head gesture, a tilt of the body, almost a fall. Lying on the floor on his side and waving his arms, he began to suggest he was brandishing a whip, a sword, then—up on his feet again—rallying a field full of troops.

King's dancing has this mysterious power to evoke character. He often seems to have a whole scenario going on in his head—you don't see the cops and robbers but you do see his involvement with them, in quick flashes, not developed scenes or actions. He speaks of this himself, as if it were a natural thing, "the thresholds of the mimetic and kinetic" running together, but most of his other dancers don't make it happen. It may be telepathy for all I know.

Blue Mountain Pass incorporates some of the movement themes of *Space City* and could be a way of carrying its ideas over from the individual to the group. King and Diane Jacobowitz, Shari Cavin, William Shepard, and Bryan Hayes engage in a series of activities that take them from inner, private body positionings to tentative probings of the near surroundings, to cooperating with other dancers, and finally into space-covering, almost random reachings and leaps. The movement language passes without comment from natural unfoldings, bouncing, running, things like that, to balletic glissades and battements and Cunninghamesque torso skews and separations. Sometimes the dancers look precisely rehearsed and timed; sometimes they all use the same material with their own timings and directional changes. And sometimes they lose their performing tension for a second, lapse into indecision, make you wonder if they've lost the thread of the dance or if there is a thread. But always they're formal, working out a prearranged pattern or solving an agreed-upon problem.

There's quite a bit of partnering in *Blue Mountain Pass*, more than I've seen in King's work lately. In a sculptural duet, he and Cavin give leaning, lunging, and balancing gestures into each other's hands, while the other two men steer Jacobowitz across the floor. Sometimes she seems to be fainting, sometimes she might almost be swatting them away. At one point everyone takes turns helping the others jump. Toward the end, both women get a chance to be carried high across the floor by two men. Curiously, none of this double and triple work looks really dependent. The contacts between the partners are peripheral, and all the people being supported look ready to stand on their own two feet at any moment.

It's form and imagination that give King's dance its conviction, not solidity or forcefulness or logic. His arguments are ephemeral, his images are gone before you can absorb them or piece them together. During this performance, which included a solo prologue, *Stand-up Comedian*, and an older work, *Wor(l)d (T)raid*, he read his lecture on astrokinetics on tape, showed a portion of the *Space City* film on a small video monitor which was left on during intermission so people could look at it up close, and inhabited calmly the environment created by the electronic/concrete sounds of William Tudor and the eerie blue-green lighting effects of Jeff McRoberts, which seemed to encapsulate the dancers and turn them into some kind of experimental beings—televised astronauts or atoms under a microscope—against the yellow electric skyline outside the windows.

In the same oblique way that he's a dramatic dancer, Kenneth King makes dramatic dances. He uses all kinds of devices and effects, contrasts and contradictions, he mixes modes and switches circuits, trusting that we can perceive as globally as he does. I've often thought King's words and symbols were sort of extraneous, or at least existed in a different realm entirely from his dance—the realm of aesthetics or metaphysics versus the immediate and physical reality. This time his nonlinearity seemed more persuasive, his different stimuli began to seem less separate, more contingent on each other. And I notice that I've changed around the order of the sentences and phrases in this article much more than I usually do. His message must be getting through.

Avant-Garde for the Opera House

Laura Dean: Music
Opera House, Brooklyn Academy, New York
Soho Weekly News, 21 May 1980

The people who walked out on Laura Dean's Music—in a steady stream for the whole hour and a quarter the dance lasted—might have been lured to the Brooklyn Academy Opera House by those breathless ads that promised the ineffable rewards of high culture. I didn't plan on that, but I was surprised by how little experimentation there was in a piece that proclaims itself, even justifies itself, as avant-garde. For some time Dean has been doing big pieces with one-word titles: Song, Dance, Spiral, now Music. It's as if she wants to excavate the elements of stage work one by one. I've sometimes wondered if that's what she's really doing, if Dance, for instance, is any more quintessentially dancy than any piece of Merce Cunningham's or George Balanchine's.

The first things Dean did, seven, eight years ago, were much more basic than her recent scrollwork. From those truly minimal materials—walking, stamping, spinning, and jumping—she's built a stock of gestures and phrases that she presents in a glamorized, even elaborate way. As Dean continues along this line, the specificity of each piece grows more doubtful to me. She seems to have added nothing to her movement lexicon for a couple of years, merely arranging the parts of it in different sequences.

Except for the program order and insignificant differences of floor pattern, *Music* looks very much like *Spiral* or *Dance* to me. Instead of using this vocabulary she's arrived at to explore new imagery or bigger ideas, Dean seems to be limiting it even more, perfecting what is essentially one closed-off, closed-in structure.

Music has four distinct kinds of action, each presented at some length, with shorter transitional sections. It's accompanied by Dean's pulsing music for synthesizer, piano, and violin. First the six dancers (Dean and Angela Caponigro, Perry Souchuk, Peter Healey, Erin Matthiessen, and Ching Gonzalez) do a continuous curling and unfolding of limbs, a repositioning and centering of the body. They're very stable, neutral, serious, never wavering as they shift weight, step into new directions, and never moving out of their lineup—three in front, three in back. They might be warming up, but after some time, the viewer can see that there's nothing particularly organic or sequential about their moves. They offer their bodies to the audience, sometimes evoking Nijinsky, St. Denis, the curves and recurves of Indonesian dance, the solid geometry of ballet.

After a long time, they slip out of the unison they've maintained so far and into individual arrangements of the same moves. They echo each other sometimes, and I thought there might be some canon or other compositional game plan in effect, but the audience around me was so restless, the plan so diffuse, I couldn't gain the concentration to discern it. Another long section was given to spinning. Usually in their original spots on the floor and again in unison, they changed their arm positions and sometimes bent over or arched back, but never interrupted the even pace of their spin.

Suddenly they were all standing close together at the front of the stage, in the same lineup, and singing wordless chords in harmony while they stepped from one side to the other. This was the only music the dancers literally made in the piece, and it seemed the most naive gesture to me, a nod to the Whiffenpoofs, but with a sound curiously unblended and unmodulated, and even made harsh by amplification and violin accompaniment.

Finally, the dance moved into active traveling and rhythmic diversification. With loose arms and knees the dancers shuffled quickly forward and back, soared one at a time in jumps along a diagonal or around in a circle, faced the audience and shook their shoulders, and did other gestural scraps from Dean's bag of patchwork. Still the phrases were brief, the rhythmic ideas square, the floor patterns invariable. Just before the end, this sequence seemed to open up as the dancers let go of rigid unison or corps-plus-soloist groupings. But what looked freer turned out to be only the illusion produced when everyone did something different in a lot of space. And the curtain fell with all of them spinning once again, back where they started, in their original cells of space.

Dean's music for *Music* is like the dance. It sputters and drones along, offering few challenges to the ear or the kinesthetic sense. Unlike Steve Reich, who collaborated with her in the early minimalist days, Dean hasn't moved into denser territories of sonority, harmony, or rhythm. Counterpoint, syncopation, and complex phrase variations are as unimportant to her work as stories or characters. She's content to let repetition be its own excuse, to let music underline the movement display rather than provoke the movement into surpassing itself.

Laughter in a Time of Crux

Bill Irwin and Doug Skinner: *Murdoch*
Dance Theater Workshop, New York
Soho Weekly News, 2 July 1980

Some of the year's best performances have been unnameable. One superlative skill like dancing isn't enough, it seems, to satisfy the inspiration of a Charles Moulton, a Bill T. Jones, or a Broadway-scale Twyla Tharp. Bill Irwin has danced with the San Francisco–based Oberlin Dance Collective, and only a dancer could have devised the routines for the two-man show called *Murdoch*. But come to think of it, only an actor could have devised them, and an acrobat, and a brainy, funny man. Bill Irwin is all of those. He doesn't do music, but that's supplied by Doug Skinner and cleverly faked by Irwin when necessary.

Irwin has the comic's gabby, confidential manner, but what he does is more profound than one-liners. Like all great clowns, he makes us believe there's a pathetic, fallible creature like ourselves underneath all the seemingly unrelated skits and characters he plays. He's always teetering between the on-top-of-it-all assurance of a stunt man and the hideous insecurity of a fall guy. Engaged in a constant drama of success and failure, he's totally committed to both. When he's winning he looks radiant, self-possessed, but when some small thing goes wrong—he knows it long before we do—something on the outside subtly crumples and you can see him thinking desperately how to recover.

In one sketch he makes his entrance on what seems to be an imaginary combination of a tightrope and a crowded subway train. Twisting and balancing brilliantly, he never gets more than a few steps along his tortuous path before being irresistibly drawn back the way he came. He struggles to keep upright, to wrench his hand or foot away from the clutching Thing on the other side of the very doorway through which he just entered. The existential quicksand always swallows him though, dragging him through the black curtains as he scrabbles against its force with his fingernails.

Irwin can do a whole variety of the vaudevillian's eccentric dance numbers and tap inventions—rubberlegs and soft shoe are especially well suited to his loose, quick frame. He can slip in and out of mime stories, like an encounter with an imaginary rival that begins with handshakes, turns into mean but unavailing karate throws, and ends with gunfire. In an encore he juggles a plate of spaghetti, saving the plate but losing the spaghetti in great ropey globs. He begins a whole dance by wiggling his eyes and sliding the parts of his face around. Irwin doesn't use fancy makeup. In relinquishing the instant identity of a clown face, he makes his own extraordinarily mobile face both more vulnerable and more expressive.

During a series of character sketches he puts on a pair of half glasses and squeezes his whole face down into his collar until he looks like Barry Fitzgerald. Then he leans over a podium and delivers, in a stream of the most glorious malapropisms, a sermon about the troubles of Job. The fact that he's oblivious of the verbal quagmire in which he's swimming is just another example of his talent for narrow escapes.

Through all his adventures, his most formidable opponent is his partner, Doug Skinner, whose stolid presence is both reassuring and sinister. Ill at ease, as all musicians seem to be in the presence of dancers, and wearing an oversized tailcoat, out-of-style eyeglasses, shaved haircut, and a long scraggly red beard, Skinner sits at the piano with his back to the audience. Stooped over, arms pulled in, almost furtive, he produces a variety of faintly mysterious and inappropriate sounds to accompany Irwin's skits. Once, he gets to play a whole piece while Irwin is changing. It sounds as though he'd initially been thinking of "My Blue Heaven" but shorted out on a proliferation of ideas before he could decide on any one key or rhythm. Another time, Skinner does a routine with a dummy that looks like Edward G. Robinson with curly bleached-blond hair. Neither Skinner nor the dummy is funny.

Skinner is that incompetent, boring, completely humorless person who seems to be in charge of so much of our lives. He's in charge of Irwin. He plays loud, rollicking introduction music before Irwin's ready, scaring him. He tells him what he's supposed to do next. He gives him a ukulele and makes him sing—sort of—a patter song, "Home in Pasadena." Snuggled up together spoon fashion, they strum their ukuleles, and while Skinner croons the verse, Irwin's toothy smile melts ever so slightly into a glint of hatred, but he's always there on cue for the refrain. At times Skinner made me so uncomfortable that I longed to like him just a little bit. But I knew he'd have to remain grim, unyielding; nothing else would incite Irwin to such excesses of danger and survival.

Traumerei

Munich Dance Project
Performing Garage, New York
Soho Weekly News, 6 August 1980

Munich Dance Project is the kind of European company that tries to make innovative, nonballetic dance but that looks, to my eyes, regressive. I wonder if one reason is that they often get their inspiration from American teachers. Experimental dancers here either disregard or flatly contradict their teachers, or, in a relatively unadventurous period like the present, they exert such individual command over their material that we don't even think about its derivation. Visualize Sara Rudner, Douglas Dunn, Dana Reitz, for instance. There's always something about New York dance that makes you feel you're out on a frontier, seeing dance redefined if not reinvented. The European dancers are less rash, perhaps not so supremely confident that any person's dance can prevail. I often feel too that I'm looking at some kind of arrested process, a mechanism ignited maybe by their teachers or the companies they knew here, which they've worked over, crafted, perfected—but haven't really metamorphosed in a personal way.

Munich Dance Project director Birgitta Trommler studied with some established American teachers and has worked with Kei Takei and other contemporaries. Her *I No Longer Dream* is an image-play that might have been done ten years ago. It's one of those very slow, ambiguous, beautiful works that's all about surfaces, all on the surface. You're probably meant to drown in it but nothing pulls at you long enough or hard enough. Not that the piece isn't long or serious; it just passes inconclusively from one state to the next, suggesting unease, but sliding away from terror. Its feeling is depressed rather than dramatic.

Dressed by Gretchen Warren in billowy white jumpsuits tightly banded at waist, wrists, and ankles, the eight dancers move as one, sometimes clumped together and breathing with a swelling-subsiding rhythm, sometimes spaced evenly or unevenly around and doing the same activity with different timing or facing different directions. They move with a soft plié and are centered close around the body, traveling hardly at all through the space. They all have a fixed, untouched expression on their faces, and they all stare straight ahead as though they don't really see. They sometimes break away from the group or assume prominent roles within it, but the movement blends so well that I take these individual outcries to be facets of the same collective "I" who dreams, or no longer dreams.

The first of three sections introduces the basic themes, which recur in slightly altered form throughout the piece. The dancers clump together and fumble to pat another person's body. They sway off balance and fall softly to the side. One person rides piggyback or athwart another person's hips. They do a martial arts sequence, sometimes slowly as an exercise, sometimes in fierce mock combat with another person. A man touches his head all over as if he's hearing voices. And there's a dance phrase, quite simple and in place, that seems to involve dancerly enlargements of some primal movement impulses: crouching, spreading, rising, sinking, balancing, and turning. Since the material is quite limited and nothing seems to be added that wasn't initially suggested, the movement grows into a sort of preliterate language that they all share in a general way and can infuse with different meanings by using different inflections.

Toward the end of the first section, a woman appears, wrapped head to foot like a mummy. Answering some irrepressible life force, she shuffles forward, crashes to her knees, strains to her feet, topples to the side, wriggles onto her back, lurches to standing, and starts again. Finally the others unwrap her, but after her limbs are freed she still repeats the horrid mummified motions. Then the others take the sashes from their waists and wind them completely around their heads, and wander around touching themselves, as if they've wrought some miraculous change.

The entire second section is a ghoulish recollection of the themes of the first, all the dancers encumbered with bandaged heads. In the third section the bandages are off but each dancer has a white face mask suggesting Pierrot, the sad clown of commedia dell'arte. One woman kneels at the back making a mask by dipping sheets of stuff in water and molding them onto her face. After once again walking, groping, falling, the dancers gather together and begin sightlessly exchanging masks.

Trommler's choice of music for this procession of images seemed based more on providing background moods than on really giving support or dimension to the dancing. Steve Reich's "Music for 18 Musicians," about two-thirds of it, accompanied the first part, and his "Music for Mallet Instruments, Voices and Organ" the last. There is, certainly, a dreamlike feeling about Reich, but there's also a very vibrant and compelling interplay of rhythms, intensities, and harmonics that often drew my attention away from the dancers, who were drifting along on the surface. The middle part had some early American hymn tunes, the kind that are sung vigorously by rather coarse voices, with open harmonies and a very square interlocking of parts. In a way, the opposite of the Reich for subtlety and sensuousness. But, like it, opening the way to a visionary experience.

Queen of the Natural

Deborah Hay: *Leaving the House*
Dance Theater Workshop, New York
Soho Weekly News, 13 August 1980

Certain women in dance, neither beautiful nor physically ideal, take such forceful hold of an audience's imagination that they become cult figures. Psychologists have not studied this phenomenon; critics treat it case by case. But it keeps coming up, so it must depend on more than isolated personalities. It's easy to understand the stardom of a beautiful ballerina or a male pinup in tights or an elegant stylist like Twyla Tharp. But Martha Graham and Mary Wigman and a surprising number of successors had neither the physical allure, the virtuosity, nor even the performing grace to impress most audiences. What they did have was magic powers.

And specifically, access to the dark side of the unknown—the occult, the forces of earth and fire, the unconscious, and the legends of the dead. The cult women in today's dance, led by Meredith Monk and Anna Halprin, have brought the layman directly in contact with these mysteries during participatory workshops, as well as dramatizing them more objectively in performance. We see only part of the spell-working in either situation. Deborah Hay's *Leaving the House* struck me in this way. The bare fact of it— an hour-long solo by Hay with accompaniment by Bill Jeffers—didn't explain Hay's cult appeal, didn't even quite explain itself. I felt the presence of other people, other meanings, a whole ritual left behind somewhere and only sketched for us.

The last time I saw Deborah Hay, it could have been in the late sixties or early seventies, she was living up in the country somewhere with a bunch of people, and they did their own version of a folk dance in Lincoln Center Plaza. It consisted of mostly walking, and the passersby didn't know whether it was a special thing or not. Even outdoors at Lincoln Center, special things tend to get done on platforms, with lights and amplification and costumes. Deborah Hay, along with many colleagues in the postmodern dance generation, wanted to blur the line between audience and dancer, to break down the idea of performance as a thing set apart. That phase of total abstinence from theatricality has passed for Hay, as for most of her compatriots, but she still seems determined to look plain even while looking sometimes quite glamorous.

The night I saw *Leaving the House*, she wore no makeup, fluffed out her black hair in sixties hairy style, and dressed in a pair of very full, white ethnish pants and a white brocade chemise top that didn't belong to her body or move with it. Jeffers, who shared the performing space in a bright spotlight, looked even more the reformed hippie with his spit-neat hair, manicured beard, impeccable tan, and whiter-than-white undershirt and trousers.

While Jeffers noodled on some percussion instruments, mostly of African origin, and recited solemn lyricisms—we are profusion, we are the feathers of birds, we are incense—Hay danced a string of movement phrases, each repeated a few times but not developed or interconnected. Some of the phrases seemed to be just displays of physicality—exaggerated running, vigorous wiggling, slow bending over. Others were infused with some kind of dramatic content whose meaning was never entirely spelled out. Arms draped over the top of her head, hips wiggling slightly, she made her mouth into various possibly erotic shapes. Sitting on the floor, one leg drawn up protectively, she looked over her shoulder with possibly pleading, possibly frightened expressions. Once she took a stick that had been fastened in the wings and crossed the space, seeming to brandish it like a weapon. Once Jeffers, posing as a courtly attendant, hung a piece of striped cloth in her hands as she ran by him, and she circled the space holding it overhead. The props didn't advance a "story" either.

A program note explained, not very lucidly, that Leaving the House was developed in a workshop. Participants made up movement based on images, which "were dropped as they became unnecessary." Nevertheless, sixty-four "images" were listed. Naturally, the audience could not memorize them before the dance started, nor link them all up to movement after it was over, so they weren't much of a clue to Hay's narrative, if there was one. The telling "images" to me in Hay's dance were evoked by the way she moves, not by the faux-naïf literality that the audience was invited to accept.

Her philosophy emphasizes ordinariness: life experience distilled to some simple, unsophisticated core. She speaks of becoming "technicians of consciousness." But what makes her worth watching, worth following, I suspect, is not at all simple or unsophisticated. It has to do with her performing concentration, with her commitment to the material at the same time as she's focusing it at the audience. She made me aware of body surfaces, especially the flatness of the foot when it makes contact with the floor and the sensuous space between the palm of the hand and one's own skin. Her poses, her moves look not so much unfinished as purposely thrown in doubt—a shoulder narrowed, a place held still, an angle exaggerated. Under the appearance of something obvious, she's really doing something quite arcane. Maybe it's the combination of things partly recognized and partly mysterious that intrigues us.

Pavement Parties

Dana Reitz: *Double Scores*, Art on the Beach
Battery Park Landfill, New York

Charles Moulton: *Motor Fantasy*, Art on the Beach
Battery Park Landfill, New York

Andrew De Groat and Dancers
Lincoln Center Plaza, New York

Soho Weekly News, 27 August 1980

There's probably never been so much outdoor dance presented as this summer, and the pavement parties run on through September, in the garden of the Cooper Hewitt Museum, the Delacorte Theater, and more. Everyone seems to use these open-air exposures differently, but from what I've seen, environmental dancing, or letting the place dictate the dance, is no more. This summer's dancers are more interested in doing their choreography or being seen by an audience than in developing dances to suit the geography. Strangely enough, Dana Reitz, Charles Moulton, and Andy De Groat all merged in entirely different ways with their scenery. Probably the spectator's eye always assimilates more than what's in the spotlight, and released from the proscenium frame, dance can create other kinds of theater. These all turned out to be city dances, though probably none of them were intended as such.

Reitz and Moulton performed on the Battery Park Landfill, a large tract of sand and tumbleweedlike vegetation overlooking scenic Hoboken. This spot is billed as a beach by Creative Time Inc., the sponsors of the Sunday evening performance series, though it looks more like a dune to me. But you do have to pay to get in, which gives it something in common with most other pieces of private shoreline on the Eastern seaboard.

Reitz's dance, *Double Scores*, continued the line of thinking that she's been on for the last several months: individual dancers' variations on a limited amount of thematic material. In theory this should bring out the personal styles of the dancers—Reitz, who's so linear that she makes even a circle look like a passage from point to point; Deborah Gladstein, who's small and moves with rounded, tactile ease, almost languorous; and Robin Hertlein, straightforward and unassertive. But in this setting the individual differences among the dancers shrank. The dancers themselves were dwarfed by the space Reitz chose to set them in. With the audience seated along a ridge of sand, the dancers used a large area surrounded by an even larger expanse of empty space. There was a sprawling, half-made frame structure of indeterminate character beyond them, and more beach and Hudson

River and crumbling piers beyond that. The setting was almost totally unfocused, and Reitz's dance, instead of focusing it, simply became another fact in the landscape.

It wasn't only scale that made this happen. The movement consisted mostly of isolated arm gestures, shuffling and lunging and digging the heels into the sand, and jumping in place. The dancers made little attempt to project this vocabulary but seemed to hug the movement close around themselves. Everything that might have accommodated the dance to the size of the dancing space was played down. The movements were big but not space-consuming; traveling more than a step or two became a non-dance activity, as prosaic and diffident as if the women were ciphers in a crowd.

For no apparent reason they would drop to the ground and lie there in melodramatic positions, then get up and walk to another spot. Sometimes they'd all be moving together—at long distance or close range—and there'd be a sudden coincidence of impulse, they'd all turn in the same direction or sink down at the same time. These moments were arresting, but a lot of the time I drifted pleasantly off to the boats going by on the river, the gulls, the traffic noises along West Street, the fisherman who ambled out along the far bank and threw in his line, my own thoughts. The dancers were like islands of low energy in the waterfront activity; only when they stopped or coalesced were they really noteworthy.

Charles Moulton's Motor Fantasy was almost the reverse—a tight bundle of high energy posed against stasis. Moulton faced his audience in the opposite direction, away from the river and toward the immense fixity of the World Trade Center. Set to A. Leroy's synthesizer pulse music, the dance was confined to a room-sized platform and was completely aimed at the audience, as presentational as a tap dance.

It was a tap dance, in part. Moulton, with taps on his running shoes, began with a shuffle-and-stamp dance, feet very close to the ground, upper body very still. It reminded me of the basic, businesslike dancing they did in some of the early black movies, with no finesse or polish about it except in what really mattered, the rhythm. Later Moulton was joined by Barbara Allen, who did some step dancing with modern-dance plastique adornments—torso shapings, arm and leg gestures. Allen's rhythms were complementary to Moulton's; her spatial patterns sometimes made modest frills around his relative lack of positional change.

The dance was in six parts, gradually making more complex use of this friendly juxtaposition of styles. But even though Moulton had all the focus that Reitz lacked, I couldn't concentrate on the cerebral aspects of his idea. I don't know why this was, but I find it hard to read when I'm outside, too. I do know that the culminating section of the dance was intricate, driving, and allowed both dancers to open up into the whole stage space. It came at me out of the blue, as demanding, as visually and rhythmically sophisticated as what I always thought minimalists like Laura Dean would work up to—but haven't seen anyone achieve till now.

Andrew De Groat and Dancers was the most advanced of the tried-and-true dance events scheduled for Lincoln Center Out of Doors, and he chose to do selections from old works rather than a new piece. There was a condensed version of *Red Notes/Get Wreck* (1978), a three-man version of *Rope Dances* (1974), and sections of a 1979 piece I hadn't seen before, *Portraits of American Dancers*.

The latter piece interested me at first because it was done to Chopin piano music and seemed to have some musical phrasing in it, rather than De Groat's usual spun-out, athletically accented naturalism. I thought he might be trying for portraits of real dancers, and Debbie Decorrevont's running, sweeping, turning dance seemed reminiscent of Isadora Duncan, Frank Conversano's muscle display suggested Ted Shawn, and Jon Harriott's wide, traveling footwork recalled José Limón. But De Groat's personality-less style demands that all real expression be submerged by the dancer, so Conversano's strength dribbled out the ends of his fingers like water, Harriott's feet scarcely seemed to touch the ground, let alone press home any emphasis.

The other eight solos didn't remind me of anybody, and the piece ended with a long simultaneous recapitulation of everyone's dances accompanied by one of Christopher Knowles's word manipulations, in this case a repeated spelling and misspelling of some name like Brick Brinzohoff, that caused my sensory system to glaze over.

The rope dances are simply spinning dances decorated by the dancer's arranging three strands of knotted rope around himself. De Groat can do it with a bouncy rhythm, Harry Sheppard makes quite complicated designs and accelerates and decelerates without a break, and Conversano turns on and off his strange, hypnotic stare and makes the dance seem dramatic though it obviously isn't.

Red Notes/Get Wreck lost whatever form I imagined it had in the cavernous Lepercq Space at Brooklyn Academy and became a stupefying recital of flingy spurts of motion and meaningless handling of props like cigarettes and fans. De Groat now seems to be mainly celebrating activity for its own sake. The audience in Lincoln Center Plaza came and went; there didn't seem to be anything special enough to look at for long, but maybe outdoor dance is for dropping in on. Like the old Trans-Lux newsreel in Grand Central, a diversion between trains.

Return of the Scream

Kenneth Rinker: *Cantata No. 84*
Dance Theater Workshop, New York
Soho Weekly News, 24 September 1980

While the controversy smolders about who got what from where in post-modern dance, a number of new choreographers have been staging a reaction against postmodern's austere formalism. Postmodernism is no longer the newest form of new dance. Not that postmodernism can be summed up in one statement, but Kenneth Rinker's new *Cantata No. 84:* "behind the moon, beyond the rain" is so forcefully not postmodern in style, form, and feeling that it's a perfect piece to look at for clearing the critical air, a perfect opener for a new season.

Over the past year or so there have been signs of rejection from people who might otherwise be postmodernism's legitimate heirs. The working premises of the last ten years—structure draped with very basic movement, or "natural" movement threaded together improvisationally, or game playing and process as a way of arriving at sequence—have begun to feel confining instead of liberating to some people, and so has postmodernism's mandate that the performer must be neutral, the choreographer a sort of functionary, both serving up the dance impartially, as if it were something separate from how they feel about the dance. What's starting to push its way through looks a lot like our old friend expressionism, the twentieth century's recurring mode of artistic rebellion.

Cantata No. 84 gets its dual title from Sergio Cervetti's eclectic but possibly Bach-based music and from some quasi-poetic words of Rinker's—a song beginning "Lost/Lost along unknown streets in the human sound track" is printed in the program. The tone of the piece, like its title, is nostalgic; it's full of allusions to the old magic days of Broadway and gives more than a few nods to Anna Sokolow. But Rinker's magic is as easy as turning on a switch, his alienation brings people together. He's fascinated with the Broadway-musical myth of how the girl next door gets transformed into a star upon the application of costumes and lights, and how the ordinary person she still is underneath becomes suddenly glamorous too. He doesn't portray individual characters or tell stories, but he shows a collective society made up of eager, competitive, mostly angry, hardly-ever-smiling faces; people working together by chance, attracted to one another fleetingly, inured to headlines, noise, fame; people who've traded in passion for therapeutic rage.

This rage is really a theme of the piece, and Rinker's way of presenting it is one of the most interesting and contemporary, if unpleasant, things about the work. The dancers seem to have ingested anger from the environment; it comes naturally to them, the way waltzing maybe did to the Viennese. They're not protesting against anything in particular, and they're not psychologically damaged cases. But every half hour or so during the show they face the audience and break into unison orgies of stomping and shouting. They celebrate hate the way chorus lines celebrate success.

A sequel to Rinker's earlier show biz invocation, 40 Second/42nd Variations, and the middle section of a projected trilogy, Cantata No. 84 begins at the end of what is possibly the final rehearsal of a show. The dancers slip in and out of everyday personas while they do a series of everyday actions and dance actions. They flirt, they perform, they change clothes, they dance marathons. The everyday actions aren't really all that casual, and the dance actions aren't overly specific, so the roles, the realities, immediately begin to blur and run together. Finally, though no figurative curtain has ever gone up, they leave after a prolonged series of bows and farewell flourishes. Only then does Rinker appear and dance, for the first time in the piece—he's been seen once before, dressed as a stagehand. And this initiates another group dance, less laced with vernacular gestures than anything they've done, but no less role-obsessed.

The dancing, especially in the large group sections, has a superficial resemblance to Twyla Tharp. I realized how far ahead of her time she was when ensembles of Rinker-people would jitter around in individual patterns that adhered to each other and dissolved again before anything in the space could coalesce into one unanimous or finished thought, and all I could think of was the fugue in Deuce Coupe (1973). But Rinker isn't big on composition; his main adventure with form seemed to be arranging much of the dance material as variations on one theme. This is stated by Beth Davis at the beginning, when she's supposedly trying out some new movement and teaching it to other dancers. It's used in all that follows and is given its—I suppose—definitive form in Rinker's superstar turn at the end.

The other thing that looked so contemporary to me was the tight, or uptight, way Rinker presents romanticized images. His ten dancers all look highly technical and pared to the bone, and so does his movement. It's often big but somehow always looks close to the body. The intensity is high all the time. The dancers often freeze in the midst of a personal gesture—tapping someone on the shoulder perhaps—and you wait in suspense, only to see the contact veer off somewhere else. They can throw movement at you with great vehemence but they're never light. They can flop and become dead weight in each other's arms, but they never seem to luxuriate in the giving in.

Even when things look improvised, I'm sure they're not. Even when they're rhythmic, they don't look musical. Rinker choreographs irregularly on Cervetti's regular beat. He sticks with the tempo but makes his phrasing on the elapsed time of the movement or on apparently arbitrary counts. This makes everything look very impulsive—and at the same time very contained. Very strange. Creatures of machines they (we) are, of electronics and media and violence. They've adapted. They're not fighting it. They're going on from here. And, feeling very much a holdout from another generation, I wonder, do we all?

Wind That Knows about War

Kei Takei: *Light Part 15*
Krannert Center, Urbana, Illinois
Soho Weekly News, 5 November 1980

Kei Takei's monumental work *Light* is now eleven years old. In dance that's a very long time, a generation. *Light* has undergone not only the natural evolution of any extended work by a single artist, but many changes of cast, revisions of choreography, and even some shifts of style and intention. Yet it remains *Light*, a series of related images about the perils and the persistence of the human race. Part 15, the newest installment, was premiered last summer at the American Dance Festival, and I caught up with it the other week in Illinois. Subtitled *The Second Windfield*, Part 15 has eight dancers working usually in pairs and a sort of stage manager (Maldwyn Pate), who prepares the stage for them, wraps them up at the end, and in between observes them from the sidelines.

In a program note, the Japanese-born Takei acknowledges—I think for the first time—a debt to the memory of Hiroshima. Though lots of other things have been suggested in the course of *Light*, Hiroshima's metaphorical reverberations seemed overpoweringly present in the very earliest parts, so much so that I've always seen the work as being primarily about survival.

Part 15 begins the same way as Part 14. Pate, dressed in black, methodically unfolds a square of cloth whose corners have been brought to the center, origami-style, many times. From a small heap of fabric, he spreads it till it covers the entire stage, then retreats to a dim downstage corner where some twigs and branches have been strewn about. As people begin to enter the arena he's laid out for them he starts working with the pieces of wood, scraping them together, chopping, hammering one against the other, always keeping an eye on the dancers. The sounds of his activity make a sort of musical accompaniment. Is he leader, servant, spy? Pate's enigmatic though very concrete presence is typical of Takei's methodology. Her characters are always engaged in very obvious tasks and processes that have, nevertheless, very elusive meanings.

The dancers enter like racehorses, full of energy and making huffing sounds. They run across the field, periodically freeze in sprinting, thrusting positions, gallop off again. As the floor cloth becomes bunched up and disarranged, one or two of them pause to squat along the edges and pull it taut carefully. One recurring theme of Light is that of the spectator/helper/mastermind, who watches the action of the protagonists—I almost said contestants—and unobtrusively sets out the course for them or repairs the damage they're doing to the landscape.

They often inflict damage on themselves too, or bear the scars of former wounds. You notice that one woman has returned clutching some kind of excrescence on her body, a lumpy brownish-greenish thing that adheres like a scab. Her movements have become wilder, and she's flung into the arms of another person. When they part, the stigmata appear on his body. Gradually more and more people acquire these growths, transferring them to each other as they embrace or wrestle, and the floor becomes littered with broken-off pieces.

You often wonder whether Takei's people are fighting or loving each other, building something together or struggling to tear something apart. Many of the encounters in Part 15 seem more physical and more intimate than earlier ones. Before, people threw things at each other, or bonked together stones that they held in their hands. Now they hurl themselves at each other, impacting in violent embraces or missing in headlong falls.

But eventually, after a mass fight in which they group into two loose teams and charge at each other, they find partners and begin a quieter task. Carrying rough poles about five feet long on their shoulders, the couples do a sort of marching dance that reminded me of people bringing logs out of the woods or hauling a captured animal between them. Sometimes they still seem to be disputing for possession of the poles, but mostly they cooperate. All the poles get piled onto one couple, then loaded in the arms of one man, who stands very still like a huge unlit bonfire.

The sound of a heavy wind has been rising, and the dancers now begin to gyrate around the bonfire, as if in celebration, but also looking tossed and scattered like leaves in a storm. Pate comes stealthily out of his den and, singing a Japanese folk song, pushes the dancers one by one up against the pile of sticks. When they're all huddled there and still, he drapes the floor cloth around them, pulling up one corner at a time and throwing it over the still shape, the way a janitor might cover up a statue before a room is painted. As the lights go out, Pate is creeping around the edges of the space, scraping two sticks together and hissing into the dark, as if to scare off predators. As always, I'm left feeling some necessary phase of a cycle has been acted out. Something has been done but not finished. Dangers have been conquered but other dangers are in store, for which the energy and the wiliness will be found. It's a bleak sort of optimism, but I know if they can survive, so can we.

After the Tea Ceremony
Unpublished notes, 29 October 1980

After the tea ceremony in Illinois, we walked out into the blustery wet morning, and as the cold air filled my lungs, I gave Kei a hug. Thinking at the same time what an unusually impulsive thing that was for me to do. I suppose the extreme formality of the thing, holding me in tight for an hour, had me so bottled up I just needed to press a human body.

Not that the ceremony wasn't full of appreciative & welcoming feelings, for Kei's performances and for all of us being there. Shozo chose pots the color & texture of *Light Part 15* for the event. But a tea ceremony is not a casual affair, nor a spontaneous one.

Camille sat in the guest of honor's seat (rather, kneeled on the cushion) by mistake and had to change places with Kei at Shozo's direction. Do they ever give tea ceremony when there isn't a guest of honor, I wondered. The whole ritual seems to be about focus—condensing & closing in the universe to one tiny room where nothing needs to be done except to pay attention to the guest of honor, the admiring of beautiful forms & sensations, and the admiring of the style of the admirers.

I felt clumsy & too large—my feet going to sleep under me—wanting to stoop over as I returned the objects to their places, though I knew I couldn't bump into the ceiling even if I stood up straight—afraid I'd make some horrible mistake of taste, not even so gross as dropping something but replacing a napkin with the fold on the wrong side.

And yet, there were moments when I almost reached a state of meditation in spite of feeling so confined, when it seemed there was nothing in the world of greater significance than me watching a man's fingers folding a cloth or sliding down the handle of a bamboo dipper.

Revolution on a Leash

Laura Dean: Night
City Center Theater, New York

Laura Dean: Tympani
Orchestra Hall, Minneapolis

Soho Weekly News, 24 November 1980

When they announced Laura Dean as one of the choreographers for the Joffrey Ballet's fall season, eyebrows were raised below 14th Street, and New York insiders, remembering Twyla Tharp's first hit ballet for the Joffrey, Deuce Coupe in 1973, wondered whether history would repeat itself. Well, history never quite repeats itself, and a lot of trains have gone by since the Golden Age of flower power. Einstein on the Beach at the Metropolitan Opera House. Dance in America. Push Comes to Shove. Probably even artists don't know what avant-garde means in the eighties. Much of what was new dance ten years ago has now been housebroken through the combined effects of media exposure and the artists' inevitable mellowing, refining, and elaborating of their own severe first thoughts. An active, two-way dialogue is going on between the lofts and the ballet stages. Watching this process take place is not the same as watching a revolution.

Night, for eight Joffrey dancers, to a two-piano score by Dean, looks very much like the things Dean's been making for her own company, with two important exceptions. The four women are in pointe shoes, and the entire piece and all its movement ideas are condensed to about half their usual length. These seem to me obvious concessions to the ballet audience, though they're not inconsistent with Dean's recent line of thinking.

Dean doesn't tax a viewer, in Night, with the mesmerizing stretches of repetition that were the original source and rationale for her work. The piece starts with about five minutes of spinning. It was through this meditative activity that Dean first spelled out her aesthetic with the circle dances of the early 1970s. Self-possessed but egoless, the dancer is a calm, centered, timeless functionary of the universe, as she revolves or treads with plain steps laid out in undramatic, logical patterns.

But a curious thing happens to this movement in pointe shoes. The body's center of weight—naturally high in a ballet dancer anyway—rises another few inches. Even the men seem detached from the ground rather than anchored in it. Velocity and tension take the place of stillness in holding the scheme together. In the remaining ten minutes or so, posing and traveling patterns, with ballet configurations like the arabesque and the grand jeté built into them, are shown—each one repeated just enough times to "read" but not enough to take us into any perceptual outer space. Rhythms are even, unaccented—emphasized, if at all, by jumps and upward-veering turns. The piece ends on a high show biz note: all the dancers face the audience and slowly raise one arm, then they finally settle assertively, feet spread, arms down, palms out, stalwart under a barrage of applause. Costumed in black pants and short kimonolike jackets, Night seems like some sort of elegant, continuous kung fu exercise, or an abstract version of a Maoist ballet.

Speed replaces contemplation too in Dean's other new piece, Tympani, premiered by her own company in Minneapolis. It's longer than Night, but instead of using time to let us savor one thing over and over, she seems impatient, makes the movements go faster, gradually hyping up our response and leading us to an almost theatrical climax. Tympani uses a set of movement modules similar to those in Night. The small ensemble, here four men and two women, begins with a slow demonstration of positions, then a period of spinning in a large circle. While three dancers circle around them, the other three gather in the center and do a set of stretchy thrusting motions, the arms pushing out into opposite diagonals from the legs, four counts per step. They switch with the people on the outside. They switch back and do the stretches in two counts. They switch. Then a sequence in one count. Naturally, speeding up the movement makes it look different, more fluid and alert. The same sequence occurs in exactly the same way in Night.

Having accelerated in pace through sequences of jumps, a section in which the dancers, spinning, whirl in and out around each other following the pattern of a Grand Right and Left, and various floor drills with stamping accents or decorative leg embellishments, the dance ends with the oppositional thrusting phrase—the dancers now moving quite fast. Lined up facing the audience, they look a bit like conjurors as the lights fade out on them.

What struck me in Tympani was how presentational it is, how much the dancers do for the audience's benefit and how little for each other. They're almost always facing front, and, when not moving in a circle, they seem to have only glancing contact with each other. Dean's concentrating now on body shapes—sinuous, curvy, arm-through-hip undulations, contrasts between close-to-the-body shuffles and widespread pliés. You can see these dances, as you see the clearly shaped and directed figures of a ballet. Dean's own dancers are more grounded than the Joffrey's, but the pulse, balance, continuity that used to enlist my kinesthetic involvement are reduced factors now. So is the infectious communal bond of strong rhythm—still to be seen in her 1976 *Dance*, which was shown in Minneapolis with *Tympani*.

Perhaps a property of minimal art is that, having once been demonstrated, it has to be built up again, made more complex, or it'll get boring. Laura Dean's movements certainly aren't unusual, and her use of block structures with little or no variation can be bombastic, possibly even condescending. Musically she's even more limited, and the tympani she's added has little more to do than underscore her square, thumping piano rhythms. There's never been much texture or subtlety in Dean's music or dance; you went to it for other qualities. In the context of the Joffrey Ballet's high-speed, ornate, popular Arpino repertory, Dean's choreography is both appropriate and cleansing. In the context of today's highly developed postmodern dance, it seems conservative, cautious, prematurely set in its ways.

The Death of Lennon

Unpublished notes, 9 December 1980

I didn't keep up with popular music after I went off to college in 1950 with my first record player and a stack of Stravinsky and Ravel. Even the freedom songs of the early liberation passed me by. I wasn't marching then. I was tied down, trying to be ordinary for the only time in my life. By the time I liberated myself it was the sixties and I was over thirty—and I knew there was no use trying to idéntify with passionate adolescents. I was trying to be *less* passionate, to be a grown-up.

Still, around the edges of the dance world, I heard music—Miles Davis on hot summer nights in New London as the crew worked & partied on stage at the American Dance Festival. Music dancers chose for their choreography, Laura Nyro, Chick Corea, the Beatles.

There were Beatle songs that could make me cry—and I didn't identify with them, didn't turn on, didn't even understand the words dissolving in electronic riptides and dozed-out carelessness. What I did understand of them was the irrepressible life force, the capacity for being amazed and unfazed at the same time, the sometimes rather beautiful salutes that could have been laments . . . blackbird singing in the dead of night.

I even sang Beatle music once, in one of the spin-offs that spread out from their phenomenal success—a wacky arrangement of songs called the "Baroque Beatles" was done for a small group by Josh Rivkin, and I was asked in as a ringer when they needed a bigger sound for a concert in Philharmonic Hall. It was a lark—I liked the Beatles for letting me go larking, which I didn't do much and don't.

I shared some of their "life-style"—because those things had always made sense to me—peace, conservation, all arts people shared those values. And some of their thing I thought was for kids. And some of it—the drugs and the hype—I hated. And Yoko Ono I never came across at all.

Yet it seemed perfectly logical to me that Yoko, the protopunk, pre-Soho avant-gardist, and John should have gotten together & created a super-rich superstar existence, and that it ended as it did. The counterculture unleashed the violence it was trying to restrain—gave people license to be anything they wanted to be, or could be, without the need to read or think or discipline themselves. Said we're all one, we're all stars. Love a star shoot a star be a star. And the stars tried to feel ordinary if they stepped from their limousines and went to the fruit store without being bothered.

Love Isn't All We Need

Wallflower Order
Dance Gallery, New York
Soho Weekly News, 17 December 1980

Of course it was only a bizarre coincidence that the murder of John Lennon took place on the same night that the Oregon women's dance collective Wallflower Order began a series of performances. Of course it was. A coincidence that I was reminded of the Beatles several times during their performance, and that all the way uptown I kept thinking how much I liked it in spite of what struck me as a confused and possibly irrelevant political pitch. And that an hour later on the news I heard about this Beatlemaniac who could legally buy a gun, carry it on a plane, hang out in a permanent crowd of celebrity-ghouls until he got his chance to effect some ultimate, sick consummation of hero worship by assassinating the symbol of peace and love who'd found happiness in New York as a semiretired supercapitalist.

It will take us a long time to digest the implications of the Lennon murder; at least I hope it does. This may be the event that finished the sixties, but what a mess the sixties have left behind, what a tangle of contradictions and ambivalence about how to solve our problems. I'm not even sure whether we're living in the aftermath of a revolution or the prelude to one.

Wallflower Order looks more like the aftermath. The five-woman group uses a pure agitprop approach to theater. Which is to say, they don't do pure theater at all but employ an eclectic array of styles, modes, and techniques in the service of communicating their values. For instance, there's Pieces of Lies, a play written by theatrical adviser Timothy Near about the kinds of female role-playing that get started in childhood. Laurel Near, dressed in a voluminous skirt and draped with more props and packages than a bag lady, rides on top of someone else's shoulders. A slightly patronizing taped voice speaks to her, urging her to get rid of all the fake identities she's been depending on. One by one she discards the trappings—and the doppelgängers, who roll out from under the skirt, cowering at having been exposed. They represent things like bad-girl insolence (Pamela Gray) and tomboyishness (Lyn Neeley). Each of these alter egos dances a solo where the supposedly protective persona gets out of control—the Isadora Duncanish romantic (Nina Fichter) gets so passionate she almost turns into a vampire, the ballet dancer driven by ambition (Krissy Keefer) pirouettes with brutal skill. Later they all dress like teenagers attending a dance and act out the same characterizations in a literal context.

The mechanics of how all this is carried out are sometimes ingenious, sometimes almost amateurishly contrived. I have a feeling both qualities were intended. The group is highly accomplished, even slick, in so many things that I can only assume that they mean to look like bumpkins when they do. Their costumes are usually ratty and unflattering—shapeless streetwear, thrift-shop finery, holes in the tights. One number, Z Ballet for Z People, looks like something cooked up by the fifth grade, with characters called Aristocrat, Bishop, Waitress, and two Karla Marx Sisters, who throw themselves at each other in aimless class warfare.

I took this piece to be a deliberately naive effort to appeal to naive audiences. The group also does sign language dances and dramatized folk tales with the same evident purpose, but with far more sophistication. There are also marching and rallying numbers and dances that illustrate political sentiments—Have you ever held hands with a woman? Many times. I held the hand of a woman in childbirth, a woman who was lonely—dances that celebrate love, dances of anger and tenderness, and even an abstract dance, where they dress in strange, Nikolais-type coveralls and pose in evocative shapes while reciting the names of endangered animal species.

They're strongest when they offer individual acting-dancing portraits of oppressed women, but these outcries have cardboard targets—the Rich Rulers, the Jailers—and point to no ways of translating anger into remedial action. When the group gathers up its collective energy, the outcome often is a brilliantly constructed inspirational song or a slogan, like Resistance, a choral recitation in fairly subtle counterpoint about fighting for whatever it is we're supposed to be fighting for. Hospital is a monologue-dance, perhaps autobiographical, by Fichter. She describes the agonies of someone who has to undergo repeated surgery for a birth defect; the piece is a desperate scream for the doctors to let her body alone. And in Prison Poem, Keefer recites the thoughts of a woman with a five-year sentence, her mind racing, struggling to stay sane.

Words are an important medium for this group, both in their overtly proselytizing pieces and in the more abstract ones. In a number of interesting performances lately, I've appreciated the depth of meaning words can add to movement. This doesn't mean that movement lacks resonance, but that dancers in recent decades have chosen to squelch its expressive connotations. At their most affecting, Wallflower Order gets maximum emotional mileage out of words and movement together.

What I found so moving about the group was its commitment. Not the political commitment, but the commitment to movement. These women move with knowledge and mastery of their own bodies. They use the full potential of their weight and momentum. Their vitality comes not from a hyped-up performing ego but from a willingness to take any impulse as far as it will go. They trust each other, but more, they trust their own activity and responsiveness. This is truly rare for American women. The members of Wallflower Order may have developed it through a communal way of working, but their example doesn't convince me I need to become a socialist or join a sisterhood. If anything, Wallflower Order speaks for the power of individual awareness, discovery, and the intelligent recognition of talents.

Friendly Occasions

Blondell Cummings
Black Theater Alliance, New York
Soho Weekly News, 23 December 1980

A woman is alone in her apartment. She's clearing up after a dinner party. It must have been a stimulating get-together because the woman doesn't seem at all tired. She methodically scrapes the plates, nibbles on a crust of bread, sips from a half-empty wine glass, interrupts her tidying up to leaf through the newspaper, drops cigarette butts one by one from the ashtray into a wastebasket, finds a two-inch joint among the debris and carefully pockets it. All the time she's preoccupied with her thoughts, which are very animated. It's as if she's reviewing the evening's conversation in her mind, maybe improving on it, adding ideas here and there.

The woman is Blondell Cummings, and this is the first sketch of *A Friend—II*, a solo dance "based on friendship experiences." The scene has much about it that rings true—the way Cummings absentmindedly munches on something she picks from the fruit bowl, the way she ambles around the room while talking on the telephone. She seems completely at home, in a way actors seldom are in a stage set, and completely absorbed and entertained by her internal dialogue. She does various dances—my favorite is one she begins on all fours after feeding the plate of table scraps to a toy dog. Slides are shown on a big screen—photographs of people's faces, maybe some of the same people I noticed sitting down in the audience. A voice reads a long list of people whose names are linked together, not always the obvious linkages either, and not always familiar names. In "Scene 2—A Crisis," she dances a long, emotional argument, I'm not sure whether with herself or with someone else, and finally, decisively, picks up the phone.

Despite the vivid realism of the atmosphere, and the clarity of Cummings's imagery, there's something about her work that I can't follow. I mean that she persuades me I'm watching this person's train of thought— but suddenly, she's projecting emotions so exaggerated that I lose my connection to the specific situation where they started. The scale of her dance matches the scale of her acting, but the two performing modes don't "read" in the same way. Since it's already an abstraction, dance of this intensity becomes generalized. What she might intend as sympathy for a dying friend looks a lot like what we saw earlier when she was possibly feeling bad about a love gone wrong.

Cummings's movement mixes facial expressions, mime, and naturalistic acting techniques with rhythmic dance impulses that surge out through the center of the body in big spasms of the torso, wrenching gestures of the arms and legs, and jazzy undulations through space. Her dances seem to be large abstractions of physical feeling-states, like blown-up photographs. In The Ladies and Me, a series of portraits accompanied by black women vocalists, there's a lurching hangover dance, and what seems like a tantrum dance, and a sadness dance, and a conversation dance that ranges all over the lot from laughter to incredulity to fear, all done in a series of equal-time stopped actions. These are virtuosically controlled and executed, and also very public, even though the emotions come from private provocations. Maybe that's another reason I feel sort of dislocated watching them.

A Friend—II ended with a little shadow play between Cummings and Connie Schrader: "Scene 3—So, what's new?" The creator of the shadow play itself isn't credited in the program, but I thought it was clever though simple—not merely a silhouette show. Two or more lamps behind the screen were made to focus on the figures from slightly different distances or angles, so that their shadows seemed to shift planes or almost look three-dimensional. Schrader is tall and thin, Cummings is smaller and rounder, and the shadow images play with this contrast, often making one shadow look unnaturally large as it pats the shadowhead of the other, who's looking very small. In one especially beautiful sequence Cummings's shadow seemed to be floating in a blurry, twinkly goldfish bowl. The episodes in the shadow play were brief, hardly more than flash card pictures, and as with the dance-drama scenes that preceded them, I wanted very much to know what was in those spaces in between.

Already, Post-Postmodernism

Marta Renzi: *What Do You Do, Dear?*
The Kitchen, New York

Robin Hertlein: *Two Down*
Warren Street Performance Loft, New York

Soho Weekly News, 21 January 1981

Postmodern dance has now spawned a second generation, which is engaged in expanding, combining, and elaborating on postmodernism's dicta. Like an earlier generation of modern dancers, only the evolution is much quicker, the post-postmoderns are beginning to look quite similar to each other although their original sources were a disparate crowd of revolutionaries. They all seem to share a desire to present movement, of whatever particular style, as a thing worth looking at in itself. They figure movement is capable of any amount of repetition, variation, or turning this way and that, and doesn't need to be delivered in a special high-performance style to be interesting. And they make few distinctions about what is appropriate movement for dance—academic steps mix with acrobatics, mime, horseplay.

Something about this flat, neutral style captures our attention. We're almost forced to concentrate on the structures and forms the dancers are showing us. But the search can pall; the performing monotone can drown the alertness we need to follow ideas or oblique narratives properly. I don't suppose Yvonne Rainer would have been insulted by woolgathering or even inertia on the part of the audience, but today's dancers seem more eager, more ingratiating beneath their offhandedness. Without being pushy, they wish to be understood.

Marta Renzi's movement is Tharpian in its quick flexibility, her choreographic form is made of small, recurring but unsequential motifs like Douglas Dunn's, and she borrows pointedly from David Gordon in a dance with a folding chair. Renzi exploits neither her precedents nor her own interpolated quasi-literal gestures and fooling-around movement repartee in *What Do You Do, Dear?* It all just passes by, take it or leave it.

The piece is a series of duets, and a finale by five couples, to five piano pieces by Thelonius Monk and a song, "Stand By Your Man," by Tammy Wynette. Renzi and Cathy Zimmerman perform all six duets. Using a lot of leggy, space-covering movement, they show you ways two people can dance together. They imitate each other, which creates all kinds of echoes, shadowings, matchings. They watch each other do little solos. They use each other for support, manipulate each other by pushing or propping up each other's limbs. The tone is impassive, but sometimes a glance passes between them, a movement looks like more than just a movement, a half-acknowledged subplot peeps through.

They make each duet into a little number by standing quietly for a second at the end, so that the audience applauds. Then they move to the sidelines where they give a show of resting—breathing hard, stooping over, taking sips from a mug—and effect small changes in their costumes. Sara Rudner has made this kind of activity an endearing part of her solo dances, but Rudner's exhaustion and recovery are natural components of a dance that's totally there and totally exposed. Renzi and Zimmerman look precious doing it—possibly because they seem so reserved and cool about their dancing itself. Though it's attached to the jazzy rhythms of the music, it doesn't really dig into the beat. I felt them riding safely above it, almost trying not to emphasize it too much. In fact, all through the dance I had the feeling of styles, gestures, characterizations referred to but not given their full stress, as if the whole thing might be too specific or too loaded that way.

After a final duet in which they peel off their costumes and immediately put street clothes on again and dance—perhaps ironically—to Wynette's reactionary sex-role message, they leave and ten dancers enter. Each couple has its own folding chair and each has a different segment of Renzi-Zimmerman's chair duet material to repeat in a loop sequence. The dance ends with a glorious avalanche of people stepping up onto the chairs and falling or jumping off. As pure movement material for people we've enjoyed in other dancers' companies—Gerri Houlihan and Mieke Van Hoek, Diane Frank and Peter Stathas, Deborah Gladstein and Vicky Shick, Art Bridgman and Myrna Packer, and Bebe Miller and Kyle deCamp—Renzi's noncommittal eclecticism finally speaks for itself.

Robin Hertlein's Two Down was considerably less ambitious, but I found it more satisfying. She offered a limited amount and type of movement material, with no stylistic or character interjections to throw you off the track. The piece consisted of a solo Hertlein made for herself last summer (Solo Replays) and a duet for herself and Victoria Marks based on that movement material. Hertlein has worked with Dana Reitz and uses Reitz's compositional device of variations on a theme. In Solo Replays she also moved like Reitz, sketching in the air around the body with her arms and then following their cryptic path with torso and legs. Duet, however, began with a long sequence for Marks on the floor, in which Marks was central where Hertlein had been peripheral, sinuous where Hertlein had been direct;

she pulled or sprang out into space instead of enclosing herself in a space.

In these two solos, so different in feeling, the dancers seemed to be deliberately working against their own types. Marks, small and compact with an angelic face, stayed firmly grounded yet spread herself along and even above the floor. Hertlein, bigger, more solid, traversed those ethereal, squiggly routes with calm fluency. But then they began to dance together and you could see similarities in shapes, in phrase developments. Hertlein almost taught you how her first solo had given rise to Marks's as they combined movement materials and motivations through a dynamic progression—slinging the gestures almost out of control, accelerating and tightening their steps to insect dancing, and lifting one another across their backs while still opening the legs as if to step. Finally they both subsided into Marks's first floor solo, and in a very long lighting fade, they slowly spiraled to a stop.

Gordian Slipknot

David Gordon: *Profile*
Dance Theater Workshop, New York
Soho Weekly News, 4 February 1981

David Gordon likes to be disconcerting. He likes to keep you off balance, divert you from whatever sequence of logic you may be following through his work. It's not precisely that he contradicts himself. Rather, he wants you to know his mind is quicker than yours, that he can find three unsuspected linkages for every one that's obvious. His new *Profile* is as unpredictable as ever, but it lacks a kind of cohesion I always found in his work before. It's a compendium of images and allusions, strung together on a base of movement. Except for a couple of narrative parts, all the literal material is reduced to terse words, gestures, or actions that make sense only when you've heard or seen what follows them. The piece slips through your mind's fingers like sand.

Gordon has always been interested in wordplay—puns, rhymes, free association, words that ooze out the ends of other words. Here the words may or may not go with the movement the dancers are doing, or words and movement may make comic sense together, but both are always delivered with a postmodernist dryness that's meant to keep the performers safe from being implicated in their material and its potentially explosive effect.

Some of the sections of *Profile* show people saying what they're doing, like the trio where Susan Eschelbach, Margaret Hoeffel, and Keith Marshall exchange places in line, step in and out of close formations, lift, hold up, and carry each other. For a while it's very matter-of-fact, even redundant. First they give their names, standing in line. Shuffling places, they announce: "Susan as Keith," "Margaret as Susan," "Keith as Margaret." Then, "Susan behind Keith," she says, getting behind. "Margaret falling," she says, falling over onto Keith's hands.

Unexpectedly Keith and Margaret are lying down embracing, and Susan, sitting on the floor at some distance, says, "Susan as the Other Woman. Woman abandoned. Abandoned woman." The shock of this transition from the banal to the suggestive barely has time to register before they're going on, into arcane overexplanations of what still looks very simple. "Susan as Keith as Margaret as Susan," she says after they've exchanged places another few times, not giving us time to wonder who is who or if it matters.

Much of the movement in *Profile* simply illustrates what the performers are talking about. Much of it is descriptive in itself, like the nonliteral gesture solos done by various members of the group against a precision formation resembling Balanchine's flying wedges in *Stars and Stripes*. The backup ensemble cadence-counts, getting up to unreasonably odd numbers like 45, 91, before the solo gesturer finishes. Sometimes there are no words and no gestures, but a series of stopped moves that bring whole stories or relationships to mind, as when a group of about eight people fall, lean on each other, grasp each other by the forearms, looking intently at their partners or equally intently away.

Gordon has often used chains of large, active movement just for itself, with no literal connotation. Here the movement of this kind seems much simplified from his earlier athleticism. Now the dancers have to do things like lunge, stretch out, topple over in one piece, take big stiff-legged steps, rise straight up on the toes, support a partner under the armpits from behind.

Rather than something especially interesting to see, this movement seems to be a way of keeping on going, even when the dancers are saying extremely loaded things. Hoeffel and Valda Setterfield have a conversation about their mothers—"Did you spend a lot of time with your mother when you were young?" "Does your mother take an interest in your dancing?"— that would be overpoweringly emotional if they weren't going through all this drill at the same time. It reminded me of the way women confide in each other while they're washing the dishes, and I thought it was the truest sustained image I ever saw in Gordon's work.

Setterfield was splendid through the whole evening, and Gordon seems to take special care to make opportunities for the quiet wit of her timing, the clarity of her gesture, the malleability of her body in a series of lifts, the specificity of her focus and her expressive but never exaggerated face.

In a final duet, Gordon and Setterfield began with the side-by-side theme we'd seen several times earlier in the piece . . . side by side . . . sidle . . . idle . . . and ended running calmly in slow motion to the apotheosis music from *The Nutcracker*. In between they played another conversational word-mime game. As they tossed the cues back and forth there were references to marital troubles and reconciliation. They seemed to be skirting danger-ous waters, falling in, climbing out again, as people do who've just had a terrible fight but have agreed to forget it. The sequence made me feel bad, as if I'd come too early for a party and seen the living room before it was picked up.

Profile is a strange, sprawling, disorderly piece. It's much less ingratiating than Gordon's former work, and while I probably enjoyed it less, I re-spected it more. It seemed serious, and subdued, as if it hadn't yet found a way to energize or propel itself without the easy glamour and jokes Gordon has relied on before. At the beginning, after a series of introductory solos by the company, Gordon danced briefly. Looking overweight and morose, even for him, he moved slowly, with a fluid sensuousness that was almost erotic. He looked totally unlike anyone else in the whole evening. He looked, for once, almost on the edge of meaning it.

Serious Fun

Gus Solomons, Jr.: *Unplay Dances*
Theater of the Riverside Church, New York
Soho Weekly News, 11 February 1981

Gus Solomons's company has eight dancers now, but in his new piece, *Un-play Dances*, there seemed to be many more. One reason is that the seven sections of the dance are arranged so that you almost never see everybody on stage at the same time, and each section sorts the personnel out in a different way from the others. This is odd; when you stop to think about it, most choreographers unconsciously adopt habitual tactics for deploying their troops. The characteristic gatherings of groups, pairings and placings of couples, setting off of solo figures against other dancers become part of the organizing principle we think of as the choreographer's style. You would be surprised, I think, to see a group of three dancers and a group of five dancers doing simultaneous but different movement in a Martha Graham dance—or a socko unison lineup in Paul Taylor. But Gus Solomons doesn't give you this kind of subliminal help.

Solomons has some Graham in his background, but his main aesthetic comes from his years with Merce Cunningham. He shares—he possibly even surpasses—Cunningham's freewheeling approach to dance construction and Cunningham's use of exacting footwork and line to maintain order in what might otherwise be a chaotic stage environment. Solomons, in addition, establishes the preeminence of spatial designs, both in the patterns the dancers follow around the stage and in the shapes they make with their bodies. Perhaps because traveling is secondary, his dance doesn't look accidental and random, which is Cunningham's way, but purposely inconsistent. Maybe that goes along with the quotation from a 1967 Solomons lecture that appeared in the program: "If work is fun, and play is work, then work is less work and play is less fun, and play becomes serious, and work becomes unplay." In any case, the dance seems to keep transforming itself into new ideas before it risks overstating any.

It begins with a rhythmic floor combination, very Cunningham, very dance-class, that's mostly stepping sideways from a wide second-position plié. The dancers work in unison, only some are likely to be standing at attention and watching as the others move. Later there are balletic, mostly in-place progressions for individuals working from open fourth positions into relevé and other balancing steps while making large arm gestures and small isolated wiggles of head, shoulders, or ribcage.

But after that there's a duet where a man supports a woman who glides from one angular position to another, and a second woman dances unrelatedly in another part of the stage. A tall man partners a very small woman and Solomons comes on mysteriously, in a red light. He's wearing voluminous harem pants—everyone has them over their briefer dance gear during some part of the dance—and with his back to the audience he seems to enfold the couple in the large circle of his arms.

If he's suggesting a genie or a benevolent god at this point, he reverts to his dancerly self immediately as the couple leaves, and does a solo with big sweeping circular gestures of arms and legs. Five dancers form a pool of labor and replace each other one at a time through the course of a long three-person dance. There's another group of five that becomes almost a classical pas de trois for a man and two women, with the other couple hovering in the wings. Three couples dance similar but not identical close-together duets at the same time, then stand still as Solomons and Kevin Coker arrive and dance an entirely different kind of duet, and that resolves, well, resolves isn't quite the word, into a group of seven dancers moving around in a circle, who look over their shoulders at Solomons, dancing all by himself on the outside.

Solomons underlines the waywardness of his structure by numbering the sections of the dance, then giving them titles that don't correspond. For instance, the fourth section is called, "4. Unplay I: Still Working." And strangest of all, his movement itself seems to put limits on the possibilities created by all those structures. Leggy and sculptural at the same time, the dancers are not only precise in space but confined, gesture by gesture, to flat planes. Though two planes may be described at once—a leg sweeping up into a side extension while the head swivels through the arc from left to right—they seldom broaden or soften into three-dimensional curves and spirals, or let loose into free space. The dancers maintain fixed focuses most of the time, often aiming their gaze into the audience, and they look more purposeful than playful.

Solomons seems interested these days in plastique, in the sculptural form of the body, and *Nile* (1980), given on the same program, models three bodies like figures on a frieze. Solomons, guest artist Susan Jean Hendrickson, and Edward Derr—all over six feet tall—make one move at a time, often in profile or clumped together so that they seem to be one. Sometimes there are pauses between the moves so that you see the poses clearly, and sometimes the dancers connect the poses without stopping.

Toward the end of the dance the men surround the woman briefly, lift her, possibly implying worship, imprisonment, sacrifice. Later they stand close together and nuzzle each other moving only their heads, before returning to their solitary posings. Mio Morales's quiet score for bells, flutes, and percussion with echo chamber and unobtrusive electronics helped throw a mood of ancient rites over the slow, incisive, and enigmatic movement.

Slings & Arrows & Runaway Escalators

Yoshiko Chuma: *Champing at the Bit*
St. Mark's Church parish hall, New York
Soho Weekly News, 25 February 1981

Friday the 13th began at 6:45 A.M. with a car crash. I didn't get out of bed to look. I could follow the crash scenario over the ruins of my sleep. The ambulance arrived. Large pieces of metal were pried off and clanked to the pavement. Chains rattled. A winch squealed, stopped, squealed again. Finally the tow truck moved off. Quiet. Eight o'clock. Time to get up. By the time I got to Yoshiko Chuma's performance it had turned into just another day in New York—a couple of spasms of paranoia, a perfunctory argument or two, no needle threaders to be had at the sewing store, entertainment on a bus provided by four lady tourists from Toronto. You know. Yoshiko Chuma knows.

Champing at the Bit was a long movement piece with accompanying sound effects and films. It reminded me of some of the more ambitious avant-garde pieces of the sixties, a sprawling mixed-media epic by Yvonne Rainer or something. Except that Chuma's work isn't haphazard. She may use found objects and ordinary movement, but she selects and shapes those things carefully. Grunginess and violence are achieved through the processes of art, not just left lying around underfoot waiting to be noticed.

The piece begins with a kind of music. Kurt Henry and Christian Marclay, collectively named The Bachelors, even (a nod to Duchamp), enter and sit down at four turntables. I think, my god, they're going to play four records at one time. They do, but not quite the way I expected. The records are "prepared"—they have pieces of masking tape on them or they've been carefully warped out of shape or otherwise manhandled to produce crazy distortions. Henry and Marclay orchestrate a repertory of squawks and scratches and mechanical hiccups throughout the performance. The sound isn't oppressive or loud, it just nags there at the periphery of your attention all the time, like the noisy elevator shaft next to my door.

There's a movie directed by Chuma and filmed by Rudy Burckhardt in familiar locations around the city. A woman has a sort of fit on the sidewalk. People in a movie audience twitch, fidget, lick their lips; the film speeds them up so they look like a roomful of lunatics. People run down UP escalators. People in a subway car engage in ballets of sidelong glances, changing seats, falling down. Sometimes passing citizens give them the eye, but no one interferes.

While the film is going on, a door opens, letting a shaft of light into the darkened room. The audience studiously tries not to notice this additional gauche behavior. But I keep glancing over from time to time and see that gradually some people seem to be entering the room. They move very slowly and precisely although they don't have to, and every time I look their position is slightly changed. There's a certain harshness, a comic-strip sensationalism about them thrusting through the cracked door, clustered together and pushing what appear to be long poles before them.

When the film is over, the lights come on and we see Chuma, Scott Caywood, Peter Cunneen, and Stephen Petronio, each with a ten-foot metal construction post. For the rest of the performance they move around these unneeded but unavoidable objects, as if they're trying to figure out what to do with them, but not as if they ever do find a use for them or get to like them. Sometimes they hold the poles upright and hang on them. Sometimes they balance them with obscure, elaborate adjustments. Cunneen lies underneath one and gingerly "walks" along it with his feet and hands, like a praying mantis upside down on a branch, till he's got it vertical, then curls his feet around till it's tilting the other way, then slides it back down to the floor. Sometimes they stand for a long time holding the poles, then drop them with a loud crash. One woman in the audience starts holding her ears every time they pick one up. Sometimes they just let the hardware lie around on the floor as they do needlessly taxing things like falling down and thrashing around till their skins get bruised.

The disc jockeys are wearing different hats every time I notice them—more and more outlandish: cowboy hats, hats made of folded newspaper, a plastic helmet, the halves of a globe. But they give no other sign of trying to be entertaining.

Periodically one of the dancers leaves and comes back with four or five more poles until thirty or so are littering the space. Some are leaning against a wall, and as another film is shown—this time it's mostly of buildings and smoke and people hustling across Penn Station—the dancers try to poke their heads between the poles and finally seem to find a way to shelter behind them. The film looks into the windows of fluorescent-lit lofts, looks at snowflakes in an unseen streetlight, looks at a cloudy sky. All the lights go off.

Chuma's tasks can seem earnest out of all proportion to the simplicity of what she's doing. In a short opening duet, *Low Bump*, she and Pooh Kaye looked almost phony, playing at playfulness, as they rolled and toddled around in artfully dirty chicken-fur rompers. But in *Champing at the Bit*, the goalless effort, the unreasonable vitality seemed appropriate, maybe even the whole idea. I think Chuma shares Rudy Burckhardt's view of the city—I do, too—as a place where people are inordinately patient with real discomfort and use great ingenuity scheming to get out of their imaginary personal mousetraps, and where the buildings are a beautiful, almost reassuring constant, a stage set for their antics.

Erotic Rage

Twyla Tharp Dance
Warfield Theater, San Francisco
Soho Weekly News, 18 March 1981

Violence and eroticism are kindred passions, according to Twyla Tharp's *Short Stories*, and it's almost a matter of chance which of them will ignite when two intense people get together. Tharp has worked with violence before. In last year's *Brahms' Paganini*, for instance, two couples wove an intricate pattern of embraces and switches with the force and speed of prizefighters. Nothing so strong as a plot motivates *Short Stories*, one of three new dances Tharp showed here during a short run at Bill Graham's Warfield Theater, but a definite charge of emotionalism propels the piece. People who've been completely absorbed with one partner whisk or fall or slam into the arms of another. The stage seethes with provocation, competitiveness, jealousy, and transitory desire.

The subtle modulation of anger into sensuality and back is the real subject of *Short Stories*, although the dance has the appearance of something simpler and more ordinary. It's made in three asymmetrical sections, its disorder as carefully structured as any serene Tharp classic. Six dancers, John Carrafa, Mary Ann Kellogg, Shelley Washington, Raymond Kurshals, William Whitener, and Katie Glasner, begin casually, dancing cheek to cheek like kids at a high school dance. Little by little their attention strays from their initial partners to someone else. It's the dancing itself that makes this happen, as they look over their partners' shoulders, circle around, graze another couple, casually reach for another hand, caress another cheek. No one's erotic vibes are irrevocably focused on one partner. The atmosphere gets steamier, open competition breaks out. The women get petulant, the men get possessive. Finally they all drift away in a temporary settlement of hostilities.

A minute later the record begins again (Supertramp's "Lover Boy") and the same characters return in an uglier mood. This time Kellogg is a solitary figure of calm. Passive, self-possessed, she ignores the pushing and shoving around her, sometimes drawing Carrafa into her island of detachment. She offers no resistance when the three men start grabbing for her and mauling her. She's thrown from one to the other and finally is left on the ground while the others stare at her in what might be remorse. This reflective moment is almost identical to the climax of Tharp's Deuce Coupe, a tableau that seemed to materialize with no explanation at all. Perhaps Tharp is offering one version of how it could have come about, the way we make up captions for old news photographs. I suspect the Events Leading to the Crime would have been quite different ones had she chosen to relate them in 1973.

In Part 3 of Short Stories (to Bruce Springsteen's "Jungleland"), Jennifer Way and Tom Rawe, Shelley Freydont and John Malashock seem older—joggers perhaps, out in the park together after work. They arrive squabbling with their mates instead of being idly romantic like the first group. They too switch partners, but these brief affairs are more like struggles for escape, and soon they reclaim their original partners after fistfights all around. The ensuing duets are truly erotic—you can almost feel their bodies in contact, experience their pleasure in yielding to each other. Then they back away, arguing again, in a reversed replay of the whole sequence with which they entered.

One of the many remarkable things about Short Stories is how much big balletic dancing is laced in among the social dancing and antisocial "story" events. Where she once concealed virtuosity by keeping it small and contained under the cool witticisms of jazz, Tharp now throws it, still in semidisguise, among the flashy aggressions of rock.

The audacious new Duet from the Third Suite (Bach's Air for the G String) is a purely formal embellishment of music so familiar it's almost hackneyed. Christine Uchida wears a purple chemise top and panties that look like expensive underwear, and purple shoes with strings crisscrossing over the ankles. William Whitener has a sort of Russian cossack loungewear in matching shades. It actually looks less vulgar than it sounds. I thought of it as designer Santo Loquasto's idea of an updated Bolshoi pas de deux.

Using the width of the stage most of the time, rather than the depth or the diagonals, Uchida and Whitener rush toward each other and stretch apart in a succession of baroque spirals and hesitations, accelerations and ritards. She seems to support his turns and balances as often as he helps hers. At the end of the music—almost a fragment it's so short—they go off in opposite directions.

A third new work was also shown here. *Uncle Edgar Dyed His Hair Red* has three pairs of women in black bathing suits, each pair posturing downstage while the others cross behind a scrim in silhouette. At a private showing last fall, Tharp said something about this dance having to do with "new ways to torture the female form," and it does look mechanical, deadpan, an attitude Tharp takes sometimes about putting women's bodies on display. The music, by Dick Sebouh, is for a Moondoggy synthesizer, and the title is still the most interesting thing about it. Except that here it was given just before the all-male version of *The Fugue*, and together they made an unusual comment. *The Fugue* seems to have some new choreography added, and looks even more elaborate and more wonderful in its combination of slouchiness, strength, and precision than when I first saw Carrafa, Kurshals, and Rawe do it at the Winter Garden last spring.

The San Francisco performances also included *Brahms' Paganini, Ocean's Motion, Eight Jelly Rolls* and the supremely elegant *Baker's Dozen*. The company looked superb, though Tharp herself wasn't dancing. They don't seem to be planning a New York appearance until fall at the earliest, so three thousands miles didn't seem too far to go to see them.

Smile and Forget

Merce Cunningham Dance Company
City Center Theater, New York
Soho Weekly News, 1 April 1981

Everybody thought this was the best Merce Cunningham season in years. Everybody else walked out grumbling. Merce Cunningham, as far as I can see, is doing the same thing he always did. What's surprising is that people still think it's revolutionary and other people still think it's offensive. Cunningham's three new works all have serviceable, jargonish titles like the labels on filing folders: *10's with Shoes, Fielding Sixes, Channels/Inserts*. The dances under each title are like fat dossiers of everything there is to know about the three separate problems, not sorted out yet. One dance I liked very much, one quite a lot, one so-so. I probably won't remember any of them a year from now.

This has nothing to do with the quality of Cunningham's work or the level of his invention, but depends more on his steadfast denial of those elements of form that give a dance an identity. I remember incidents in a Cunningham dance, like the scene in *Roadrunners* (1979) where he's trying to get dressed and has to keep snatching up his pants and shoes and scurry to another part of the stage because a woman (now Megan Walker) is dancing a big florid passage that lops over into his space. Narrative isn't the only way we remember things in a dance, but some kind of sequence or intentional alteration of the space gives a context to steps that are otherwise abstract.

The units of dance intelligibility seem smaller than ever in *10's with Shoes*, but my feeling that it's a trivial dance probably comes as much from its environment as from the goofy, disconnected, mechanically up-tempo dancing. Mark Lancaster's set encloses the stage with panels in bright shades of green, blue, and yellow with white squares painted on them. It reminded me of wallpaper for a kid's room. For the score, Martin Kalve put together sounds of domestic life—babies crying, dogs barking, muffled conversations.

By this time I question the experimental nature of the music by John Cage and his disciples that Cunningham permits to be heard against his dances. There's an infinite number of sounds in the universe that could be put together and manipulated in an infinite number of ways, but that doesn't mean we have to hear all of them. Cage's own ever-so-cute score for *Fielding Sixes* consists of Irish reels played on violins and more incongruous instruments (flute, trombone, harmonica) by Paddy Glackin and Matt Molloy, then overdubbed, slowed down, speeded up, and made as discordant as an alley full of yowling cats by Cage. Initially I had an extreme resistance to this dance, to the layers of rhythmic dissociation within the score and between the score and the dancing. Enough of the traditional music remained intact so that you could hear its strong lilt, its danceability; and the tension between that and the dancers' unheeding skittery, spurty steps made all the rhythm disappear.

Later I could see that the dance had been choreographed on a 6/8 meter like the music, and there were times toward the end when they almost became synchronous. At these times if not throughout, Cunningham was clearly embroidering the rhythm with syncopations, suspensions, doubletimes, and I wondered for the hundredth time what kind of crotchetiness makes him want to obscure this vital connection that's so natural to him.

Channels/Inserts, like *Fielding Sixes*, uses almost the whole company, fourteen dancers, but where *Fielding* is isolated, spacey, a mass of quirks, *Channels* is dense, coherent, and even flowing. David Tudor's radio-noise score supports this feeling with its sustained buzz and hum. There's more time for breathing in the movement than in most recent Cunningham pieces and a greater number of similar elements to help you grasp the action.

For one thing, in much of the first part of the dance, there's at least one doubled movement motif going on. Few enough dancers are onstage together so that you can see two or three of them are always in unison. They face the same way, too, or mirror each other, so the doubled image asserts itself. About midway, the group seems to separate into couples, always returning with the same partners, and you conclude that the whole dance was a couple dance even though it wasn't. Perhaps this is because Alan Good and Lise Friedman have a long duet by themselves and are seen alone at the end.

Unlike the double work at the opening, the couples don't emphasize unison but work as complementary partners, the men supporting the women in very extended or arched balancing shapes, lifting them in ways that require a lot of body contact. They wrap their arms around the women's middles and pick them up, the women throw a leg over the men's backs or hips.

In the midst of all this close work come two large, space-covering sections. One of them is like a classroom exercise in grand jetés, except that each dancer changes direction in mid-jump and the stage seems to be filled with flying arcs. Later there's a sequence of tiny solos for all six men, followed by a sequence of larger solos elaborating on the first set. They're all made of twisting, acrobatic jumps and all different, showing off the particular qualities of each man.

After a rather stiff and severe opening night, the company warmed up, and by the second week they were looking more animated than I've seen them. Many of them came across for the first time as dancers who enjoy what they're doing, which of course gives the audience pleasure too. Give dancers enough time and they can handle anything, even the exactitudes of Cunningham's fast, finicky choreography. Sparked by the irrepressible Louise Burns, they looked at each other, smiled, took small liberties with phrasing. After nine years, Chris Komar appeared relaxed for the first time onstage, really appeared the accomplished dancer he's always been. Karole Armitage smiled once. Some others who impressed me were a couple of newcomers, Judy Lazaroff and Robert Swinston, and Joseph Lennon, who looks dark and forbidding but who throws himself into propulsive movement with great power and risk.

Treetop Telegrams

Simone Forti: *Jackdaw Songs*
Performing Garage, New York
Soho Weekly News, 15 April 1981

Many experimental dancers in recent months have been playing around with narrative, or playing around the edges of it. Stories are still out— remember the bad old days of "modern dance"—but we often see discontinuous units of action in a dance that could be parts of the same story, or the symbolic tokens of a story that remain a long time after everyone's forgotten its facts. Simone Forti says her new *Jackdaw Songs* is an arrangement of movements that seem to her to have communication possibilities; she says the piece is "moving more toward theater," beyond, I suppose, the unstructured physical expressiveness of her previous work. Forti is known for extending human movement range by the incorporation of animal-like gestures, focus, and weight distribution. But she isn't just imitating animal motion. I think she's able to get into the mind of an animal as well. This means folding back layers of her own evolutionary development to revive some of the faculties no longer needed by Homo sapiens—long-distance eyesight, for instance, or an acute sense of smell and hearing. Forti behaves like an animal of superior intellect who can't read, write, or speak.

We might think that limits her, but maybe she's trying to show that our ability to conceptualize gets in the way of other talents. Forti thinks animals communicate deliberately and well, and she's begun building up semitheatrical events out of the preliterate movement material she's explored before. *Jackdaw Songs* is a series of possibly related group actions that are not quite animal, not quite human. The idiom of the piece keeps shifting, and so does the identity in which the performers are supposed to be known to the audience.

In one sketch, they're like invisible stage managers. Holding long fronds of dried reeds or bamboo, they create an atmosphere like the shore of a lake. The reeds rustle as the dancers move from place to place. Later someone holds two slabs of galvanized metal cut in oval shapes and glides them around the bases of the reeds like fish in shallow water. In another sketch, Forti "swims" along the floor, pumping her arms and wriggling her body, her legs trailing inert behind her. Instead of manipulating a prop fish, she is a fish.

There are animal dances, like one in which several people behave like creatures in cages at the zoo. And there are movement progressions that seem solely intended to create metaphors: five dancers huddle close together while a sixth climbs up and over their bodies; later Susan Rethorst makes a "journey" over the humps and hollows of their backs as they dash from the back of the line to the front, to make more ground for her to cover.

During the first part of the now-she's-the-mountain-now-she's-the-mountain-climber section, an unseen voice recites a litany of greetings and other comments. "How well you're looking. So fat." "It's such a long way." "Down here!" Things like that. In the second half of the piece these same messages are repeated while three projectors show slides of a colony of cats living in what might be a Roman ruin. Of course, the words then become Klibanesque captions.

Rethorst and Richmond Johnstone transmit another whole series of instruction-messages while eating their lunch on a very long plank balanced like a teeter-totter across a sawhorse. These signals have no verbal equivalent, but their kinetic content is immediately apparent and often hilarious, as Rethorst and Johnstone lean, sway, inch forward, or scootch back to keep from letting either end of the board bang down to the ground. This seesaw episode is probably the most successful in the dance—possibly because it's the most recognizable situation. But it's also an example of the extreme differences in types of theatrical material Forti puts together. The audience's problem is how to synthesize it all.

At another point Forti and Johnstone do a dialogue as quasi-mythic figures. She threads long thin flexible wands through the sleeves of her shirt until she seems to be surrounded by her own little house. He wears a shirt festooned with crumpled-up balls of newspaper. She glides bonelessly on the ground; he throws himself in demonic fits. Lying on the floor, they clasp hands above their heads and struggle spasmodically a couple of times. Then he whirls away and she thrashes as if trying to rid herself of his power.

For the dancer-actors in *Jackdaw Songs*, the problem is not merely the switch from playing ordinary movers to animals to spirits to abstractions, but switching their consciousness as well. They can't just work instinctively, as they could in Forti's early animal improvisations, because they've got these theatrical characterizations and tasks to carry out too. Some of them couldn't manage it credibly. Musician Peter Van Riper had a couple of moments to himself, including one extraordinary solo where he played the soprano saxophone while spinning, but mostly he padded from one spot to another and never became quite integrated in the piece.

I thought sometimes Van Riper was trying to approximate the way Forti-as-creature feels out the territory before she picks a roosting spot. But no one adopts these attitudes as thoroughly and naturally as she does. At the end of the dance she turned into a small, close-to-the-ground animal. Finding a wooden baton, she played with it and examined it very seriously, never using the human's oppositional thumb. At the very last minute she sat behind a low table and grasped the stick, applied it to the table surface, and drew a large arc. You could almost see millions of years pass before your eyes.

Modern 101

Elisa Monte and Dancers, Dance Umbrella
The Space, City Center, New York
Soho Weekly News, 22 April 1981

Most modern dance companies still organize themselves around the work of a single choreographer, even though that choreographer's imprint may not be particularly notable. Generally if anything else enters the repertory, it's a fledgling hatched by a company member, or a sample of historical modern dance. Elisa Monte is doing something different. For her Dance Umbrella performances she surveyed four distinct approaches to modern dance developed during the past decade. The program looked and sounded fresh to me; its ideas and impulses hadn't stayed out in the sun too long and congealed.

The dances were Monte's *Treading* and *Pell Mell*, Cliff Keuter's *Woodblocks*, Molissa Fenley's *Direct Effect*, and Sara Rudner's *Our Duet*, and what they had in common were their propulsive, repetitive scores and a performing style that kept the dancers' energy concentrated within the compass of the dance rather than walloping out at the audience. But the demands of each choreographer were surprisingly different from the others', and Monte's company couldn't quite convey the full distinction among movement qualities. This is a common problem for modern dancers in repertory; I've just never seen such a contemporary range all together.

When Fenley danced one of the roles in her own piece, the contrast between her and David Brown and Terese Capucilli was striking. The dance, an excerpt from Fenley's *Energizer*, is driven, frenetic, a ceaseless charge of motion set to a fast, pulsing score for synthesizer by Mark Freedman. I've never seen Fenley's work before, and I found the piece friendlier, less masochistic than some new wave dance, perhaps because Fenley always has a lively expression on her face and a rhythmic invigoration in her step. She seems to be enjoying the marathon she's prescribed, not trying to lash herself into a catatonic rigor.

There's quite a lot of controlled variety in the movement, especially along the big-to-small scale, and the torso and arms make gestural accents on top of the ceaselessly traveling progress of the feet. Fenley is less definite in space than Monte's dancers—or I should say more careless of where she throws her movement. Her gestures are less fluid, more articulate and

segmented. You see every move as a percussive event. Brown and Capucilli elide the gestures into one another, ease more gradually into and out
of the beat. I also noticed that Fenley thrust very consistently and instinctively into the offbeats, the second beat of the measure, while the other two
seemed irresistibly drawn to come down on the first beat. Fenley dancing looks unconventional, willfully contending with the music, while the
others let themselves go along with it.

Monte's response to pulse music—the complex and textured "Music for
18 Musicians" of Steve Reich for Treading and "Poppy Nogood and the Phan-
tom Band" of Terry Riley for Pell Mell—follows an earlier modern dance
aesthetic that sees the dance as independent of its musical environment.
Monte spreads across the longer phrase of the music rather than working
off its insistent supporting beat, making a stretchy, sculptural movement
with few accents and little emphasis on traveling through space. There's
a tension between dance and music, but it's different in Monte's dance
from Fenley's; you feel her dancers suspended over the sound rather than
actively embedded in it.

Monte has added a trio section to the duet Treading, and the piece now
progresses from its initial images of people rooted on a small base and
molding their bodies within the familiar immediate space they can feel, to
larger groupings and gatherings with excursions of reaching, spiraling, and
swinging. Only once did I see the dancers travel somewhere beyond their
own centers. Monte's dance, despite its preoccupation with body shape,
has moments of undefined drama—sudden sharp changes of direction, intense visual searchings into the distance. In Pell Mell, which is so slow and
controlled it's anything but dramatic, a quartet very gradually coalesces
from individuals, then couples, and inches its way across the space and out
toward some goal that the audience can't see, their quest growing more
arduous as it continues.

In Cliff Keuter's solo, Monte manipulates about eight five-foot dowels
around a garden of small geometric objects, by Keuter, while one of Charles
Marie Widor's organ symphonies exclaims in the background. Monte alter-
nately carries the sticks above her head like a giant sunburst, turning herself
into a sort of icon, and hauls and shoves them around as if they're some
kind of farming implements. Finally she sticks them all into a box like oversized pencils and slowly scrambles toward the audience with her hands
and feet balanced on bricks. Keuter's work is often cryptic; this one is a lot
sparer in its movement than things I've seen of his before, and somehow
more comprehensible because of it.

The Sara Rudner duet, accompanied by Michael Sahl's fast disco-Latino
music, had Monte and Brown just dancing, in a loose, vernacular way that
avoided character but lacked style. I think here more than in any of the

works, their uniformly spongy attack smoothed out the accent. They obscured the subtle differentiation between stops and starts, taps and stomps, that Rudner herself handles so virtuosically.

I wish dancers who do repertory would give us more responsible program copy. Monte's was short, and sometimes wrong, on dates, music titles, stuff like that. She didn't inform the audience specifically that *Treading* will be danced by the Alvin Ailey company this spring, or that *Our Duet*, from *For an Hour or So*, was a sort of preview, since the complete work won't be premiered by Rudner until next month. I don't see the point in omitting this kind of information. After last week's blockbusting Early Years of Modern Dance festival at SUNY-Purchase, maybe I'm supersensitive to history, but maybe it's time modern dancers admit they have one.

Marathons and Mudpies

Emerging Generation Companies, American Dance Festival
Duke University, Durham, North Carolina
Soho Weekly News, 22 July 1981

Emerging Generation is how the American Dance Festival described the five downtown choreographers it presented in a week of performances at the North Carolina State University campus in Raleigh. The use of a collective rubric to encompass the likes of Bill T. Jones, Charles Moulton, Molissa Fenley, Johanna Boyce, and Marleen Pennison tempts us to look for what they might have in common, but I can't equate them on any level; maybe this means there are no clear trends at the moment. The term, however, is nicely neutral, avoiding the implication of avant-garde, experimental, or even slightly demanding work but evoking an energetic, ambitious march into the future.

Aside from Pennison, all the EG choreographers do use various devices of an earlier avant-garde, proving once again that yesterday's breakthrough is today's box office. All the dances were accessible, entertaining, and made use of modernist tactics that would have shocked us years ago—nudity, repetitive pulse, nonsequential phrasing and unstructured sequences, nondance movement, semi-improvisational tasks and games, weird juxtapositions of styles and media. I didn't see Bill Jones's new work, *Social Intercourse*, in completed form, but the other premieres offered nothing I hadn't seen their makers do before and no further enlightenment on the nature of the modern dance frontier at the present time.

Charles Moulton's trio *Expanded Ball Passing* combines his precisely timed ball-passing routines with larger traveling and gestural movements. A. Leroy supplies a metronomic synthesizer score overlaid with random cuing notes, and Moulton follows it exactly, so you see a very regular rhythm, sometimes doubled to produce tiny baby steps or head shakes, sometimes halved to slow the pace down to a stroll, and changes in the activity that occur at irregular intervals. Each of the dancers, Moulton, Beatrice Bogorad, and Barbara Allen, has a tennis ball, and the balls periodically get rolled, lobbed, and handed from one to the other without a break in the rhythmic continuity. For some reason, maybe because the dancers have to manage traveling from place to place and jiggling their heads, arms, feet in time to the music as well as passing the balls, the piece didn't seem as ingenious to me as Moulton's simpler ball-passing dances. There the activity is so industrious and concentrated that the machinery takes on an endearing humanness, like the robots in Star Wars.

Moulton shares with Molissa Fenley the athlete's determination to last longer, to make the task harder, so the perfecting of it will be more triumphant. Where Moulton's charm lies in his relaxed approach to this, Fenley's attraction has to do with intensity. Obsessive and contradictory, her dances are hard to tell apart though her movement is easy to remember. The new work, Gentle Desire, is in two sections, "Gentle Desire" for Fenley, Deni Bank, and Lynne Allard, and "Peripheral Vision" for Fenley alone. The first part seems to have faint echoes of movie Westerns in its galloping rhythms and tossed gestures, while the solo seems a bit twistier and engaged with the space behind the body.

But what you really see in both of them and in all Fenley's dances is this nonstop movement, almost always traveling on a regular synthesizer pulse (by Mark Freedman), with the arms making large decorative shapes around the body on the same pulse. Some of the shapes are interesting, some of the steps are more heavily accented than others, but they all have the same value—which eventually equals no value. This is one of the contradictions. Fenley drives so hard at each movement you think she must be going for emphasis, but each succeeding emphasis negates the one before. She's always moving across the space, but she never makes you feel she's arrived anywhere. Her movement is simultaneously presentational— externalized—and preoccupied with changes in the shape of the body. She seems to be neither absorbed with the sensuality of it nor anxious to project its full force out to the audience. To me, her dance looks like a person running away from something, or a dance running away with the dancer.

Marleen Pennison doesn't seem to be intrinsically interested in dance at all, except as an illustrative language. Her theater piece, Free Way, is a cliché about guys in love with cars in the fifties. The girls flirt and the guys show off. The plain girl gets the klutzier guy. The other guy then wants her and there's a struggle for possession. She ends up with a kid and one of the guys. He spends most of his life sliding under the chassis while his pal leans against the garage and kibitzes. She pities herself a lot and feels trapped. The piece reminded me of one of the more sodden morality plays of early women's lib.

The idea of a dance in a swimming pool suggests Billy Rose's Aquacade, Esther Williams movies, a kind of show biz that might be healthier for you than hanging around stale, dark theaters. Johanna Boyce's *Waterbodies* is like an Andy Hardy flick transposed from the school gym to the neighborhood Y. You can just see her getting her friends together and saying, "Gee, we'll get the pool, and we'll have live music, and we'll sing . . . and wow, we'll have a show!"

Johanna Boyce is really into recapturing the enthusiasms of youth, but she doesn't want to spoil them with the skills of maturity. *Waterbodies*, for the audience, is vicarious regression. You watch the nine performers doing their group bouts of blowing bubbles, falling in with a splat, splashing and ducking each other, doing the dead man's float. I could relate to it; it made me want to go into the pool. Later the group does some rudimentary formations—holding hands and ducking under, following each other around in a breast-stroking circle. At one point, gasping a little, they sing a gargly tune in four-part harmony. This seems to be the apex of theatrical organization for the night, and afterward the swimmers drift away and climb out of the pool and leave one by one, the way they came.

During the piece, colored spotlights played over the pool from the darkened galleries. At intervals a double screen showed underwater films of the performers paddling around. And the whole thing was accompanied by five women harpists poolside, who played watery music under the direction of a large, serious man in shirtsleeves. When it was over, I wanted a swim more than ever.

Comforts of Hell

Bill Irwin: *Not Quite/New York*
Dance Theater Workshop, New York
Soho Weekly News, 22 September 1981

Somehow it seems right that Bill Irwin came to town on a night when New Yorkers had been more battered than usual by floods, blackouts, transit chaos, and political skulduggery. It seems right that an overflow audience arrived anyway to greet him. He's a sort of hero of the ashcans, a saintly version of your neighborhood bum. Irwin is the kind of clown who survives by persistence and sheer grit. The fact that he also happens to be clever, even intellectual, doesn't give him any advantage in his race with the Ultimate, it just prolongs the indignity. In his new piece *Not Quite/New York*, he's beset by challengers, loses to them all, but after the winners have left the ring he's still there, shuffling dejectedly in a fading light.

We see him first in running clothes. Confident as a young adman, he sprints into the room, stands center stage, and does a cool, efficient little movement combination—a hinge backward into an interrupted fall, a few tight gestures, a pivot into a loping circle around the space. He tries this a few times, then goes up to a wardrobe trunk and takes off his streamlined warm-up jacket. Underneath he wears a white dress shirt three sizes too big for him.

He's ready to start again when the door opens and Charles Moulton comes in, dressed just as he is and carrying a suitcase. They eye each other; you think at first Moulton is late for a rehearsal and Irwin, in charge, is being patient but annoyed. With a long look and a cold nod of agreement, they both begin doing Irwin's running combination. Right away it's apparent that Moulton hasn't come to work with Irwin but to steal his show. Mid-course he takes a flying jump that isn't in the plan. Unnerved, Irwin keeps on going, but from that moment on you know he wants to keep this guy from getting the better of him.

Moulton leaves after he and Irwin put on identical white bow ties and pairs of baggy pants and hats the color of sludge. Irwin fiddles with a big box that looks like a crude homemade hi-fi and gets it to play some music, ragtime on a guitar. He starts dancing a rubberlegged version of the combination but the music fails him. While he's tinkering with the controls on the box, Moulton comes back and they do the routine again. They both put on matching too-big vests and suit jackets. The more daring Moulton is, the more Irwin comes unglued, tripping over his own feet, getting off on his timing, till Moulton swaggers out.

While Irwin is trying to practice a dance to Dixieland, another man (Michael Moschen) comes in and takes a white ball out of a black three-by-five card box. They start tossing the ball; then they're taking turns doing tricks with it. Irwin is a pretty good juggler but Moschen is a champ. Doug Skinner, the next rival, brings a ukulele, and they strum and sing a duet about the Charleston. But Irwin starts taking the words too seriously and Skinner lets him know he's screwing up—and in front of the hard-nosed New York critics, too. Irwin tries to ingratiate himself after Skinner's exit by doing a soft-shoe dance, but something horrible keeps dragging at his foot, threatening to suck him into the wings unless he scrambles with all his might to stay onstage. Tommy Sellars, who now arrives, plays the accordion while roller-skating. After a few go-rounds, Irwin's convinced Sellars is chasing him, decides to put on skates himself, thinks better of it when he see Sellars toss off some stunts. Left alone, he's driven into a fit by his own music machine.

The obsessive nature of this piece—always the challenger, dressed just like Irwin, the initial skirmish when it looks as if they might at least come out in a draw, then the humiliating defeat, the failure at even his own dance—lets us know this is the way life is. It's going to go on and on; only the acts will change. The more extravagant Irwin's alter egos get, the less it matters that he can't match them and the funnier his efforts at keeping up.

The idea that his adversary is himself seems an important part of Irwin's clown persona. In Pantalone and Harlequin, which is basically a series of skits accompanied on piano, toy xylophone, slide whistle, kazoo, and tambourine by Doug Skinner, he plays at least two sets of dual characters: the curmudgeonly old Pantalone and the street-smart Harlequin who trumps him; and two dueling Gentlemen from Verona, a tall, lordly one and a scrunched-up fat one. Irwin seems to be saying it's not just the faulty products of civilization that can defeat us, the recalcitrant pots of spaghetti or defiant sound systems, but our own grandiose ambitions. Staying alive, he seems to be saying, is the most absurd of our notions, and the most necessary.

When he's run out of skits, Harlequin subsides into a trunk and watches Moulton, Moschen, and Sellars glide by, assured, glamorous, and potent as ever. Irwin smiles sadly. He's wondering if he could parachute off the Empire State Building.

Apocalyptic Circus

Twyla Tharp: *The Catherine Wheel*
Winter Garden Theater, New York
Soho Weekly News, 13 October 1981

The Catherine Wheel is a tremendous work, brilliantly conceived and dazzlingly executed, and I'm glad I did not have to review it after one performance. Twyla Tharp has put so much into it that each viewing takes you into new territory even though you thought the ground was already familiar. The dance is so densely constructed that every member of the audience probably perceives it in a different way. It isn't that Tharp hasn't got a plan; she has so many, all intertwined and sprawling on top of each other, that it's impossible to say for sure what the ballet actually is.

Tharp seems to have begun all over again to make her last big opus, *When We Were Very Young*. *The Catherine Wheel* is an entirely different concept, but it does have the same screwy, belligerent family watched over by a corps of sometimes hostile, sometimes idealized counterparts. Tharp took out the autobiographical tone—and in fact took herself out of the piece—which enables her to turn the family's discontents outward, into a kind of parable about idealism and corruption, love and hate, fun and fatality, and about how sometimes one thing wears the face of its opposite. The elusive dream of perfection that kept luring the discontented mother to leave home in *When We Were Very Young* is now personified as a Poet (John Carrafa), who's at first blissfully innocent, then just as blissfully gross.

The story now goes like this: Mom and Dad (Jennifer Way and Tom Rawe), after a few moments of bashfulness, start climbing over each other in lust and latent anger before she even gets her wedding veil off. They acquire two dopey kids (Katie Glasner and Raymond Kurshals), a Maid (Shelley Washington), and a Pet of uncertain species (Christine Uchida). Before you know it, they're all squabbling. Mom teaches the kids to dance, takes them out on the road as a traveling act, which is only a wiggle away from being their pimp. Meanwhile Dad makes passes at the Maid, later humps the Pet. Everybody in the family is after this golden pineapple, which gets bigger and bigger as it invokes more grandiose desires. The Poet wants it most of all. Being a natural creature, he can't tell the difference between worshipping the pure and the beautiful and becoming a raging sensualist, which he finally does, feasting orgiastically on the forbidden fruit with Mom.

Commenting on the family's descent is a chorus of anonymous dancers dressed in bandit-chic—black layered practice/warm-up clothes with red ankle warmers that look like boots and red half masks that they can push up to resemble headbands. They're led by Sara Rudner, unmasked, all in red and dancing as if she's being consumed by flames, who foresees everything, suffers everything, and doesn't appear at the transfiguration.

Because there is a sort of happy ending. After the last, biggest sex battle, the chorus cleans up the shards of violated pineapple with a broom dance, and Mom, Dad, and the kids deliver a metaphoric lesson. The parents dance a duet that is one sinuous embrace, curling and twining around each other with the greatest possible body contact, their only untroubled encounter in the whole evening. Then they drift into a waltz, only to be interrupted by the kids, diving between them in a continuation of their perpetual sibling wars. In telegraphic succession, the parents two-step, Charleston, lindy, twist, and frug, their dance harmony always splintered apart by their offspring. This is the history of the world, Tharp is telling us—love begets discord but keeps popping up again.

After that, a long dance sequence brings the principals together with the chorus, and they all change into golden costumes like what the gods might wear to play tennis. They begin yet another sequence, their hostility transformed into speed—maybe they're angels on speed, dancing at the outer limits of human powers, and after a lull and a windup, the curtain falls on Christine Uchida leaping into yet another dimension.

To outline the plot of The Catherine Wheel is only to create, almost artificially, a way to talk about the dance as a theatrical experience. For more than an hour without a break, you're blasted with nonstop dancing and reckless mime, superimposed on sets going up and down, moody projections, literary and balletic references, symbolic props, and David Byrne's rasping, accusatory music. Tharp's most remarkable works always seem to have too much going on. You know you're always missing something, which gives her dance a special excitement, like a pile of unopened Christmas presents. In The Catherine Wheel the stage looks pressured, ready to explode from all it contains.

While I can eventually cope with the confusion, I'm less happy with the excess, although of course excess is what the whole thing is about—excessive love, desire, and fulfillment. As Byrne sings in the "Golden Section" (all the parts of the dance have titles in addition to the titles of the songs that accompany them, but I won't go into that): "We goin' boom boom boom—That's the way we live—And in a great big room—And that's the way we live." Even excessive dancing, maybe.

Tharp's humor, which can be deft and understated, is sardonic here. The family take pratfalls as easily as they throw one another about with furious judo. People fornicate as aggressively as they fight. When the Maid howls in indignation, you're not sure whether she's mad because Dad goosed her or because he likes the Pet better. All the characters are drawn large, busy, and unreflective. It's hard to love any of them, even Carrafa, whose altar-boy credulity is compromised from the start by his determination to get his hands on that pineapple. His slow, solicitous duet with Uchida is the only truly serious moment in the ballet, a meeting of natural forces—air and earth—and its growing eroticism ends when Carrafa discards her for the next bigger pineapple.

Although the characters aren't stock types at all, they have a cartoon quality that I guess is Brechtian more than anything else. The dance as a whole has a look of expressionism—hard-edged and cruel even when it's most beautiful. During the whole first part, the space is impeded by twenty-four poles that are never needed, until the air clears and everything turns to gold; they make their point only by being taken away.

Santo Loquasto has made a series of set constructions that look like the engine drawings of Leonardo, wheels, braces, pulleys, extremely intricate in design and ambiguous in purpose. They either get in the dancers' way or menace their safety. The most horrid one is a contraption that hangs a few feet off the floor with spikes protruding from its undercarriage. Rudner has a bagful of lumpy objects that might be hunks of pineapple, and as she dances with the chorus, she shoves it up onto one of the spikes. At no particular time, the machine rejects it with a grinding of chains and a clang. She picks it up and impales it again. You think of the finality of jail, the guillotine, bombs not merely dropping from the sky but being forced down onto people's heads.

Jennifer Tipton's lighting shrouds the dancers in miasmic brightness, carves them into glaring silhouettes, and sometimes echoes or foresees what they're doing with distorted images projected in shadow play on the backdrop.

David Byrne's score matches the dance in loudness and relentless motion. I especially like the pieces without words, like the broom dance ("The Blue Flame"), which was based on an African bell pattern. But I felt a discrepancy in style between the music and dancing. Byrne's punkish throbbing rock is rough, intentionally lower class, his lyrics half articulate, made of vernacular phrases strung together. They sometimes make a stoned kind of sense, and they sometimes can't even be heard. Tharp's dancers, on the other hand, are finely bred, precise even in abandon. They give you a feeling of extreme dexterity and delicacy even when they're throwing themselves around or engaging in punching bouts. You feel they're using their skills to the fullest, while Byrne often seems to be suppressing his.

Tharp's company now can dance with their faces as well as their bodies, even those who don't play specific characters. They're astonishingly good actors. I especially enjoyed Carrafa's ingenuous acceptance of treats and treachery alike, Uchida's satisfying defeat of Rawe after he's grabbed her once too often, and Way's feisty, quick-witted opportunism.

Finally, it's the fantastic dancing that supersedes all the other inventions in The Catherine Wheel. The ending is like another whole dance, still competitive but no longer so deadly aggressive. As usual, Tharp generously gives everyone a solo, embedded like a cherry in the swirls of dancing. As they go spinning, flying by, in aerial pairs, interlocked but shifting groups, split-second counterpoint, their virtuosity makes you think the dance is not about the apocalypse after all, but the millennium.

Scrollwork

Trisha Brown and Company
Opera House, Brooklyn Academy, New York
Soho Weekly News, 3 November 1981

Trisha Brown's dance is now so fancy it looks almost precious. Surprising when you consider that not so many years ago she specialized in utilitarianism. On the stage at the Brooklyn Academy Opera House, Brown's three recent pieces showed her choreographically in a strange state of not quite being what she used to be, and not quite pulling off what she perhaps wants to be. The establishing of aesthetic baselines, or style, is always an important matter for modern dancers. The more they depart from the familiar territory of academic ballet, the more convincing they have to be about where they are. Because once we're outside our usual experience, we need markers, consistent clues about what the choreographer expects of us. Performing on the stage of a beautiful theater tells us one thing. Doing it in silence may cause a tension of opposites. Only the dance itself can tell us why.

Trisha Brown has worked through a very plainspoken, conceptual sort of dance making toward a greater concern with the body's plasticity. Game structures, improvisational wit, and the occasional awkwardness that came from something unfinished have dropped into the background, while an increasingly refined and detailed movement sequence has become prominent. There may be messages, a grand design, but I tend to get lost in the dense tracery of the surface.

The surface is made of movement, as it always has been with Brown, although she now employs striking if not distracting peripheral effects, like Robert Rauschenberg's jumbo-size slide show of images only a photographer would notice (Glacial Decoy)—brick walls and palm trees and boxcars—or his eminently undanceable strapless nightgowns made of white accordion-pleated papery material with matching armlets. With most of their bodies concealed, the four women in Glacial Decoy (Brown, Eva Karczag, Lisa Kraus, and Vicky Shick) seem to be engaged in an endless series of weighty displacements—pushing, shaking, sinking, dropping, hiking up some limb or joint in order to start a progression going through the body that results in a new design. They enter and exit frequently, but once on the stage they don't move around it too much, each keeping to her own side until the last few moments of the piece, when they start to exchange territories. The movements and the shapes may recur in a thematic order, but there doesn't seem to be any way to predict when this will happen.

In Brown's new piece, Son of Gone Fishin', you can see the whole body, more or less complemented by Judith Shea's bright blue and green costumes that look like what your mother made when you had to be a brownie in the school play. With Donald Judd's monochromatic backdrops descending and rising behind them, the dancers look even more arm-and-leggy than they did before. As they activate new shapes by pushing or flinging out a body part, the torso wriggling or exhaling to accommodate these changes, the movement looks very indulgent—lush and goalless. I think it must be far more absorbing for the dancers to do than for us to see.

Green-spotlighted in the orchestra pit, Robert Ashley is seated at a console that looks like a Mighty Wurlitzer, and the first sounds that come out of the loudspeakers are sort of rhumbaish. But before you get too nostalgic for old movies, you start to hear sounds like fiddles, harmonicas, distorted voices, and other electronics. Ashley hardly seems to touch the organ keyboard, but I notice him changing one of his fine array of stops once in a while, and Kurt Munkacsi is in the pit with him but I can't see what he's doing. Son of Gone Fishin' is Brown's only dance with a score, and the score seems merely to coexist with the stage events.

For a long time Karczag, Kraus, Shick, Diane Madden, Stephen Petronio, and Randy Warshaw seem to be doing unrelated individual movements, but eventually some phrases appear to reflect or ricochet off others, and there's even a moment of semiunison. Maybe the dancers are all using some of the same movement material, but I can't tell if they're allowed any discretion with it or if everything is set in advance. Trisha Brown comes onstage for the first and last thirty seconds of the piece, not enough time for me to grasp what she's doing at all, except that she might possibly be dancing to Ashley's music.

In Opal Loop/Cloud Installation #72503 the choreography's visual drift and indefiniteness finds an artful counterpart in Fujiko Nakaya's multisourced stage fog and Beverly Emmons's stormy lighting effects. For the first part, Brown, Karczag, Kraus, and Petronio skitter around pretty independently.

Suddenly—by what cue I couldn't tell—they all sit on the floor at once, then begin working in strict paired unison.

When I see Brown dancing alongside the others in this work, the whole movement style becomes rational to me. Brown does the same movements, but every gesture is related to space; every sequence takes her traveling, even adventuring; every shift in rhythm is a clear change. You never doubt her logic for a minute. *Opal Loop* ends abruptly with a unison pose. Like the other two pieces, it's over just as something is introduced which could give the dance a new direction. Maybe this is Brown's way of emphasizing a certain kind of arbitrariness, a stylistic hybridization; or maybe it's just her way of leaving a path for herself into the next dance.

Overdrive

Senta Driver/Harry
87 Fifth Avenue, New York
Soho Weekly News, 8 December 1981

Senta Driver's new dance, Missing Persons, batters unmercifully at the places where people feel the most sensitive. Some dancers, New Wave types, assail the audience with noise, speed, generalized sensory provocations. But Driver's raw material is the behavior of strong emotions—fear, compassion, anguish, desperation; you can't sit there and just be randomly aroused by it. I guess you could break down; my reaction is to resist it. It's not that I'm immune to emotions but that these symptoms of personal crisis are so monolithic, so perfectly wrought, so dissociated from cause or effect, I simply don't believe in them, although I suspect one thing Driver's trying for is believability.

In Missing Persons and in Reaches, given on the same program, Driver seems to be working with elements that underlie performing but that aren't prominently perceived, like the emotional coloration, the dancer's fortitude, endurance, intensity. She makes these things the main event. I can scarcely remember the shapes of her movement, almost never the sequence of her movement events. I remember a lot about how it feels.

For instance in Missing Persons the five dancers play out several curious episodes accompanied by angelic English voices singing sentimental Victorian songs. Then Driver does a long solo of the most extraordinary difficulty while a baritone, then a soprano, sings "Drink to Me Only with Thine Eyes." The contrast is appalling. I can see her wrenching her body around to the side violently until she pulls herself off balance and almost falls. I can see shuddering contractions of the center body, see her arms and legs rotating inward, the ball of one foot raising the whole body into a looming tilt.

The rest that remains with me is a sense of her moving frantically, pain-fully, and at the same time with great care, in waves of unconsolable feeling, until she subsides to a reclining position, upper body resting on her fore-arms, staring fixedly at the space a few feet in front of her, the fingers of one hand stretched out not quite touching the floor. She stays frozen like that while the other dancers move around her, sometimes bending down as if to see what they can do for her. She doesn't pay them any attention, and they don't do more than make the gesture.

Some of the events in Missing Persons I could sketch on my program be-cause they went on for a fairly long time. Driver balanced on her stom-ach, legs and chest curving up off the floor, and brushed at the floor vig-orously with her fingers. Nicole Riché lay on her back, legs straight up in the air, and Rick Guimond rested, stomach down, on her flexed feet. They meticulously touched fingers, one at a time—a game on a precipice. Riché, Guimond, and Andrew Honeychurch formed a sort of Pietà arrange-ment—one supporting, one lying back, one touching—all three fixed but almost off balance, looking away from each other, and maintaining only the smallest amount of contact, cantilevered like Chinese acrobats. Every-thing in Missing Persons "reads" dramatically. People stand in clusters, not quite together; someone runs into their midst and they all fall outward. Duet partners tug till one falls against the other; she leans on him, then presses, maybe pushes him down; maybe he pulls away. Why they're doing it, and more than that, why they're doing it so effortfully, is never known.

Driver's movement seems overwhelmingly gestural to me. Almost any part of the body is capable of channeling through space on some errand of its own and pulling the rest of the body with it on an improbable path. Sometimes, perhaps in order to save itself from vertigo or upset, the body is mobilized against the gesture. But never does the body let loose with the full follow-through that the gesture implied. The dancers look massive and odd, like those mythological beasts with wolves' heads and eagles' wings and scales. You can't imagine them doing anything useful for all their interesting attributes.

Every time I start pursuing one of Driver's ideas, I run up against contra-diction, irony. I mean, I can see why she might be brushing at the floor, but not why she'd be doing it on her stomach with her legs in the air. She seems to take pleasure in pushing balance to the point of risk—and then finding a way to become stable. She makes up illogical rhythm patterns and then punches them heel-toe into the ground as if they were folk dance.

Reaches seems to be about the conventions and conditions of perform-ing. After its premiere last spring at the Kitchen, Driver talked about having built it for a space with a "double front," where the audience sits along two adjoining sides of the room. I was surprised. I hadn't thought of the dance as being oriented to any particular "front." This time I thought what she meant by front was the side to which the dancers present their most engaging and energized faces. From the moment they enter the space—intense, almost militantly prepared—the dancers are trying to win the audience, to impress us with their power and intelligence, to communicate the idea of communicating. They enact games in which the significance is not how the game comes out but how it's played, and rituals that are imposing but not transcendent.

I think Driver has pushed her dancers' abilities so far that they're beyond admiring. It seems as if all the risk, all the testing, has taken place long before, in the studio, and that now they're on top of it all. Dancers are amazing how they can do that. Twenty years ago, no modern dancer could get a leg above her waist. Now a six o'clock extension is no big deal. Driver's dancers have taken all the supposition out of their work. They seem to be saying, "See, this is like a person who's dancing," or sometimes, "This is a person dancing," but only in rare fleeting moments, "I am dancing."

Tharp Down the Line

Bebe Miller and Dancers
Dance Theater Workshop, New York
Soho Weekly News, 15 December 1981

Bebe Miller belongs to the third generation of Twyla Tharp dancers—she's in the company of Nina Wiener, who danced with Tharp in the early seventies. Her work combines many of the ideas about dancing that Tharp set in motion with some current philosophical strictures about dancing to which Tharp no longer subscribes, or never did subscribe. Miller and the five dancers with her on this program (Barbara Boolukos, Hope Mauzerall, Lisa Wallgren, Erin Thompson, and Stephen Peters) are cast very much in the Tharpian body image: small, delicate, androgynous, and beautifully proportioned, with a proud but not pushy vertical carriage. They can move off these assured centers on strong legs, detailing gradations of size, speed, and timing with step patterns full of skids, hops, teasing stumbles, tight spins, and holds. The body often seems flung carelessly out into space during turns and jumps, seldom modeling itself around or into space. Sometimes a deliberate gesture splatters against the flow of motion—a hand or a foot angling around the body, a head thrown to the side. But mainly what we're aware of is the goingness of the movement in all its fluctuations.

Unlike Tharp, Miller seems primarily concerned with dancing, not with composing dances. The four short pieces on the program had small differences in tone, character, or floor design, but were all made of telegraphic phrases with more or less equal value that succeeded each other in no particular order and had no special developmental or kinetic point to make outside themselves. Although it isn't improvised, it has the quality of improvisation: you dance what comes into your mind, as thoroughly and precisely as you can, and only that, and only then. You don't need to do anything with it—prolong it, embellish it—though you might repeat it later as a sort of home base from which to start out again.

Square Business, one of two new group pieces, had four punkily dressed women moving around the edges of a performing area that was squared off by four lights hanging close to the ground. Sometimes they crossed along the diagonals; sometimes they stood facing one another close together in the center. There was an embryonic solo or duet for each dancer. The other new piece, *Jammin'*, had six dancers in army fatigues, shirts, shorts, moving mostly toward the audience in unison groups of different sizes, and ended with a duet for Miller and Erin Thompson that was also unison and faced the audience.

Miller did two solos. *Tune* (1978) began with the stance of social dancing (the music was a waltz-tempo number by Van Morrison) that expanded into larger, more flowery movement. In *Solo: TaskForce* (1981) she wore a mannish costume—shoes, pants, pink shirt, narrow satin tie—and moved in silence, dancing into postures that might once have been street behavior but were gentled into something less edgy. *TaskForce* reminded me of Tharp's 1970 *The Fugue*, not so much for its vernacular feeling as for its clarity. Miller, like Tharp, has the ability to let you see every move distinctly. In this solo, and in her duet with Thompson, which was set to some rhythmic singing by an unaccompanied black female group, she came closest to suggesting some other world that might exist outside the immediate dancing moment. The ability to be referential, and personal, has gone way down on dancers' lists of priorities. What they want to do is dance superbly. What they don't want to do is put a great personal burden on their dancing, to shape the dancing in ways that will influence the audience one way or the other, to be "loaded," coercive, to make us remember or get steamed up or think about any related thing. I enjoyed Miller's dance a lot. Like a train ride through pleasant country, it offered passing images, demanded nothing, and—I suppose intentionally—left nothing of any kind to go on with.

Exhibit A and Possibly B

Meredith Monk: *Specimen Days*
Public Theater, New York
Soho Weekly News, 5 January 1982

Meredith Monk's *Specimen Days* has been in the making for three years; maybe that's why the piece seems to have several unrelated themes. Monk's method of operations is fragmentary anyhow, and with elements of different scale, pitch, and character comfortably butted up against one another or laminated in sometimes baffling simultaneity, it doesn't much matter while you're watching that the ideas don't quite mesh. Nothing less expansive than entire cities, wars, or historical eras seems to satisfy Monk's panoramic vision, and this time she turns her attention to the Civil War. As usual she views it with the microcosmic eye of a poet, the sweep of a high-soaring bird. Images so familiar they're almost clichés seem new again in the sketchy, childlike outline or theatricalized miniature of her staging.

One possible center of the work is two families, one Northern and one Southern, who live similar lives though each has its own customs—gestures so well known they've become repetitive and barely functional. At dinner the Northerners spoon their soup toward the outside edge of the plate, make elaborate preparatory motions with knife and fork before attacking their food. The Southerners say grace with hands folded on the table and heads bowed, eat with many flourishes and gracious social asides. The children carefully copy everything their elders do, and later, when someone is dying, try to keep back their terror by reciting what they can remember from their lessons. Both families lose somebody in the war, but somehow both return intact to their dinner tables after it's over.

These are not any particular people, notable for their individual histories, but symbolic types, specimens I suppose. And they are observed and recorded in various ways. There's a photographer (Gail Turner, dressed as a man) who comes and sets up a big box camera on a tripod, ordering his subjects to hold still for fifteen seconds while he makes a picture. Monk herself plays the composer Louis Moreau Gottschalk, who lived in the South but was sympathetic to the Union side. Gottschalk made a great success touring as a concert pianist, and then wrote all the local color he'd seen, but almost none of the agony, into his light, danceable music. Monk, dressed in black trousers and a velvet frock coat, sits and ruminates at the piano, plays, writes a few notes, sings, but the music is her own chanting, rocking distillation of gut feelings—musical belly laughter, soothing murmurs, sobs. Once she dances a long shuffling journey accompanied by abstracted gestures of piano playing, receiving the applause of an audience, greeting well-wishers—duties of a touring celebrity.

Then there's a technocratic type in a lab coat (Pablo Vela), who's sometimes a lecturer demonstrating the statistics and assets of the actors. "Number 1 and Number 3, step forward please. Incline from the waist. [Numbers 1 and 3 bow.] Thank you. You may retire." He brings on a black man (Cristobal Carambó), gets him to display his teeth, measures his head, reporting 16 centimeters ear to ear, 22.4 centimeters from crown to chin. Is he offering a slave on the auction block? Giving an anthropological paper? Suddenly Vela places his hands on Carambó's midsection, pauses dramatically, and pronounces, "Hunger." At the end of a long war scene, Vela coolly walks over the battlefield spraying the havoc with disinfectant.

Vela seems to represent the sanitizing, alienating effect of science on history—but then Monk's Gottschalk illustrates that art can do the same thing, and so does the objective journalism of Turner's Matthew Brady. From time to time a screen is brought in, once so that Vela can show a series of slides made of picture postcards—Paris, France; Peking, China; Easton, Pennsylvania. What begins as a travelogue suddenly incorporates those pictures of the families that were taken earlier, and also pictures of battlefields and exhausted troops.

It's mostly through Monk's music that the passions and sorrows of real people keep breaking through their fixed, flat tintype representations. From time to time the cast assembles to sing wailing, summoning, whimpering solos and choruses, sometimes from offstage, sometimes ranged in neat rows. Feelings flame to the surface, then quickly burn out. Robert Een sits completely still for a long time, as if posing for the camera, then he slowly gets up and smashes the chair.

Contrasting with the formality and stillness of these abstract characters is the montage of scenes showing the war itself. Turner and Vela, dressed like dime store Abe Lincolns, stand on soapboxes and orate silently while the chorus chants from different parts of the room. Een and Carambó, dressed as soldiers, dart in and out, shooting, falling, carrying one another off, managing to represent both the Union and Confederate armies by changing from blue to gray caps when they're offstage. Meanwhile stage managers are setting up tiny tents all over the space. Then the Abe Lincolns and the soldiers are gone, and from the wings big black rubber balls are rolled across the space, knocking over the tents. The effect of a room full of broken toy tents in a pale light is devastating, not at all cool or scientific.

After the war, the deathbed scenes, and the reassembling of the families, Monk has interpolated her movement-singing piece Turtle Dreams, perhaps simply as a return to severe formality. There has been a turtle in Specimen Days, actually—the star of three short films by Robert Withers. This engaging reptile is first seen plodding through a swamp, then hovering over a map of the United States, and finally blundering down the streets and over the elevated tracks of a miniature city. I couldn't figure out any way this went with the Civil War, though I enjoyed the films.

The last turtle film interrupts Monk, Een, Paul Langland, and Andrea Goodman in the middle of their dance, but their singing goes on behind it in the dark, with musical cries of pain and confusion and mourning. When the turtle's journey has finally taken it to the moon, the screen is cleared away to reveal an unfolding tableau in which the quartet continues singing, now with small fluorescent lights hanging across their chests.

Vela and Turner, now in modern dress, stand on soapboxes and exhort, sometimes clutching their sides as if they've been wounded, but continuing their silent orations. Four women in hoopskirts revolve at the periphery of the space. The other characters walk backward, slowly, across the rear of the space. At this point there are about three different sounds—the *Turtle Dreams* quartet singing, the chorus in the background, and Steve Lockwood's organ ostinato underneath it all. Nicky Paraiso leaves the other organ he's been playing and crosses to Monk's piano, where he sits and plays a lilting Gottschalk waltz. And that's the way the piece ends, in a cacophony of clashing sounds and people in motion, in which each sound, each group, has a distinct character and a clearly perceived pattern. Only a mind like Meredith Monk's could have no qualms about putting them all together.

New Dance in America: An Excess of Success?

Ballett International (Cologne), January 1982

New dance in America has become so successful that it often looks a lot like the very systems it claims to oppose. I use the term *new dance* because it has continuity and irony. It reminds us of the conscious dance innovations of the 1930s at the same time that it invokes the immediate present. The dance of our time is always the new dance, though it may not be "modern" in a modern-dance, modernistic, moderne, postmodern, avant-garde, or experimental sense.

Despite the enormous variety and quantity of new dance being done, most of it shares certain rather regressive properties with American culture. It is emphatically technical—not necessarily in the sense of virtuosity, although we could hardly classify Twyla Tharp's or Merce Cunningham's dancers as anything other than virtuosos. I mean that most new-dance choreographers require a very specific and acute technical capability from their dancers, whether it's the mathematical concentration of Laura Dean,

the tremendous endurance and physical totality of Molissa Fenley, the spatial and temporal exactitude of Kenneth King, the playful engineering and
athleticism of Charles Moulton or Bill T. Jones, the controlled, attenuated
body imagery of Eiko and Koma, the stevedore strength of Senta Driver,
the shrewd sense of improvisation and bodily placement (Trisha Brown,
David Woodberry, Dana Reitz), the ability to look ordinary while doing
something out of the ordinary (David Gordon), or any of several other specialized demands that a choreographer makes on those who execute his
or her ideas. None of the styles mentioned above might look technical in
terms of some academic criteria for dancing ability. All of them grew out of
various aspects of the determinedly nonacademic, iconoclastic statements
of the 1960s. The fact that so much development has occurred indicates
how right the revolutionaries were in thinking that modern dance and
ballet had become too limited in possibilities. Yet the new dance of today
hardly looks casual or spontaneous, or without limits. In fact, in spite of its
liberated antecedents, it often looks decidedly uptight.

It doesn't look "democratic" either, although the original postmoderns made an ideology out of bridging the gap between performers and
audience. Today's new dance is stylish, often quite dazzling or grandiose
in its presentation—from big works like Lucinda Childs's *Dance* with its
proscenium-size film by Sol LeWitt and its large electric score by Philip
Glass; to smaller works like Karole Armitage/Rhys Chatham's punk rock
essay on *Drastic Classicism* or Ken Rinker/Sergio Cervetti's expressionistic,
fragmentary dramas.

Though its forms and structures may be nontraditional, new dance now
looks even more slick and almost mass-produced than the academic dances
it superseded. From Merce Cunningham on, new dances have not had to
spring romantically from some original art concept, but could simply re-
cast the latest version of the choreographer's thought process. Each dance
of Cunningham's doesn't try for a new medium of expression, a particular movement language (a goal that the traditional modern dancers often
had in mind). It pursues movement ideas from the point where he left off
in the last piece, or takes up the same idea in a slightly different working
frame. One doesn't distinguish most present-day Cunningham dances by
their particular movements or spatial arrangements, but by the sounds,
costumes, stage designs that offset them.

New dance is often showy, appealing to the eye, an overwhelming thrill
to the senses. Yet the performing style is almost universally alienated, self-
involved. Dancers pay attention to what's going on in their own bodies,
their immediate sensory environment, but they don't go out of their way to
communicate to the audience what they perceive. They don't "editorialize"
and they don't rely on an external music to color their phrasing. Space and

design along with emotional or personality projection are low on the list of performance priorities. Sensuality, physical mastery, intellectual control, and an internalized, often metronomic sense of time are high. The performer is center stage, either impassively coexisting with other production elements or manipulating them. Total theatrical work as in dance drama or even mixed media is out. Even highly responsive ensemble work is likely to impress us with the exceptional abilities of the individual dancers rather than the group effect—and this a generation after the discrediting of stars and egotistical performers.

Eyebrows were raised recently at some remarks from Trisha Brown to the effect that she was tired of trying to lead her audience into her dance; she was going to do what she felt like doing whether anybody understood or not. This rampant individualism was considered by some a serious breach of Marxist theories of accessibility. But the fact is, despite—or because of—its popular appeal, new dance is virtually apolitical, or worse, noncontroversial. What gets argued about now, if anything, are questions of style, taste, sensibility—whether a thing is too long or too repetitious or too pretty, but not whether it's art at all, whether it's dangerous, threatening, undermining to important social values. Even those new-dance choreographers whom the audience finds less obviously congenial are accorded a respectable preeminence.

Maybe this means we have no important social values left, or that artists aren't concerned with addressing them right now. New dancers and audiences are communicating with each other quite well, and the sector of the dance population that one might expect to find outside the pale of conventional arts patterns is not starving today. They are benefiting from a cultural lag and an intellectual complacency of society's making as well as their own.

It always takes new ideas a while to seep into the American consciousness. Serious art ideas have a particularly hard time in our culture-obsessed but frivolous climate. Dance, even new dance, has been discovered by the media, the gossip columnists, the buyers of coffee-table books, the consumers of subscription hit shows and high-art concerts. Partly due to their own eclecticism and disregard for history, dancers have erased most of the distinctions that used to segregate the modern-dance from the ballet audience. Now even new dance is marketed by subscription, flung on the community in gala festival packages, and celebrated on TV.

Punditry has also discovered it, but the heaviest theorizing seems to be years behind the times. Intellectuals are talking about new dance as if the Judson Church aesthetic were still its motivation. The audience that looks for the latest avant-garde turn-on shows up eagerly at new-dance performances, but what they're seeing isn't very outrageous. Very few new dance choreographers are concerned any longer with such basics as body image (what should a dancer look like, what does a dancer do and not do), formal structures (how do you translate the idea of repetition or nonsequentiality or simultaneity into a process that bodies can do), demystification of the art or the artist, or presentation of dance as a thing in itself independent of narrative, virtuosity, tradition, or other coercions. These issues are no longer in question. Audiences accept that a dancer can do anything and still be a dancer. New dance now doesn't need to be destructive or instructive or corrective or liberating or ennervating or even infuriating.

Those were very much the concerns of new dancers when the 1960s were questioning a lot of our other basic social and cultural apparatus. That revolution, however, is through for the moment. As in much else of American life, what it seems to have liberated in us is an enthusiasm for the opposite. Dancers aren't more creative but more productive. They look less like the audience, more like a superspecies. They say less to more people. If they are still on the fringe, it's an affluent fringe. Respectable journals cover novice loft events and Trisha Brown performs in the opera house. As these dancers' lives become easier, they're so exposed, so committed to a regular output, that they don't experiment. They don't ask the hardest questions.

So perhaps new dance isn't very new at the moment. Now, when we really need a revolution, dance is more conservative across the board than it's been in thirty years. It's even hard to see where the next new dance will originate. Possibly with someone unclassifiable and elusive like Douglas Dunn, who's always stepping just beyond the reach of those forces that work so devastatingly upon the maverick mind—analysis, delineation, organization, reward. Or perhaps it will come from Twyla Tharp, who has those things firmly at her command and is still willing to risk them. Or perhaps we'll have to go through a severe retrenchment as government subsidies dry up. Then we'll find out which work really needs to be done. Most of it will be conservative of course, but some of it will be small and fierce and make us uncomfortable. Wherever and whenever it comes, a few people will find it and recognize its strangeness. It will be the new dance.

Relativity

Lucinda Childs: *Relative Calm*
Opera House, Brooklyn Academy, New York
Soho Weekly News, 12 January 1982

Lucinda Childs has worked with musical and scenic artists before *Relative Calm*, but Jon Gibson and Robert Wilson seem aesthetically more compatible with her diffident sensibility than her previous collaborators. In her last big work, *Dance* (1979), Sol LeWitt's larger-than-life film of the dancers and Philip Glass's hyperelectrified score seemed to blow up Childs's ideas to such outsize proportions that the dancers became almost subordinate to the overall sensory blast. Small detail disappeared, and meditative perpetual motion was goosed to a galvanic drive. The three elements in *Relative Calm* allow the Childs imagery to extend itself without undergoing such a shift in values.

Minimalism has always had the potential of going either way, I suppose—toward hard rock and glitter, or toward computerized randomness bordering on surrealism. Somehow Wilson's bizarre, delicate visuals and Gibson's intuitive, jazz-influenced approach to pulse music have a loosening-up effect on Childs's work, make her seem a little more amenable to "interpretation" than in her ultrasevere previous work. Any stage event creates tensions, expectations, contrasting tempers in us even if they're not intended. Childs in the past has made me feel she'd rather I didn't give in to them.

The hour-and-a-half *Relative Calm* begins with an image of timelessness. Behind a scrim as the audience enters, eight dancers in white are sitting on the floor, knees up, resting back on their hands, all facing the same way, in a silvery-blue light. Stars wink in the blue distance and a crescent-shaped luminous object sails slowly across the scrim. The sound is a quiet drone with almost toneless flutters like the stirrings of a field at night. During the whole first section of the dance this mood is sustained; the light grows dimmer, then brighter. It feels like some all-night ritual dance, a solemn celebration.

This section seems to be concerned with the deployment of the dancers in a long, intricate, but fiendishly rational sequence. They begin in the same spots where they were sitting and return to those spots after many crossings and repositionings that stress the stage diagonal from up-left to down-right. Their movement is academic, uninflected, built on bold walking steps to the steady beat of electric keyboards. Out of the walks come lunges, step turns, and later jumps, but the dancer's body is held absolutely flat, arms rotated outward slightly, chest open, head front. You begin to see the movement as pure rhythm, direction, floor pattern, not specific steps at all.

I know I'm supposed to focus on these evolving lineups and pairings, the syncopated skip that breaks into the regular beat at irregular intervals, the counterpoint between dancers moving with slow and fast steps. But especially at first, I keep coming back to the body attitude, the really odd way Childs's dancers move. Except when resting, they travel at a pace that is not only constant but pressured. They lope across the space as if skipping weren't fun but urgent. They're in a rush but held back at the same time. It's like some kind of race with elaborate handicaps.

In the second section two pairs of dancers share the space, circling with big sideways steps and jumps, tilting from foot to foot like rocking toys. Two at a time the first quartet, Jumay Chu, Daniel McCusker, Meg Harper, and Andé Peck, are replaced by Priscilla Newell, Garry Reigenborn, Carol Teitelbaum, and Tertius Walker.

The music keeps a steady rhythm of six, six, and five counts overlaid with loud chiming chords, and a series of unsettling events occurs in the background: a star sputters and goes out, garbled radio voices softly break through the music, curved shapes flash onto the background and disappear. Peck jogs on with a blasé white dog on a leash. A little girl in street clothes comes and takes the dog away. The projected arcs on the backdrop form into schematic rings that scoot across the horizon. Later they assemble in neat columns like math problems, and are swiftly wiped away. No explanation is made for any of this, but it doesn't seem to harm the dancers so we accept it, too.

Part 3 is a solo for Childs to Gibson's taped saxophone, overdubbed twice or more so that a short phrase played at irregular intervals is echoed or overlapped by another one, not quite the same. Wilson's triangular chunks of white light on the floor and the cyclorama frame her and carve up the space differently as they subtly change in intensity and angle. Childs begins center stage and moves back and forth along the opposite diagonal from the one the dancers used in Part 1. Like the others, she keeps her body very straight, pivots all at once, focuses directly toward the end of the diagonal and nowhere else. Her dance seems like a series of sudden accents—sweeping arm gestures, unforeseen backtrackings, and hitches into the air—punctuating the implacable momentum of her forward step. When, once or twice, her body bends or crouches over the legs, she appears unreasonably vulnerable—you almost expect her to fall.

The group returns in the last section to take its interweaving formations into backward running steps with wheeling pivot turns. Although the movement is more open than before, the sense that nothing can disturb their progress is the same. And this time there is something to disturb it, Gibson's music, which splatters discordant, almost bluesy sax and keyboard chords against a frenetic bass rhythm. Dots and dashes are projected on the backdrop like messages in an unknown language. A dark blue haze seems to settle just above the floor. The dancers keep plowing through it, transformed and totally undeterred.

Mediadance

Twyla Tharp: *Confessions of a Cornermaker*
Soho Weekly News, 19 January 1982

Twyla Tharp directed her setting of three recent dances, the *Bach Duet*, *Baker's Dozen*, and *Short Stories*, proving once more that given the resources, a choreographer who's committed to television can produce videodance that's remarkable in its own right, not just a reduction of stage work that emits whiffs of the stronger stuff. Tharp introduces the dances herself, dressed in jeans and a baggy Irish sweater, squinting into the wind on a stony beach. Quite a switch already from Patrick Watson's impeccable, impervious Mr. TV Host on the recent tape of Balanchine's *Davidsbündlertänze*. And her comments on the dances are equally disconcerting. I imagine Tharp scripting these things like a writer. She knows there are many things one can say about a given dance, so she picks one provocative observation and couches it in arresting language, hoping to get our attention. Tomorrow she might say something entirely different.

She explains the designation "Cornermaker" as describing her obsession with couplings, with the way things come together and go apart. She has, she tells us deadpan, "a singular filthy-mindedness." She says she choreographed *Baker's Dozen*, one of the most gorgeously crafted modern dances ever made, after completing a movie (*Hair*, from which her choreography was largely excised), and needed a catharsis from the "waste" she saw in the commercial filmmaking process. *Baker's Dozen* was about "economy," she says, "not to be confused with stinginess."

Twyla Tharp's mind as displayed on this tape is exotic enough to spend at least one viewing on her verbal ideas alone. But her direction of the dances is even more astonishing. Both *Bach* and *Baker's* are shot in a white space, almost a void, where floor merges with back wall and the dancers seem like crystalline figures on display. *Short Stories*, the violent, sensual dance about partner switching, has dark backgrounds and seems filtered in henna-colored light.

For the *Bach*, a duet she says is about keeping the dancers apart as much as together, she uses cameras that seem to be placed near each other. The cameras don't move much, but in the editing she "wipes" from one to another to show you a slightly different view of the dancers, Christine Uchida and William Whitener. Using a wide-angle lens, which telescopes depth distance, she can keep one dancer in the foreground while the other quickly gets very small moving upstage, appreciably larger while coming nearer. The *Bach Duet* hasn't been shown in New York, but when I saw it last spring in San Francisco, Tharp used a single horizontal band of the stage to suggest this apart-together duality. In some ways the video works even better.

Baker's Dozen is a big piece, using twelve dancers and a lot of large group patterns. Here Tharp pans in and out with the camera, but chooses to omit some of the choral counterpoint and full-stage sweep in favor of getting closer to small groups of two and three dancers. A work as intricate as *Baker's Dozen* really has to be seen live, but Tharp's video captures some of its lovely good humor, its style.

Tharp speaks of *Short Stories* as a piece of social criticism, but even without her savage descriptions ("tribal bloodletting," "a society so inbred they eat themselves"), the dance is devastating. Here she gives up any attempt to show a stage work, or even a stage. People meet, embrace passionately, shrug away, swoop down on another partner with the predatory disinterest of a flock of blue jays. The camera pans from one couple to another restlessly and avidly, pausing to appraise the glint of an eye, the yielding of flesh. The editing cuts right across the movement, underlining what is already harsh and interrupted. Unlike their counterparts on *Dallas*, the dancers look blameless, serious, and utterly real.

Excavating Judson

Judson Dance Theater, 1962–1966
Grey Gallery, New York
Soho Weekly News, 9 February 1982

There's an eerie, static quality to the photographs of Judson Dance Theater (1962–66) in the commemorative exhibit at NYU's Grey Gallery. Dance is never carved in stone, even at its most conservative, but the iconoclastic gestures of such experimenters as the Judson dancers look particularly bizarre when frozen into images and displayed twenty years later. The photos of Al Geise, Robert McElroy, Peter Moore, Terry Schutte can give us a great deal of information about how these dancers presented themselves—their wacky genius for costume, their sensual gift for theatrical as well as natural environments, their fetishes for rope, plastic, spray paint, and crumpled newspaper. The scores—like Steve Paxton's photo montage of men in action, clipped from magazines and threaded together to make a movement sequence—show them engaged in a process of clearing away the existing apparatus of dance making and constructing whole new sets of tools. The hours of taped interviews give us the participants' reflections on what they were doing from what seems like the centuries-later eighties.

But the essential quality, the philosophical underpinning of the whole enterprise, was movement, instability, impermanence, with a deliberate prospect of change. Even the newly reconstructed pieces—I saw tapes of Paxton's *Flat* and Elaine Summers's *Dance for lots of people* excerpted—seemed strangely out of place. But Robert Whitman's *Flower*, in footage of the 1965 original version especially staged for camera, gives a sense of how the Judson stuff might have looked to its own audiences. There's a kind of avidity for shock in it, a childlike attraction to color and texture, a meticulous craftsmanship in adorning the body with layers of lush artificial growth. These same ideas, by the way, were being pursued in different ways beginning in the mid-1950s by Alwin Nikolais down at Henry Street Playhouse, though we can scarcely think of the two theaters in the same breath now.

The Judson retrospective will continue in April with four performances of reconstructed work, and the whole thing gives us a lot to think about with regard to the course dance history has taken within our viewing lifetime. The organizers of the Grey Gallery exhibit, Bennington College faculty members Tony Carruthers, Wendy Perron, and Daniel Cameron, have unearthed enough material for years of study; the exhibit catalogue, with articles by Judson-generation critic-advocate Jill Johnston and latter-day critic-chronicler Sally Banes, only indicates its scope. For skimmers, the gallery exhibit may titillate. If you want to explore this kitchen midden of the avant-garde, better allow at least an afternoon.

The Aesthetics of Brawn

Elizabeth Streb
The Kitchen, New York
Soho Weekly News, 9 March 1982

One branch of the postmodern revolution has led to a preoccupation with the body as spectacle. Like gymnastics or baton twirling or skirt dancing, this work focuses on what the performer can do under certain restrictions. Particular props, structures, costumes are applied to limit and to extend the sphere of movement simultaneously, and the object is for the dancer to display her skill in overcoming these self-imposed handicaps. Usually this lends itself to short, brilliant escapades, like vaudeville acts, rather than to sustained choreographic invention. Although the total performing time of Elizabeth Streb's concert was only thirty-five minutes, my interest in what she could do had waned before the end.

Streb's ploy is to keep repositioning herself on special tilted platforms in as many ways as she can. There turn out to be a lot more ways than I would have imagined, but it matters surprisingly little. In a new piece, *Ringside*, Streb, clad in tomato-red unitard with yellow elbow pads, hurls herself athwart an eight-foot bright blue disc. Sliding, slithering, crouching, folding up and springing open, she maneuvers across the surface with a bumpy, spasmodic rhythm. She dives toward the downside, perches for a moment, clings to an upper edge. Despite the lighthearted crayon colors, she looks like some creature who lives permanently and discontentedly in a cage. At the end she rolls off the high end of the platform and disappears.

Fall Line, Streb's piece from last year, with Michael Schwartz, now has three parts. They first scramble over a plywood board about the size of two Ping-Pong tables, roughly following a crisscross grid of colored tapes laid out on the board. They lunge in and out of each other's paths, run up in unison, roll down diagonally. They have the efficient bodies of tree-climbing anthropoids, stretching out and gathering together their limbs to suit each precarious new landing. They take out little trapezelike gadgets fastened to the top of the incline, which enable them to hang and leapfrog each other and work even harder at their Sisyphean labors. Finally, they trudge up and up and up the hill, tiptoe down the edge, trudge up, slide down.

Streb's work is a logical development of certain experimental trends of the past twenty years—the dancer-as-athlete idea, and the various approaches that stipulated moving in some strange juxtaposition with natural elements or accomplishing difficult tasks that would require new feats of physical mastery or just new ways of moving. Streb seems to be taking up where Trisha Brown left off when Brown turned her experimenting to dance movement itself. Brown's equipment pieces of the early seventies—*Walking on the Wall, Man Walking Down the Side of a Building*—put the performer to the test of maintaining his equilibrium, both physical and psychic, while engaged in the most dislocated kind of work. I also remember a piece of Brown's (*Planes*, 1971) where dancers inched from one cutout hole to another on a vertical wall, in a flattening white light. Streb's visual perspective is similarly distorted; the background and the figure assume an unnatural relationship, both to each other and to the audience. We're looking neither into a picture, nor down at it from above, but at something crazily in between.

Where Streb's work differs from its predecessors is in its evident motivation. She's not really trying to test out the body by tossing it into some unknown waters, sink or swim, but to put the body where it can demonstrate conquest, even virtuosity, in an altered but governable universe. There are many tip-offs to this: Streb and Schwartz can, after all, fall or slide around the ramps any way they want; if they make a mistake they risk bruises but not broken bones. Not death. Their idea is to look as handsome as possible—pointed feet, Streb's little gold earrings, and all—and at the same time enhance the effortful quality of the work. The platform in *Fall Line* is miked, for instance, so that every prehensile footfall, every squeaky grab of the palm jars you audibly. Streb makes huffing and puffing faces like a TV wrestler.

All this had an increasingly unpleasant effect on me, despite its cleverness. I kept seeing further elaborations on hard work, punishing exercise for its own sake, and no ease, no respite, as the dancers returned to the uphill battle again and again. The audience was raptly attentive. Which only shows that one person's anxiety dream is another person's fantasy.

Vanguard Meets the Mainstream

Philip Glass: *Satyagraha*
Opera House, Brooklyn Academy, New York

Twyla Tharp: *The Catherine Wheel*
Winter Garden Theater, New York

Hudson Review, Spring 1982

As the 1981–82 season got under way, economics and creative inertia appeared to have overtaken the avant-garde. After nearly two decades of development, the postmodern dancers, whom we have most associated with protest, resistance to tradition, the smashing of old forms and the devising of new ones, are now veterans, possessors of companies and reputations, of managers and disciples and literary apologists. What they have that the modern dancers whom they deposed did not have is a high degree of public visibility. If not precisely popular, the so-called postmoderns have gained access to the culture's most official modes of recognition—the news media, the opera house, and public subsidy—a condition that never was enjoyed by this country's first generation of dance revolutionaries. The reasons for this shift are, I think, largely extra-artistic; just because Laura Dean is on television, we aren't necessarily becoming more sensitive to experimental dance. In fact, the successes of Philip Glass's opera *Satyagraha* and Twyla Tharp's rock allegory *The Catherine Wheel* suggest that our concept of avant-garde needs redefinition. Postmodernism is probably the most important development in dance since the early 1930s, when Martha Graham, Doris Humphrey, and others formulated the antiballetic approaches to composition and movement that collectively came to be known as modern dance. Although the term *postmodernism* is already in dispute, I am using it loosely to mean the whole tendency to break with what were perceived as the worn-out and decadent conventions of modern dance. Not just the rebellion of one individual against his or her teachers or the refurbishing of frayed ideas, it was a radical break and one that spread across a whole generation. For a while new choreographers were saying no to everything, including choreography. During the seventies this phase quickly passed. Technique, formal structure, narrative, character, even emotion returned, purged of romanticism, couched in vernacular idioms, and relieved of the modern dance's psychological freight. The initial negation, shock, and anarchy became a basis for the development of new forms, even new formalisms.

The postmodern revolution occurred at a time when the performing arts were being given every inducement to partake of mainstream opportunities. Purposely or by accident, the improvement of the dancers' lot defused much of the political unrest that triggered their rebellion. Federal, state, and local subsidies got spread to a wide diversity of artists, and in turn spread their work to a less specialized public than they might have attracted without assistance. Public and private subsidy brought the art of the salon and the loft—as well as the art of the opera house—into everyone's television set, and suddenly an audience of a few dozens or a few hundreds grew to millions. The television age has brought about the fusion of two previously irreconcilable concepts; high art and mass art effected a merger.

At first this process had nothing to do with the artists: it was a function of production, distribution, and marketing. The costs of art were once borne by the upper classes, who then could keep their protégés as more or less private ornaments. Now arts subvention was largely taken over by public agencies, and the new taxpayer-patrons got to have "their" culture by tuning in Live from Lincoln Center or mobbing the Picasso exhibition or building their own little Lincoln Centers with their own little ballet companies right there in River City. This kind of art producing is simultaneously elitist and populist, exclusive and democratic. It seems to hold out the possibility of serious work being done, serious ideas being dealt with, certainly serious community events being brought forth, but in fact the size and diverseness of the audience, the cost, the built-in drag associated with institutional planning, scheduling, and subscription campaigns, all bring about a leveling of the art process, a fixing of values that should be flexible, a protecting and hardening of aesthetic realities. The artist working in this climate doesn't deliberately set out to talk down, but he must be conscious of accessibility.

One of the most interesting changes wrought in this period is the growth of the audience's capacity to perceive artwork. Twenty years ago the ballet and the modern dance had virtually separate audiences. There were certain proprieties, certain contractual niceties to be observed between dancers and audiences. And there was the assumption that dancing was definitely an acquired taste. Very much as a result of the postmodern revolution, there's a great deal more range in the forms, activities, messages that popular dance can offer now. We've had rock ballets, nude ballets, homosexual ballets, protest ballets, and even postmodern ballets. No movement language seems too precious for today's dance audience; no ideology too threatening.

And since this is true, it isn't unusual to find the experimentally based postmodern dancers working in highly visible situations. With the expansion of the dance audience has come a need for material. Dance is a field in which recovering old works is difficult; no historical repertory exists that can automatically feed the producing organizations as opera or symphonic repertory sustains the music establishment. New choreography is the lifeblood of dance on every level from the traditional to the far-out. The postmoderns, being instinctively more resourceful and original than anyone, are gradually being sought to supply the ballet repertory. And while the legitimate theater continues to flounder, Tharp produces a month of her own at Broadway's Winter Garden. And the Brooklyn Academy decides that it is more practical to present four "Next Wave" artists in its two thousand-seat opera house than to afford them the leeway of the smaller, less economically productive, nontraditional room where they have performed in the past, the Lepercq Space.

*

At least one artist refused Brooklyn Academy's invitation, but Laura Dean, Trisha Brown, Lucinda Childs, and Philip Glass accepted. All of them offered works that enlarged on very simple ideas for which they first gained attention. With the exception of Brown, who treated the situation as she would any theater performance and whose plain, close-around-the-body dances emerged somewhat diminished in scale, they all multiplied various aspects of their work. The length, number of participants, production values mounted to epic proportions in the case of Glass. It's not inappropriate that this should happen. Dean, Childs, and Glass have all worked with incremental material. Structure in their works is based on repetition, the setting up of ostinato rhythms that become hypnotically predictable. The power and shape of the work depend on how these rhythms are changed. Dean's work shifts suddenly in large blocks, from one movement pattern and floor design to another, and the length of the interval between changes becomes an issue. Glass and Childs work with making inner changes: shifting rhythms within a steady pulse create coloristic effects and sometimes disturbingly unpredictable and subtle dissonances.

What many experimentalists of the seventies responded to was their need, and ours, for uninterrupted time, to think, to meditate, to absorb the essence of an event. Cycles, loops, phasing, and numerical repetition were all devices that relieved postmodern dance and music of the excitations found in traditional development-climax-recapitulation structures. Glass's opera about Gandhi had all the trappings of spectacle, and this too is a legitimate product of minimalism, contradictory though that may seem. Robert Wilson's productions of the seventies demonstrated that by inducing a dream state in the viewer with an almost static, prolonged, and minutely changing visual scene, he could make the most remarkable things happen, the most incongruous clash of elements seem plausible.

Satyagraha arrived in Brooklyn after its delirious reception in Europe had been ratified by the American critics at Artpark last summer. The sold-out audiences in Brooklyn impressed *Village Voice* critic Gregory Sandow as being made up of "the people who talk about Werner Herzog and Twyla Tharp . . . sophisticated people who don't normally pay attention to classical music," and Sandow thought this was because the work represented just the infusion of new ideas that classical music needs. It seems more likely to me that *Satyagraha*'s appeal indicates Glass's increasing conventionality, rather than his innovativeness.

Satyagraha offered an unbeatable mix of cultural cachet and safety, with its large, beautiful, and tastefully uncluttered staging; its Handelian-sized orchestra and chorus; its churchy, chordal, and always resolved harmonics; and its easy-to-comprehend action centering around high-minded characters and historical dilemmas. Far from being obscure, the work used many of the devices of conventional opera to achieve typically operatic effects: realistic gestures, poses, props; massed choruses that traveled in formations to produce a collective and disciplined sound; and tableaulike arias interspersed with descriptive but nonsung activity. There were spectacular engines—a printing press, two wagons bearing effigies of Hindu gods—that you got to look at long enough to apprehend their symbolic as well as their decorative value. And brooding above the main action there was in each act a different presence—Tolstoy, Tagore, and Martin Luther King—a character not directly involved with the plot but symbolic of some philosophical connection to past, present, or future.

In fact, the only element in *Satyagraha* that represented a radical departure from the known practices of spectacle was time, which Glass uses in extremely altered ways. Not only is the musical line conceived as a multiple of small repeated units, but the extended length of each musical idea gives the effect of stopping time, or attenuating it into some intangible other dimension—history, or even thought. The slow, meditative pace and the pictorial staging were derived from Robert Wilson's *Einstein on the Beach*, on which Glass collaborated, and other Wilson epics. But Wilson's visual effects are staggering in their inventiveness, weird and gigantic and often totally cryptic. Nothing in *Satyagraha* even comes close to being theatrically daring, not after the precedents set by Wilson. People who even now would find Wilson outrageous see a house built onstage in *Satyagraha*, but it represents only the building of a house. I remember the ominous, irrational force of Wilson's images: the gradual, inexplicable burning down of a house in *Deafman Glance*, the mad atomic-computer-assembly-line at the end of *Einstein*.

One more thing about *Satyagraha* that seemed regressive to me was its politics. The story was about Gandhi's pacifist efforts to abolish discrimination against Indian nationals in South Africa before World War I. In the final scene, workers stage a sit-in and are carried off unresisting by government troops. Then they're apotheosized as a crowd of onlookers, or a heavenly choir, at the assassination of Martin Luther King. You don't have to know anything about Gandhi to realize that his protests have had little lasting effect on racism in South Africa. And the race wars are far from won in America, too. In 1981, it seems to me, we can only look at the liberating efforts of the seventies with irony. The martyrdom of these men accomplished little except to give us the satisfaction of glorifying them now. Nonviolent protest is as politically dead and safe in the eighties as Prohibition, which makes it a perfect pseudo issue for the mass theater. Who could be against it?

*

Politically and in quite a few other ways, Twyla Tharp slips it to the middle class in *The Catherine Wheel*. Slick and provocative and insidious, the piece throws our hedonism in our faces, shows it to us for the attractive, pernicious force it is. The main elements of *The Catherine Wheel* are staples of pop culture: a loud, nagging rock score by David Byrne; a battery of feverish effects—lights, glitter, smoke; knockout dancing of the highest technical quality and the meanest intensity; and a cast of characters that sets a slapstick family of libertines against a sinister, abstract corps de ballet. Entertainment, 1980s style. But beneath the high tech and the punchy laughter is a deep alienation, a sense of betrayal and futility, and finally a presentiment of a hyperactive if not blissful tomorrow.

The family members go in for self-gratification, from sex to aggression, and carry on in the most violent way imaginable even when they're making love. They're lured by a vision of pleasure, a golden pineapple that grows bigger the more they play with it. Sara Rudner as the leader of the chorus first plucks it out of a golden pineapple bush, worshipping it like a holy object, then letting it loose to incite the family. Later the most innocent of the characters, the Poet, plays with it the way the Blackamoor in *Petrouchka* plays with his coconut-totem. But it's clearly an evil spirit, not a benevolent one, and everyone's desires are eventually frustrated, if only because there's a bigger pineapple just around the bend. The violence escalates into orgiastic battles, until the parents do a dance of resignation, as if admitting this has been going on since the beginning of time and will continue. Rudner seems satisfied. She returns the pineapple to its golden altar, and magically the characters and the chorus reappear dressed in golden costumes.

They dance a long coda with breakneck speed and cruel virtuosity. No longer violent, they're still driven. A bleak sort of optimism but perhaps a realistic one.

The Catherine Wheel is disruptive, jarring. The story of the family doesn't proceed in consecutive episodes or even intelligibly sequential ones. For an intermissionless hour and twenty minutes it attacks us in bouts of interrupted, overlapping narrative. Sometimes the plot is foreshadowed by silhouettes projected on screens behind the action. Sometimes it's commented on and given an even more hostile and personalized meaning by the chorus. Intricate, precision-tooled machines with unknown functions hover overhead. Stage drapes fly up and down constantly, slicing up the space which has already been mined with twenty-four metal poles as high as the proscenium. Things get thrown through the air and left littering the floor. Costumes are made of layered, unidentifiable garments, like ragamuffin dancer attire exaggerated until their movement is hidden and obstructed. Whether acting or dancing, the performers work at higher than necessary levels; they mug, fidget, ram into the movement, rage to be heard. Tharp is turning the postmodern dictum of impassivity inside out. You don't want to get to love these dancers, she seems to suggest. But instead of making them "objective" or "neutral," she makes them so overexpressive that we have to keep them at a distance or be flattened by their power.

Throughout the twentieth century, theater styles have tended to swing from naturalism to artificiality, although Broadway and television have adhered consistently to the naturalistc mode stemming from Stanislavsky's theories of acting. In Satyagraha, despite formal structures, Glass is edging toward naturalism. His literal treatment of the plot, the affecting though restrained performance of Douglas Perry as Gandhi, and the general lack of strangeness or dislocation make us feel comfortable, even involved. The Catherine Wheel, on the other hand, is a very firm statement of nonrealism, a new kind of expressionism perhaps. Certainly the piece is more allied to Brecht, Kurt Jooss, or George Grosz than to Dickens or Antony Tudor or even Jiri Kylian. Tharp doesn't want to encourage our sympathy or stroke our certitudes. She wants to make us angry, batter our senses. She doesn't want to put us to sleep, she wants to wake us up. It's astonishing that some dancers think she's gone commercial, and that commercial audiences think she's such a kick. The Catherine Wheel continues Tharp's long career of subversion. If she's turned gloomy and down on the culture, maybe it's time for us to do the same.

The Death of Some Alternatives

Ballet Review, Fall 1982

Everyone knew the Soho News was in trouble. Marginal was its middle name, from the time it was founded in 1973 by a rock promoter without enough experience in the newspaper business to know how much capital it was going to take to start a weekly in New York in the posttelevision age. Everyone at the paper knew, in those last few months, that the British press moguls who had rescued it from its most recent financial precipice had run out of patience and were trying to dump it. There was a chance they wouldn't find a buyer. But somehow I always figured the Soho would scrape through again. So when the hotel clerk in Bucharest handed me my editor's cable on 17 April (SOHO NEWS FOLDS LOVE LOIS), I felt all my systems stop, as if a great paralyzing cloud had settled around my ribcage. It was like the sudden death of a friend.

I started working for the Soho News in the fall of 1974. Although I desperately needed a place to review dance in New York, they didn't pay anything the first year, and I had my pride. I wouldn't work for nothing. For the next three years I got ten dollars a review—usually a long time after the review was published. Offered a lucrative job on New York magazine, I left in 1978, but a little more than a year later I was back. I preferred being an underpaid downtown dance critic to being an underused media fixture.

I never did make a living at Soho, although the fees were raised little by little—instead of paying for my carfare, they ultimately paid the rent. We critics remained stringers, ineligible for the benefits that staffers at last extracted from management—insurance, severance pay, unemployment credits. I got a book out of it—most of my second collection of reviews was published first in Soho—but that didn't pay anything either. I didn't resent the low pay at Soho. In some perverse way I liked the feeling that nobody owned me. We built a rather freewheeling dance section that covered obscure events as often as it ignored prominent ones.

I was lucky enough to work under four editors at Soho News who were all good dance writers and all consistently supportive of my work. They were Rob Baker, Robert Pierce, Sally Banes, and Lois Draegin. The other regular critics who wrote the dance pages with me included Robert Greskovic, Jean Nuchtern, Tobi Tobias, Nancy Goldner, and Allen Robertson. Nathaniel Tileston joined the paper to take pictures of what I and the others reviewed, and he was later joined by Johan Elbers.

My first article for the Soho News was about the debut of Gelsey Kirkland and Mikhail Baryshnikov dancing together, in Winnipeg in 1974. The Soho News didn't send me to Winnipeg, or anywhere else, though I wrote reviews for it from Philadelphia, Princeton, San Francisco, London, Los Angeles, Minneapolis; from Durham, North Carolina; Middletown, Connecticut; and Graz, Austria. Not making a living writing for *Soho*, I spent a lot of time traveling around doing lectures and other assignments, and whenever I saw some interesting dance somewhere, I'd send back an article. They'd print it, even though that event might never be seen in New York. I had the news reporter's appetite for covering the irrecoverable; in dance, I found, you do it every time. In 1981–82, neither Baryshnikov nor Kirkland danced a full season; and as for the partnership whose first tremulous moments I glimpsed in Winnipeg, it had already ripened into perfection by the time they played New York a few months later, and it soured not long after that.

The next thing I did for *Soho* was another one-of-a-kind event: Douglas Dunn's *Exhibit 101*. In this singular performance piece, Dunn lay in the top of a wooden structure that completely filled his Soho loft. For four hours a day, for two weeks, he just put himself on display there and let the audience come in and observe him any way it wanted to. By 1974 the stark, shocking, often formless dance experimentation of the sixties had mellowed into something an audience could grasp more easily—well, sometimes uneasily. The avant-gardists were no longer trying to prove that the conventional modern dance had expired as an arena for innovation. In their initial vague gestures of protest, their demonstrations of personal anger and personal indulgence, they had been stumbling upon some pretty interesting ideas, and people who had been busy saying no began to pursue specific themes of experimentation, to set up more controlled and complicated conditions for their work. Dadaistic theater pieces, happenings, and open agendas were evolving into close-knit, clever improvisational ensembles like the Grand Union, structured activities in untheatrical places like Trisha Brown's environment and equipment pieces, and planned events so bizarre they were guaranteed to destroy our inkblot reactions.

Though of course we didn't know it, 1974 was a time of transition. Ideas were coalescing into what would, a few years later, start to be called postmodern dance. Reviewing for a weekly paper, I didn't think my job was to assess trends or name movements, but to report on things one at a time, trying to locate the particular oddness that distinguished each one. It would be time enough in a year or five years to see that some ideas led up blind alleys and some quickly developed into more elaborate, polished groups of things that could be called styles. I wanted to preserve a first impression of these events, even if they might give rise to things much more imposing. This seemed a doubly urgent responsibility in the experimental dance field because new dancers since 1960 had been determined not to subordinate their creative needs to the traditional demands of repertory and formal company structures, not to aim for repeatability in their dances. I never expected to see any experimental work again after its initial performances.

When Bennington College recently began a series of events commemorating the twentieth anniversary of the experimental Judson Dance Theater, I didn't expect to see the spirit of Judson revived. Never mind that St. Mark's Church in the Bowery has replaced Judson as the sanctuary for new dance, or that the original Judson rebels are now middle-aged—and some of them are even stars, a designation that would have excommunicated them from the movement twenty years ago. The Judson revivals made especially clear the attrition that time wreaks on a dance, only here we were seeing more than the loss of detail, of stylistic nuance, of the original impetus that makes a dance captivate us in its initial moments and that never quite infuses it so fully again. Because the Judson dances were so representative of the sixties counterculture, their reenactment in 1982 also gave dramatic evidence of what twenty years have done to our thinking, to our style.

Even to speak of reviving Judson is to perform an act of transformation, for the essence of the movement was its relevance, to use a sixties word. Judson dance cannot be thought of except in relation to its dance context. It was a forum for asking questions, the answers to which would change everything. In 1982 it's no longer in doubt whether you can dance in a nonproscenium space, whether you need a formal dance technique to do a dance, whether the outcome of a dance must be known in advance by the performers, whether one dance action has to be followed by the action it most naturally provokes. In fact, the answering of these kinds of questions effectively disposed of them. To make a real revival of Judson today, you'd have to ask new questions, but work on them with a Judson frame of mind.

One of the most important reforms that the Judson dancers and their cohorts in the sixties wanted to bring about was to reanimate dance for both the dancer and the viewers. They began with the most drastic premises: a dance didn't need to consist of highly accomplished movement, or any movement at all. Anyone could dance, anything could be dance. If you resisted the idea, you'd still have to consider it. Deborah Hay, one of the explorers of this territory, made dances of walking and other simple, tasklike sequences. Her 1968 work *Ten* was done at St. Mark's as an intermission piece, which the audience was invited to "watch and not watch as they please." The ten performers used a horizontal and a vertical pole as props to which someone would attach himself or herself in simple ways, like leaning against them, and more complicated ways, like wrapping one leg around the pole and bending till the performer was almost off balance. Then another performer would approach and try to copy the first one's pose exactly.

Very soon this gambit would indeed become something you wouldn't want to watch, but then you'd be forced to confront the issue of what is interesting to watch. I remember in Hay's early pieces that the plainness of the actions and the unstudied way her people did them made me very conscious of each person's body and way of moving. There was often a lot more individuality to be seen in this kind of performance than in the ballet, where everyone was striving to look alike. What was interesting about Hay was not only the movement differences but the strong sense of performance, despite her elimination of what were thought to be performance essentials.

Then, at some point—I think I can actually nail it down to the first time I saw *Angie's Waltz* by Andrew De Groat in the fall of 1977—the individual nondancer was dramatized and made a star. Frank Conversano, a pudgy, bouncy man who looked more like a gas station attendant than a dancer, was given the same things to do as De Groat's by then very adept company, and he performed the way children do before they've learned there's something called professional. Judson's naturalness had become "naturalness," and I guess it wasn't surprising to see Hay's dancers in 1982 exaggerating the whole process of imitating their cohorts' poses—looking with stage-serious eyes, examining a leg, stooping to get a better view of the arm placement, easing themselves very carefully into place, as if draping around a pole were really a tremendous feat.

Almost all of the Judson revivals that I saw seemed to have grown sharper dynamically and visually than the originals. Some of the creators felt they were seeing their ideas fully executed at last. Lucinda Childs recently asserted that her solo *Carnation* was exactly the same dance she'd done in 1964, except that she now had a different performing attitude. To the viewer at St. Mark's this made the piece, in which she performed deadpan rituals with unlikely props, seem hilariously dramatic and nonsensical, where it had originally been very dry and serious. Yvonne Rainer told me that when she did the first performance of her *Trio A* at St. Mark's—she hadn't danced it in almost a year—she'd completely neglected the possibility of disabling stage fright. Although *Trio A* was meant to be performed by all kinds of dancers and nondancers, to reveal their movement as a personal and natural spontaneous act, stage fright was not now an acceptable limitation. So Rainer did the dance all over again on the spot.

Steve Paxton was interested in natural, improvised movement as a way of stating the relationships between performers and as an obvious solution to the problem of the open-ended scenario. Later, in *Lazy Madge* (1976), Douglas Dunn found out how to use real choreography, even choreographic phrases, and still not predetermine the program of the dance. He simply let the dancers decide when to go out and do their preset movement bits, where to make each contribution within the fabric of time, space, and the other dancers. Actually, Merce Cunningham had tried doing this earlier, during the sixties, but it made his dancers too nervous.

Paxton followed a nontechnical course, which eventually developed into a full-blown system of movement called contact improvisation. Contact is a duet form in which the dancers, through an extremely delicate, maybe even psychic, sense of touch, weight, and placement, can get in tune with their partners and do highly physical, impeccably timed, unplanned movement sequences without hurting themselves or each other. By 1981, when I copied the following from an ad in a dance publication, improvisation had become a product: "Intuitive Dance Improvisation is a way for dancers to explore personal movement sources in a systematic sequence of classes. Attention will be given to clarifying impulses that lead to dancing intuitively. Through the work dancers will develop a dependable technique for capturing the spontaneous."

Paxton's *Jag Ville Gorna Telefonera* excerpt (1964) was originally made for himself and Robert Rauschenberg and based on poses taken from photographs of athletes and other active men. Rauschenberg, of course, was not a dancer, though he performed in many of the sixties events. In 1982, done by Stephen Petronio and Randy Warshaw at St. Mark's, the piece was an expert performance, theatrically acute and physically resilient. Paxton has instilled his natural, catlike grace into the moves of his disciples: jump, rebound with a compact roll to the feet; wait, totally centered and at ease, till the partner lunges at you; adapt to his weight without even visibly bracing. The dance looks beautiful now, accomplished, and, as a historical reference, incongruously slick.

What the St. Mark's revivals didn't have that Judson and the whole counterculture had was a dedication to the unknown. I knew a journalist who was taking mescaline in 1961, not to get high, but to explore places his conscious mind had barred him from. He thought it would make him a better writer. Avant-garde dancers in the sixties understood movement as a thing that wasn't perfect, that couldn't be perfected, a thing whose value as a performance medium depended on its fallibility, and on the unforeseen consequences of any action. Their movement, though it was made of the everyday actions all people share, often looked self-conscious, because they put themselves in the unaccustomed position of being on show. They forced an expressional neutrality, tried to smooth out the dynamic ups and downs, so that we would see the movement as some objective thing, appreciate it for itself, see its inherently differing mechanics on different bodies. But there was still a lot that was personal to what they did—the roughness and hesitancy of natural rhythms, the lapses in the flow of invention, the dying out of momentum when it isn't goosed up artificially, the erotic and theatrical energy released when the dancer leaves off his or her customary protection of technique and performing attitude.

You could see all this at St. Mark's in Elaine Summers's documentary film *Judson Nights*, and I thought for the hundredth time that all new dance should be filmed at its inception, and the most experimental dance should be allowed to lapse after that. Summers's footage had another important, vanished quality of Judson nights: it looked unfinished. The work of those days wasn't amateurish, but it was often purposely left unresolved. There was a certain rebelliousness in this, a deliberate messiness to counteract the too-neat solutions of the fifties. But people also wanted to acknowledge that dance could be mysterious, unknowable; they were willing to be obscure; they were in a hurry to go on to something else. They were learning to let go; they were teaching us.

Inevitably, I suppose, dance came around again to virtuosity, to the dancers doing it better and more uniformly and looking less like the danceless, awestruck slobs in the audience. Looseness—we soon called it flow—became a technique, along with the natural body line, the noncommittal expression, and the quick reflex. The sixties accustomed us to choreography absolved of composition, stars relieved of personality. With a few more options, and a few less, we're back again to what works.

At the Soho News I began to realize my pieces were hardly ever about trying to describe completely new phenomena anymore, but about placing things in relation to their precedents. It was my first time describing a revolution subside, and it wasn't as much fun. So I started writing more often about film and video dance, and about non-Western dance, and art-music-theater events connected with dance. They went on printing it. I felt secure, though the paper was a mass of shifting sands around me. Political issues and their partisans came and went. Style was mod, then punk, then retro. Gay was in. Gay was out. Style was in—style, finally, was all.

They printed good stuff sometimes—Jane Perlez on the media, Tim Page on new music, the Red Chef's recipe for bluefish chowder. But the paper never was angry enough for me, or argumentatively sharp enough. Brash and ambitious when it began, kooky and sleazy by turns later on, it always seemed to be too much about fashion and not enough about journalistic necessity. It was done in by poor management and absentee owners and the rising value of the Soho real estate on which it stood. It was done in by a lack of readers and a lack of advertisers, and by a general failure of confidence in newspapers. Most of all, it was done in by the death of the counterculture, along with the more politically activist Real Paper in Boston and the arts-oriented Bay Guardian in San Francisco, and who knows how many lesser papers.

Now there are plans for new periodicals around New York—highbrow monthlies and flashy style sheets, with great hopes and important backing. But so far there's no sign of any new forum for the fringe mastermind, the inarticulate reformer, and the fugitive spectacle. I guess we'll have to wait till we need one again.

Selected Filmography

DURING THE LATE 1970S DOCUMENTATION of dance performances became a standard practice. The downtown dance presenting spaces such as Dance Theater Workshop were especially sensitive to the ephemeral nature of new dance, and video records were made of a large number of the works commented on in this book. The following filmography includes as many of the works I described directly as are available to be viewed, as documentary records, at the Dance Collection of the Performing Arts Library at Lincoln Center in New York. Such works are identified by the abbreviation L in parentheses. In addition, it includes important films available to be rented or purchased (distributors' information is in parentheses).

I have not viewed all these record films and videos, and the quality will vary. Readers are advised to check the library's catalogue for additional film titles. The choreographers or their agents may be able to supply additional film information to those doing archival research. In most cases, I have included only those dances discussed in this book, rather than trying to encompass all the dances by a given choreographer, even for the period covered by the book. Dates following the film titles are the dates of film release, not the dates of the choreography.

General

Beyond the Mainstream (1980)

NET/Dance in America survey of postmodern dance. Includes excerpts from dances by Trisha Brown, Yvonne Rainer, David Gordon, Kei Takei, and Laura Dean and contact improvisation. (L)

Dune Dance (1980)

Postmodern compositional techniques and countercultural spirit, filmed outdoors on Cape Cod. Dancers include Sara Rudner. Directed by

Carolyn Brown. (Dance Film Archive, University of Rochester, Rochester, N.Y. 14627)

Judson Dance Project (1982)

Five documentary performance tapes from the 1982 reconstruction project undertaken by Bennington College and performed in New York. A set of related videotaped interviews with the participants is listed under "Judson Project" and the choreographers' names. (L)

Making Dances (1980)

Seven postmodern choreographers, with interviews and rehearsal and performance footage. Included are Douglas Dunn, Meredith Monk, David Gordon, Trisha Brown, Lucinda Childs, Sara Rudner, and Kenneth King. (Blackwood Productions, 251 W. 57 St., New York, N.Y. 10019)

Choreographers

Trisha Brown

Water Motor (1978). (Dance Film Archive, University of Rochester, Rochester, N.Y. 14627. Also from Film-Makers' Cooperative, 175 Lexington Ave., New York, N.Y. 10016)
Dancing on the Edge (1980). Performance at Bennington College, Bennington, Vt. Includes *Opal Loop, Water Motor,* and *Locus/altered.* (L)
Accumulation with Talking Plus Water Motor (1986). (L)

The Trisha Brown Company has begun distributing Brown's tapes and films. A listing of available titles can be requested. (Trisha Brown Company, 225 Lafayette St., Suite 807, New York, N.Y. 10012)

Remy Charlip

Remy Charlip Dance Company (1977). Performance at Dance Theater Workshop, New York. (L)
Dances—Remy Charlip (1978). Made for WGBH, Boston/New Television Workshop. (L)

Yoshiko Chuma

Champing at the Bit (1981). (Rudy Burckhardt, 50 W. 29 St., New York, N.Y. 10001)

Merce Cunningham

NET/*Dance in America* (1977). Includes excerpts from several current dances, plus *Video Triangle,* created for this production. (L)
The Cunningham Dance Foundation distributes about twenty-five films

of Cunningham's work, and updated catalogues are issued periodically. (Cunningham Dance Foundation, Media Department, 463 West St., New York, N.Y. 10014)

Laura Dean

Tympani (1981). Made for KTCA-TV, St. Paul/Minneapolis. (L)

Andrew De Groat

Angie's Waltz (1978). Performance at Entermedia Theater, New York, February. (L)

Angie's Waltz (1978). Performance at Delacorte Theater, New York, September. (L)

Cloud Dance (1979). A film by Robyn Brentano and Andrew Horn. (Film-Makers' Cooperative, 175 Lexington Ave., New York, N.Y. 10016)

Senta Driver

In Which a Position is Taken and Some Dance (1977). Performance at Entermedia Theater, New York. Includes Sudden Death. (L)

Pièce d'Occasion and Board Fade Except (1977). Performance at Entermedia Theater, New York. (L)

Second Generation and Exam (1977). Performance at Entermedia Theater, New York. (L)

Sudden Death (1980). Performance at American Dance Festival, Duke University, Durham, N.C. (L)

Missing Persons (1984). Performance at Riverside Church, New York. (L)

Dance Preludes: Harry (1986). Documentary by Dennis Diamond. Includes rehearsal and performance segments from Missing Persons and Reaches. (Video D Studios, 29 W. 21 St., New York, N.Y. 10010-6807)

William Dunas

The Trust (1978). Performance at Dance Theater Workshop, New York. (L)

Simone Forti

Jackdaw Songs (1981). Performance at Performing Garage, New York. (L)

David Gordon

Chair (1975). Performance in Tokyo. (L)

Chair (1975). Rehearsal. (L)

Performance at Dance Theater Workshop, New York (1978). Includes Chair, What Happened, and Mixed Solo. (L)

10-Minute TV (1982). Performance at Dance Theater Workshop, New York. Includes Dorothy and Eileen, What Happened, and Close Up. (L)

Trying Times (1982). Performance at Dance Theater Workshop, New York. (L)
TV Reel (1982). Studio performance. (L)

Grand Union

Performance at Guthrie Theater, Minneapolis (1975). (L)

Deborah Hay

Leaving the House (1980). Performance at Dance Theater Workshop, New York. (L)

Bill Irwin

Not Quite/New York (1981). Performance at Dance Theater Workshop, New York. (L)

Margaret Jenkins

Copy (1980). Performance at Cunningham Studio, New York. (L)
Videosongs (1980). Performance at Cunningham Studio, New York. (L)

Kenneth King

Dance S(p)ell with Telaxic Synapsulator (1978). Performance at Brooklyn Academy, New York. (L)
RAdeoA.C.tiv(ID)ity (1978). Performance at Brooklyn Academy, New York. (L)
Space City (1981). A film by Robyn Brentano and Andrew Horn. (Film-Makers' Cooperative, 175 Lexington Ave., New York, N.Y. 10016)

Bebe Miller

Performance at Dance Theater Workshop, New York (1981). (L)

Meredith Monk

Quarry (1975). Five-minute film-within-the-dance by David Geary. (The House Foundation for the Arts, Inc., 131 Varick St., Rm. 901, New York, N.Y. 10013)
Ellis Island (1979). Seven-minute film used in the dance Recent Ruins. (The House Foundation for the Arts, Inc., 131 Varick St., Rm. 901, New York, N.Y. 10013)
16 Millimeter Earrings (1980). A reconstruction of the 1966 dance, filmed by Robert Withers. (Robert Withers, 202 W. 80 St., #5W, New York, N.Y. 10024)
Ellis Island (1981). Twenty-eight-minute version. (Ken Stutz, The Stutz Company, Berkeley, Calif. 94710)
Turtle Dreams (1987). Ten-minute film sequences used in Turtle Dreams and

other works, including *Specimen Days*. (Robert Withers, 202 W. 80 St., #5W, New York, N.Y. 10024)

Meredith Monk/The House issues a complete listing of all Monk's films and their sources. (The House Foundation for the Arts, Inc., 131 Varick St., Rm. 901, New York, N.Y. 10013)

Charles Moulton

Motor Fantasy (1981). Performance at Dance Theater Workshop, New York. (L)

Judy Padow

Tuesday Project (1977). Performance at Dance Theater Workshop, New York. (L)

Rudy Perez

District 1 (1976). Videodance made for WGBH, Boston. (L)

Yvonne Rainer

Trio A (1978). A film by Sally Banes. (Dance Film Archive, University of Rochester, Rochester, N.Y. 14627)

Kenneth Rinker

Cantata No. 84 (1980). Performance at Dance Theater Workshop, New York. (L)

Sara Rudner

As Is/Layers (1977). Performance at Entermedia Theater, New York. (L)
Dancing Parttime (1978). Performance at St. Mark's Church, New York. (L)

Elizabeth Streb

Fall Line (1981). Performance at Dance Theater Workshop, New York. (L)
Fall Line (1982). Videodance by Michael Schwartz. (L)

Kei Takei

Light Part 5 (1976). (Dance Film Archive, University of Rochester, Rochester, N.Y. 14627)
Light Part 10 (1976). Videotape by Doris Chase. (L)
Dance Three (1977). A film by Doris Chase based on a theme from *Light Part 9*. Chase made several films with Takei and other dancers during the mid-1970s. (Film-Makers' Cooperative, 175 Lexington Ave., New York, N.Y. 10016)

Light Part 9 (1977). Performance at the Cathedral of St. John the Divine, New
  York. (L)
Light Part 10, 12, 13 (1977). Performance at Entermedia Theater, New York. (L)
Light Part 1–15 (1981). Marathon performance at the Dance Gallery, New
  York. (L)

Twyla Tharp

Making Television Dance (1978). (L)
Hair (1979). Feature film by Milos Forman with choreography by Tharp. (L)
Confessions of a Cornermaker (1981). (L)
Sue's Leg (1981). NET/Dance in America. (L)
Tharp Scrapbook (1982). Made for Hearst/ABC ARTS. Includes excerpts from
  Hair, 1903, Short Stories, and *Baker's Dozen.* (L)
The Catherine Wheel (1983). NET/Dance in America. (L)
Baryshnikov Dances Sinatra (1984). Includes ballet version of *Sinatra Songs.* (Kul-
  tur Video, 121 Highway 36, West Long Branch, N.J. 07764)

Robert Wilson

Einstein on the Beach (1984). Performance at Brooklyn Academy, New York.
  (L, permission required)
Einstein on the Beach (1986). Documentary about the collaboration between
  Wilson and Philip Glass on the piece. (Direct Cinema Limited, P.O.
  Box 69799, Los Angeles, Calif. 90069-9976)

David Woodberry

Edges/Invisible Dance (1981). Performance at the Kitchen, New York. (L)

Index

Keuter, Cliff, 151; *Woodblocks*, 150, 151
King, Kenneth, 9–11, 39, 52, 54, 80, 109–11, 169; *Blue Mountain Pass*, 109, 110; *Dance S(p)ell*, 54; *RAdeoA.C.tiv(ID)ty*, 9–11, 54; *Space City*, 109–10; *Wor(l)d (T)raid*, 110
Kirkland, Gelsey, 184, 185
Kitchen (Broome Street), 11, 65, 77, 91, 92, 96, 135, 163, 176
Knowles, Christopher, 121
Knowles, Timothy, 28–29
Koegler, Horst, 1
Komar, Chris, 62, 102, 147
Kovich, Robert, 53, 62, 102
Kraus, Lisa, 161
Kurshals, Raymond, 27, 104, 106, 108, 144, 145, 157
Kushner, Robert, 42, 43

La Barbara, Joan, 42, 43
The Ladies and Me (Cummings), 134
Lancaster, Mark, 146
Landrover (Cunningham), 100, 101
Langland, Paul, 168
Lazaroff, Judy, 147
Lazy Madge (Dunn), 32, 187
Leaving the House (Hay), 117–18
Lecture-Dem in Geeneewannaland (Jacobowitz), 81
Ledesma, Jorge, 29
Lennon, John, 130–31
Lennon, Joseph, 147
Lepkoff, Danny, 12, 41
Leroy, A., 97, 120, 152
Levey, Karen, 10
LeWitt, Sol, 169, 171
Light (Takei), 44–46, 47–49, 85–87, 125–27
Limón, José, 121
Line Up (Brown), 18–20
Litz, Katherine, 71
Locale (Cunningham), 100; film, 102–4
Lockwood, Steve, 168
Locus (Brown), 3, 19
London Contemporary Dance Theater, 1, 2
Loquasto, Santo, 107, 145, 159

McCusker, Daniel, 80, 173

McRoberts, Jeff, 111
Madden, Diane, 161
Mail order dances, 38
Making Television Dance (Tharp), 37
Malashock, John, 144
Man Walking Down the Side of a Building (Brown), 177
Marclay, Christian, 142, 143
Marks, Victoria, 136–37
Marshall, Keith, 137–38
The Matter (plus and minus) (Gordon), 89–91
Matters of Fact (Driver), 29
Matthiessen, Erin, 112
Mauzerall, Hope, 164
"Mediadance," 98–99, 102–4, 174–75
Meditation (Charlip), 39–40
Medley (Tharp), 24
Memorandum (Driver), 29
Menaker, Shana, 42, 57
Miller, Bebe, 136, 164–65; *Jammin'*, 165; *Solo: TaskForce*, 165; *Square Business*, 165; *Tune*, 165
Minimalism, 4, 7, 40, 47–48, 56, 59, 73–78, 79, 81, 93, 113, 120, 130, 172, 180
Missing Persons (Driver), 162–63
Mixed Solo (Gordon), 59–60
Monk, Meredith, 28, 48, 54, 81, 98, 99, 117, 166–68; *Quarry*, 99; *16 Millimeter Earrings*, 98, 99; *Specimen Days*, 166–68; *Turtle Dreams*, 167
Monte, Elisa, 150–52; *Pell Mell*, 150, 151; *Treading*, 150, 151, 152
Morales, Mio, 141
Moschen, Michael, 156, 157
Moss, David, 62
Motor Fantasy (Moulton), 119, 120–21
Moulton, Charles, 96–97, 113, 119, 152, 155–56, 157, 169; *Expanded Ball Passing*, 152–53; *Motor Fantasy*, 119, 120–21; *Thought Movement Motor*, 96–97
Mud (Tharp), 24, 25, 26–28
Mudsong (Jacobowitz), 81
Munich Dance Project, 115–16
Murdoch (Irwin/Skinner), 113–14
Music (Dean), 111–13

Nagrin, Daniel, 69

Marcia B. Siegel's books include *The Shapes of Change—Images of American Dance, Days on Earth—The Dance of Doris Humphrey*, and two earlier collections of dance reviews. She teaches in the Department of Performance Studies, Tisch School of the Arts, New York University.

Nathaniel Tileston did graduate work in photography at the Art Institute of Chicago. In 1970 he came to New York to work with Martha Swope. He began photographing dance for the *Soho Weekly News* in 1976, and his pictures were also seen there with William Harris's theater reviews and Wendy Perron's performance reviews. Photographs from the same period covered by this book were featured in one-man shows in 1980 at Dance Theater Workshop and 1981 at the International Center for the Arts in London. In 1982 he and his wife Susan moved to Nova Scotia, where he makes photographs and is active on the board of the regional theater.

Library of Congress Cataloging-in-Publication Data
Siegel, Marcia B.
The tail of the dragon : new dance, 1976–1982 / Marcia B. Siegel ; photographs by Nathaniel Tileston.
Includes bibliographical references and index.
ISBN 0-8223-1156-9 (cloth). – ISBN 0-8223-1166-6 (pbk.)
1. Modern dance—History. I. Title.
GV1783.S53 1991
792.8—dc20   91-522 CIP